Helen Harper
Pig and a Sack of Stray Cats

RoseDog❤Books
PITTSBURGH, PENNSYLVANIA 15222

The contents of this work including, but not limited to, the accuracy of events, people, and places depicted; opinions expressed; permission to use previously published materials included; and any advice given or actions advocated are solely the responsibility of the author, who assumes all liability for said work and indemnifies the publisher against any claims stemming from publication of the work.

All Rights Reserved
Copyright © 2007 by Helen Harper
No part of this book may be reproduced or transmitted in any form or by any means, electronic or mechanical, including photocopying, recording, or by any information storage and retrieval system without permission in writing from the author.

ISBN: 978-0-8059-8974-8
Library of Congress Control Number: 2006938386
Printed in the United States of America

First Printing

For more information or to order additional books,
please contact:
RoseDog Books
701 Smithfield Street
Third Floor
Pittsburgh, Pennsylvania 15222
U.S.A.
1-800-834-1803
www.rosedogbookstore.com

The Ice Cream Supper Miracle

"Guess what! Guess what!" I yelled to Grandma and Pa as I burst through the screen door into the kitchen where Grandma was beatin' chocolate cream frostin' for Pa's favorite cake coolin' on the sideboard."

"There's gonna' be an ice cream supper. See, I've got a flyer right here and they're puttin' ' em up all over the county. Ya oughta see the fence posts, bet ever one has a flyer on it and they're all colors. Jillions of colors. Look! I picked out a blue one."

I danced 'round the kitchen table chantin' the exciting news. "An ice cream supper. An ice cream supper."

"Ice cream social, honey," Grandma smiled.

"Yeah, there's gonna' be one."

Her and Pa smiled at one another.

"Choat's cows are all down by the road starin' at all them flyer's and one of the bulls is standin' there pawin' the ground and bellerin' at a red one. He sure is mad. Do ya s'pose cows can read just a little, Pa?"

"I doubt it sprout," he murmured absently.

He was smokin' his pipe contentedly, watchin' Grandma ice the cake and I was standin' behind his chair with my head draped over his shoulder.

"Jeepers, I screeched," I almost forgot the best part. Guess where it's gonna be. You'll never guess where it's gonna be."

"May as well save my breath then," Pa chuckled, reachin' out to snag me as I circled the table once more.

"Try, Try!" I laughed happily. "You too, Grandma."

"Well, let's see," she began, "Is it at…?"

But I couldn't hold the news a second longer. "It's at Pig's house. Can ya imagine? It's at Pig's house. Boy is he lucky," I laughed excitedly, hookin' a finger through the chocolate frostin'.

"Just where I was gonna guess it would be," said Grandma smugly.

"Let me see that flyer, young lady," Pa said, "before it's in shreds." He began to read out loud. "An ice cream social will be held at the Walter Lawrence farm, south of Tunnel Hill, July 4th at 7pm. Fireworks at 10pm."

"Fireworks!"

"Must be an echo in here Net," Pa laughed."Fireworks is what it says here kiddo."

"Who's puttin' it on? asked Grandma.

"Says here it's the Baptist church."

"They're in bad need of a roof, I know that," Grandma observed, swirlin' globs of frostin' into fancy loops. "Emily says it leaks somethin' awful."

"You don't say," Pa murmured, his eyes still on the cake.

"She said they have a dozen buckets settin' all over the place ever time it rains."

"Now thats a shame, Net. We have barn raisins' and house raisins' all the time, no reason we can't have a roof repairin'."

"No reason a'tall, " Grandma said, pattin' Pa on the back.

I had the strangest feelin' that the Lord and Grandma had planned this conversation all along. She had a habit of takin' the long way 'round to reach the short end of somethin', and it seemed to always get her to where she was goin'. At that time in my life God was a grand, mysterious being - who lived beyond the clouds past the deepest blue of the sky that my eyes could see - whose power was beyond my ability to imagine; but I felt safe and secure in his love cause he and Grandma were personal friends and I was Grandma's precious child'.

Next day me and Pig put our heads together, marked the calender and made a long list of all the excitin' games and activities that made ice cream suppers so popular with kids and grownups alike. Friends, neighbors and kin would come from many miles away to catch up on the news, wonder over the new babies, and inquire for those folks that had died in their absence. They would reminisce on the loved one, sharin' memories and funny happenins' stored up over a lifetime, their laughter and their tears mingling in a joyous memorial to the deceased. I'd sit and listen, enthralled with the wonderful stories and wonder what they might say about me if I died. Try as I might, I couldn't come up with much of anything that would interest anybody.

Room for the visitors would be made in various houses and they'd stay a few days before making the long trip back to their own homes.

"It's a whole week till the fourth," Pig moaned.

The days slowed their normal passage and began to creep along like sorghum mollasses on a winter mornin'. To kill time we talked incessantly of all the goins' on, made long lists of all the games that would be played, like Andy over, Fox and dog, softball, hoop and paddle and my favorite, football, where somebody most always got hurt, or worse still got a broken arm or leg.

Pa and Grandma had put their foot down on football since I was knocked out my first game, so I had to content myself with runnin' up and down the field screamin' encouragement to Pig and our team. To lessen the severity of my disappointment, Grandpa took two tin cans, put a handful of pebbles in them and the racket they made rattled the opposin' teams nerves and was enough to wake the dead, as Grandma put it. A year later Pa added two cowbells to my arsnel which made the fracas might-nigh unbearable and caused such anxiety among the cows some of them stopped givin' milk.

The fourth dawned clear and sunny and by noon it was a scorcher. We were all up at the Lawrence farm settin' up long tables, with new lumber laid across saw horses. The Baptist preacher was there and asked the Lord's blessin' on the social and 'specially on that lumber that would later be used to shore up the roof. He also asked the Lord for enough money from the social, to buy the shingles and I knew from the happy smile on his face, he expected the Lord would provide the shingles also. From that time on I began to think of the Lord as one big, endless storehouse.

"How come everbody asks the Lord for everthing?" I asked Grandma.

"Well, not everybody gets what they ask for," she said, raisin' her bonnet to stare thoughtfully out over the fields dancin' drunkenly in the heat waves,"Cause they ask wrongly. If we live as the Bible tells us to live and obey the commandments, then the Lord provides our need, no matter what it is. The big word here, honey, is IF. Obedience first, provision second."

"I sure do want a bicycle for Christmas," I said.

"There's another important word, child," she said seriously. "Want."

"I think I need one, Grandma, cause I walk my legs off sometimes gettin' where I wanna go and with a bicycle I could get there faster and it would be more fun too." I hung my head. "Guess I just used the want word again. Reckon the Lord's not interested in how much fun I have."

"Oh, but He is child. He wants not only the best for us but also what makes us happy. HE don't just provide enough to keep body and soul together but heaps His riches on us accordin' to His grace."

"Well, if He could see his way clear for me to have a bicycle, I'd sure appreciate it."

"Then why don't you just talk to Him about it tonite when yer prayin'." she said, smoothin' the oilcloth table covers over the rough lumber..

I walked to the barn scratchin' my head where my straw hat had chaffed it, thinkin' on all Grandma had said. Maybe I would talk to the Lord about that bicycle, then again, maybe I wouldn't. What if I caught Him in a bad mood from bein' pestered by wants from folks that didn't need. It'd be just my luck to ask at the wrong time and then I'd stand out in his mind forever as that wantin' Fitzgerald kid. I decided to bide my time and lay low for awhile, at least till the church roof was done. When I got to the barn Pig and his dad were loadin' apple crates in the wagon to be put around the yard for folks to set on.

"Only six more hours," I told Pig happily, "and we'll be stuffin' ourselves with ice cream.

"Yeah, but what'er we gonna do till then?"

"Well, there's swimmin'. We can take a bar of soap and kill two birds with one stone. All we'll have to wash when we get home is our feet."

"Yer always thinkin', kid," he grinned.

I helped them set the crates up 'round the yard then me and Pig trotted off down the road toward the lake. When we got to Inez Shaeffer's house she was settin in the porch swing with jillions of rollers in her hair. Anyone older than me and Pig would have sent her screechin' 'outa sight. Course ole Pig was only a year younger than her but he never made eyes at the girls, and that in Inez's oponion, put him just a few years past infancy.

I was no threat cause I wore overalls, let my hair hang natural and never bit my lips nor pinched my cheeks to make them red. Poor Inez was trapped under all that platinum hair, a pretty face and a closed mind. She'd stopped bein' a little girl with her first peek in a mirror and I felt sorry for all the fun she was missin'.

"Come for a swim with us ," I invited.

She looked shocked but managed a smile. "Not today. My hair's done up for tonight and I wouldn't want to get it dirty. Is your mom doing your hair?" she asked pointedly.

"Nah. Just a brush and a few licks with the curlin' iron, I reckon."

"What are you wearin', Helen Ruth?" she asked sweetly.

"Overalls," I replied.

Her eyes swept over me with pity then she smiled sweetly. "Momma got me a pink lace dress from that new shop in Marion and you wouldn't believe how much it cost." She sighed as though the weight of the world was on her shoulders and a dress that expensive would be more than she could bear.

"I'll bet it's pretty," I smiled as me and Pig walked on toward the lake.

"Who does she think she is?" Pig said angrily.

"Don't pay her no mind, Pig. She's at that silly age and can't help herself. Look how hifalutin' her mom is, not that I'm faultin' her for that cause she's really a nice lady... but I reckon Inez just naturally had to pick up some of that."

"I don't care how many excuses ya make for her," he grumbled. "She was bein' 'uppity, no two ways 'bout it."

"Well, it don't bother me none. I'd rather have fun than set around worryin' 'bout my hair all the time." I stared at Pig. "Can ya picture me all done up in curls and bows, settin' prim and proper on a chair pretendin' to be a lady when I'd rather be out playin' all them fun games that will be there tonight?"

"Horrible picture," he agreed. "Sides, I like ya just the way ya are. I specially like ya bein' my best friend."

"Blood friends to the end," I replied solemnly.

We left the road and crawled under a barbed wire fence into Bowman's pasture and took a deeply rutted cattle path that twisted like a serpent down the hill. At the bottom of the hill the lake shimmered in the hot sun, its cool water beckoning to us. We broke into a run, laughin' and screamin' joyously, with not a worry in the world, blissfully happy in our innocence. Friends to the end was what we swore one day; Pig carefully cuttin' the end of my finger, then his own. We joined our blood together in an everlastin' bond of friendship.

That afternoon we got to the Lawrence farm early so the grownups could get started with the preparations. A couple dozen dairy milk cans were clustered in a circle and a truck from the Harrisburg ice company was backed in beside them. I heard the driver tell a farmer that he had over a thousand pounds of ice on the truck. Course he'd stay for the doin's since the ice couldn't be kept outside the truck. All the kids would get their share of ice chips when they started packin' the freezers, and we enjoyed that almost as much as the ice cream itself.

The women were fillin' wash tubs with milk and sugar and dozens of eggs and with both Mr. Watkins and Mr. Raleighs vanilla, then stirrin' the rich mixture into a smooth, creamy confection. As fast as they mixed up a tubful, the men laddled it into the freezers and began packin' ice and salt 'round it. When they turned the cranks the cannisters would grate and rattle and hang up on big pieces of ice till a smoothe ice wall formed then it would settle into a soft raspin' hum.

Grandma slipped me and Pig a glass full of the delicious cream then shooed us away. "No time to have young'uns underfoot," she grumbled with a twinkle in her eyes. By then people were comin' in droves and we searched every face, wonderin' who they were and how far they'd come. There was a lot of laughter and huggin' and kissin' as families renewed old friendships and were reunited with loved ones. The men unloaded freezers and cakes and pies and the women tied aprons around themselves as they hurried to help with the mixin.'

Pig wandered off with Ray Neely but I was havin' too much fun watchin' all the activity so I crawled up in a wagon and perched on the seat where I had a birdseye view of everthing. The long tables were nearly full and folks sat here and there on th' apple crates catchin' up on the news, their ears tuned hungrily to the sound of ice cream bein' made.

I finally tired of the talkin' and wandered down toward the apple orchard where it was cool and shady and I could set on a limb and dream of the fun we'd have in a short time. Suddenly I heard angry voices and slipped behind a tree to listen. Grandma always said people who eavesdrop, hear no good of themselves. After listinin' to them a few minutes I sure believed that now, but what I saw when I peered around th' tree sent me hurryin' for Pa.

"Come quick, Pa! Pig and Ray are down in the orchard tryin' to kill each other."

"That's pretty serious kiddo. What're they fightin' about anyway?"

"Well, it's kinda silly," I hedged.

"I've been known to enjoy somethin' silly now and then," he drawled.

"Well, ya know they're auctionin' off a cake for the prettiest girl tonight."

"Heard about that," he smiled.

"Ray said Inez Shaeffer is the prettiest girl in the county and he's gonna bid on the cake for her."

"Sounds reasonable. She's pretty alright."

"But theres more, Pa."

"I'm listenin' kiddo."

"Well, Pig said Helen Ruth's a pretty girl too, and.... Ray laughed real big at that and said I look like a freckle faced, skinny, long legged colt"

"I'm sorry you heard that honey. Did Ray know you were there?"

"No. I heard them talkin' and stayed behind a tree, but the minute he said that ole Pig lit into him."

All this time Pa's walkin fast thru the orchard with me trottin' to keep up with his long legs.

"Ray's a sight bigger than Pig," he said, "and..."

"But Pa," I interrupted, "Pig thinks he can lick anybody, even Joe Louis,"

"Well, I reckon the boy's a mite short on common sense, but ya can't fault 'im on courage."

At that time of year it was still bright day even at seven-thirty in the evening; but the sun was already castin' long shadows through the apple trees, and smearin' crimson streaks all over a sky full of clouds. Pa was squintin' at the shadows, his eyes dartin' here and there lookin' for the culprits.

"There they are Pa," I yelled excitedly, pointin' to a pile of flailin' arms and legs sprawled on the ground, "but looks like ole Pig's doin' the killin'," I said in disbelief.

"Reckon ole Joe might have a worry or two at that," Pa chuckled as he began pullin' Pig off Ray.

"I reckon so," I laughed happily, bustin' with pride for brave ole Pig whose courage exceeded his common sense.

"Well boy," Pa said to Ray, kneelin' down for a close look at the damage, "looks to me like you'll be fine in a day or two. You got nothin' worse than a bunged up nose which I reckon you probably had comin' to ya for sayin' Helen Ruth looks like a colt."

Ray's shocked face turned deep red as he looked sheepishly at Pa, then at me.

"I reckon you owe my Grandaughter an apology son. Ya know, it's mighty hurtful for a young lady to hear such a remark, 'specially from a handsome lad like yerself."

I could see ole Ray caught that handsome part. He mumbled a sorry in my direction, and Pig bristled angrily, since he felt ole Ray was insincere. Pig sure looked a sight with his spike hair pointin' in ever direction, blood on his hands and dirt all over his overalls.

Pa was still squatin' by Ray. "I expect son," he drawled thoughtfully, "you've had an unkind remark or two 'bout them ears of yours."

"Yes sir, I have," Ray admitted, a startled look on his face.

"I thought so," Pa mused. "But to my way of thinkin'," he said seriously, "they'er fine lookin' ears and thats a fact."

"Ya think so, Mr Hundley?" asked Ray in astonishment.

"I do indeed." He studied Ray's ears with great interest, with me and Pig holdin' our breath waitin' for some great revelation. Finally he spoke and not even a leaf on the apple trees made a flutter .

"I'd say they're a lot like Ceasar Agustus' ears. Ya know 'bout Cesar I'm sure," Pa said matter of factly. "He was known fer his noble head, ya know. I reckon they made thousands of busts of his head; still do to this day and you can see them in a museum if you ever get to the big city."

"Is that a fact, sir" Ray stammered.

"Sure as day follows night," declared Pa.

I took another look at Ray's ears but they still looked like elephant ears to me.

"Now, you take my rather good size nose," Pa smiled. "Some folks have likened it to a donkey's nose, but I'm mighty proud of my nose, since some of the most Royal of Royals had noble noses of generous proportions. Did ya know that, son?" he asked Ray conversationally.

"I never did, Mr Hundley."

"Well, I don't care what anybody says Pa, I've always admired yer nose."

"Very nice nose, Mr. Hundley," Pig agreed.

Ray grinned up at Pa. "I've never seen a nicer nose on anybody, Mr. Hundley."

"Well, I sure do thank ye all for the nice compliments," Pa smiled, puffin his pipe thoughtfully "but I think it's time for a nice bowl of ice cream all around... that is after you boys make a stop at the water trough to clean up."

Ray got off the ground and brushed at his overalls and Pig just stood there sayin' nothin'.

"Back in the days of knights and gentlemen," Pa said soberly, "a fight usually ended with a handshake, unless one of the combatants was dead, of course; but you lads look to have a few more years ahead of ye, so I reckon a handshake will show ye to be of noble intent."

I was about to get sick over all that noble stuff Pa was talkin' on, specially since I couldn't see a speck of change in ole Ray; but to my surprise Ray reached out his hand and Pig took it. They both had silly smiles on their face as we walked out of the orchard toward that bowl of ice cream bein' cranked that very minute in one of the dozens of ice cream freezers from all over the county.

After we'd eaten two big bowls of ice cream apiece, the kids all got together to start the games, knowin' one of the main events was a couple of hours down the road. 'Course that was the big auction for the cake that everbody was talkin' about.

Inez Shaeffer was dazzlin' in pink lace, her platinum hair piled on top of her head in curly splendor. She sure was pretty settin' there all prim and proper on her chair, waitin' her turn on the stage of excitement. Ray, of course was goggle eyed and even ole Pig had an admirin' look on his face.

"Ya oughta bid on that cake for Inez, Pig," I told him.

"Are ya silly or somethin?' he sputtered.

"What's silly 'bout sharin that cake with Inez?" I replied.

"Well, nothin', I guess, 'cept I don't think I'd enjoy that a lot."

"Never know till ya try," I said casually.

"Knock it off, kid," he said irritably. "If I had all the money in' th' world I wouldn't buy that cake fer Inez and have to set fer an hour listenin' to her act growed-up."

Soon, Inez and the cake were forgotten as we played our hearts out, yellin' and screamin' at each other. No one got hurt in the football game and I was itchin' to get in it, but Grandma was keepin' a watchful eye in my direction and I knew Pa was lurkin' somewhere closeby.

The football game finally came to an end with Pig's team barely squeakin' to victory. He limped off the field and sprawled in the grass, exhausted and dirty, but happy our team had finally won a game. They'd skunked us the past two years runnin' and a powerful lot of bad feelins' had built up.

"Boy, that was some game," he laughed, " but if we'd had you in there kid it wouldn't have taken so long to win."

"Maybe next year Grandma will let me play," I replid sadly.

"My bet is she'll never let ya play 'cause she likes yer face the way it is." He looked at me critically. "I can just see ya with cauliflower ears, a split lip and smashed nose. Imagine Inez lookin' like that," he giggled.

"With all that platinum hair piled on her head and a flower behind her ear," I added. We fell on the ground and laughed 'till our sides ached.

"You fergot the pink dress," he screamed, rollin on the grass.

Finally, he hauled hisself off the ground and held his hand out to me. "Let's go drown ourselves in ice cream, kid."

We made a bee line for Grandpa Lawrence who was dishin' out five cent bowls full of ten cents worth of ice cream ."A nickle a bowl fer this fine cream," he said, "and mighty generous helpins' too, I might add. I reckon yer two nickles might buy a couple of them shingles fer the church roof," he beamed at me and Pig.

We stood there uncertainly, not sayin' a word, while he eyed us suspiciously.

"You younguns' got any money," he frowned.

"No sir," said Pig.

"As I recollect," he said pointedly to Pig, "you picked strawberries this year fer Coy McCuan and he was payin' three cents a box. Now that's good wages boy, so what did ye do with all that money.

"It's in my bank Grandpa. I been savin' up fer somethin' special."

"Well, I can't think on anything more special than the church roof... and you little miss," he said, eyen' me sternly. "Did you come fer a free ice cream handout like ye do fer Ma's chicken and dumplins'?"

"Well sir, I reckon I can go get a nickle from Pa."

"Never mind!" he said, dismissin' the subject. "This bowl's on the church, so to speak, and the next one's on yer Pa, little miss. And if yer still

hungry after that, then maybe I can scrape up a mite more. Now off with ya while I tend to my business."

We sat on the ground, our backs against a tree, and watched the activities. Jillions of lanterns hung from rope strung from tree to tree, their flickerin' light castin' scary shadows into the darkness, makin' the horses and wagons clustered in the field look like giant monsters creepin' outa the night. The long tables were crowded with folks from all over the county, who had come for the fellowship as much as the ice cream. Kids played around the tables, yellin' and makin' a nuisance of them-selves, stoppin' just long enough to grab a mouth full of ice cream.

"Hope yer Pa is as charitable as Grandpa," Pig said, lickin his spoon, "cause I'm still hungry."

"Don't see why not since it's on the church, so to speak," I giggled.

"What special thing are ya savin' up for, Pig ?"

"Oh, just somethin."

The Auction

Pa stepped up into one of the wagons that had been pulled to the front of the yard and for a long minute he looked out over the crowd with pure pleasure on his face, then he stomped his foot for silence. Laughter, loud talkin, and yellin' kids gradually dwindled off into silence as every eye turned to him.

"Well now, that's better," he twinkled. "Wouldn't guess right this very minute, with all this quiet, that there's a party goin' on, but there is and we're havin' a great time. Amen?"

A great shout of Amens rang out over the field and down into the wooded valley below. I'd have liked to be standin' at the schoolhouse on the far hill to see if I could hear it there.

"And this party's not over yet folks, not by a long shot. As a matter of fact, we're just beginnin'; but we've come to an important event and I reckon everbody, specially the young folks, can hardly wait to get it started."

In the wagon beside Pa, a couple of apple crates were holdin' somethin' big with a cloth coverin' it. Pa reached down and carefully removed the cloth, and the crowd gasped with admiration. It was the finest lookin' cake I'd ever seen and as big as a dishpan. Pa eyed the cake admiringly for a minute, then addressed the crowd.

"Ladies and gentlemen!" This beautiful cake was made by our own Amelia Dalton, -better known as Meelie- who's famous for her good-lookin' cakes as well as for her splendid tastin' cakes.

Pa turned a smilin' face on Amelia. "Stand up Amelia and let everbody see a prize cake maker."

There was thunderous applause of appreciation, and Amelia glowed, her face pink with happiness.

"Look at them wonderful roses there," Pa went on in amazement. "Why I'd swear them roses were growin' there of their own accord."

His gaze lingered on the roses. I looked over at Amelia and she was so puffed up by Pa's compliments, I thought she might bust. Her eyes sparkled in a face wrinkled and worn with age, but her wonderful smile made her look like a young girl again.

Pa had a knack for bringin' out the best in people and makin' them feel worthy, and I knew Amelia would live this moment over and over again for years to come. I looked at Pa standin' there in that wagon, tall and handsome, his face wreathed in good humor, eyes bright and lively and that Roman nose he claimed to be so proud of, and I knew I'd never love anybody more than Pa.

"Now, this cake's a work of art if I ever seen it, and it's purely a shame to eat this cake, but somebody's bound to, and I aim to see it don't go for a piddlin' amount to one of you cheap skates out there."

Everbody laughed.

"Yes sir, this cake's worth yer best effort gentlemen, so dig deep in yer pockets. After all this is for a good cause and I can't think of a cause more worthy than a new roof fer the Baptist church. 'specially since the pulpit's most always under water these days. Hear tell the Reverend's so nervous preachin' with all that water pourin' down on 'im, he's cuttin' his sermons short." Pa laughed heartily. "I guess there's a blessin' even in a leakin' roof."

The crowd roared agreement and several men slapped Reverend Moore on the back who was standin' off to the side, a big grin on his face, enjoyin Pa's banter as much as anybody.

"One of you pretty girls out there," Pa continued, "is gonna share this cake with the lad who has the most money.

They all laughed at that.

He looked appreciatevily at the cake. "Why, I just might bid on it for my own pretty girl. I don't want to hear no snickerin' from you young bucks neither. She's still my girl today as much as she ever was when I courted 'er.

The crowd cheered wildly, enjoyin' his nonsense.

"I'll bid twenty-five cents," someone in the crowd yelled.

Pa scowled in his direction. "Two of you able bodied men take that smart aleck down to the pond and feed 'im to the fish. Reckon that'll eliminate one cheapskate outa the bunch. Th' rest of you tight-fisted, penny-pinchin' lads better look alive; there's plenty of room in that pond fer the lot of ya."

A skuffle had broken out among the men and everbody broke into laughter and whistle's as one poor lad was dragged, kickin' and yellin' toward the pond. His body was suspended between two strappin' men, one holdin' his feet, the other his arms and just before they threw him in, he yelled, "I'll bid five dollars, Mr. Hundley."

"Hold it!" Pa ordered the executioneers. "Bring that lad back up here." They walked along side the young man as he shuffled thru' the crowd and stood before Pa.

"Did I hear ya say five dollars, son?"

"Yes sir," he mumbled, lookin' at the ground, "but... I maybe oughta said two instead but seein' that muddy pond gettin' closer and thinkin' on my new pants and all... I reckoned Ma would likely kill me if I muddied 'em, so my mouth up and said five when it should'a said two, but five's what my mouth said and five's what I'll bid."

11

Pa fell over on the wagon seat, laughin' so hard the wagon was shakin, and the whole crowd howled and carried on for five minutes. Finally Pa got hisself under control, wiped the tears outa his eyes and gazed admiringly on the young man who was shufflin' in embarrassment, his face a deep red. Pa jumped off the wagon and put his arm'round the lad's shoulder.

"Now here's a man who stands on his word, folks, even when his mouth over rules his common sense." More laughter broke out, but Pa went on talkin' over it and soon it was quiet again "And, to my way of thinkin', a man's word is his bond, and it's a right honorable thing to be known as a man of yer word. I'd be horored to shake yer hand son," he said, pumpin' the young man's hand vigorously.

Several ladies ran over and hugged the boy and the men reached out to clasp his hand as he made his way through the crowd.

"I have five dollars gentlemen, and I don't reckon that young man will be upset a bit if one of you makes it six. Who'll make it six? Yer buyin' shingles for the Lords house," he reminded them, "and while the biddin' started out a sight higher than expected, don't forget that when ye cast yer bread upon th' waters, it don't come back to you void." He gave Grandpa Lawrence a wicked smile. " I reckon them waters are a heap cleaner than that muddy pond of yers, Eli."

Pig's Grandpa laughed and shook his fist at Pa. Five-fifty was bid and Pa took it and started off again toward six dollars.

"Why, there's three dollars worth of frostin' on this cake," he said, "and at least two dollars worth of elbow grease to beat it up. Who'll give me six?"

I gasped as Ray yelled out, "Six dollars fer Inez Shaeffer, the prettiest girl in the county.

Inez fairly trembled in her lace dress and tried to look demure. There was a proud glitter in her eyes and I saw ole Pig kick the tree he was standin' by, then scowl at Ray. The price of the cake inched up a quarter at a time as various men bid on it for their favorite girls, until it reached seven dollars and fifty cents. That was a fortune for most anything sensible, but outrageous for a cake, even a fine rose covered cake. Emily's handkerchief fluttered nervously as she fanned herself, her mouth open in disbelief at the bidding on her masterpiece.

Then I nearly fell off my apple crate as a voice thundered, "Eight dollars on the prettiest girl in the world, Helen Ruth Fitzgerald." It had sounded like Pig's voice but it couldn't be. Pig never had eight dollars in his whole life. I shot a look at him and his lips weren't movin', so who said that? Then ole Pig looked Ray straight in the eye and smiled the biggest smile I'd ever seen and I knew it'd really been Pig, and my heart was hammerin' so hard I couldn't breathe and why on earth hadn't I worn a dress and curled my hair, for this was the most excitin' dream I'd ever had in my whole life, only it wasn't a dream and everybody was starin at me,'specially Inez ,whose face was frozen in shocked disbelief. Where did Pig get that kid of money, I wondered, my mind in a jumble. Was this the somethin' special he had saved up for? I tried desperately to add up how many boxes of strawberries at three cents a box, he had to pick for eight dollars.

Ray gave Pig a murderous look, the handshakes and noble intent of a few hours ago forgotten, then he yelled, "Eight-fifty."

"Nine dollars," Pig said so fast I thought I'd imagined it. Pig was outta his mind, no two ways 'bout it. He'd be workin the rest of his life to pay for that cake. I expected his mom and dad to swoop down on him any minute, but they were standin' off to the side with big grins on their faces.

But Grandpa Lawrences' heaped up dippin spoon was frozen in midair above Mrs. Jacksons' empty bowl, his mouth gaped open with shock and I could tell he was worried 'bout Pig's finances too.

Pa beamed on the two boys. "Looks like we got ourselves a horse race here folks. You men gonna let these youngsters outbid ya on this cake?" he chided.

"I come to bid on a cake, Mr. Hundley, not ta buy an automobile," someone yelled out.

"Me too, Mr. Hundley," said another voice.

"Them boy's aire outa their mind," opioned a weatherbeaten farmer.

"It's a powerful lot of money, and thats a fact," Pa agreed, "but it's fer a good cause and I reckon the Lord works in mysterious ways. The money for this cake, no matter who buys it will cover a fair size portion of that roof."

"I have nine dollars," Pa continued, his baritone voice piercing the nite, "do I hear nine-fifty?"

"Oh Lord," I prayed, let someone bid nine-fifty on that cake so Pig won't have ta go ta jail. I looked hopefully at Ray but defeat was spread all over his face as he looked longingly at Inez, the object of his undying love; but the object of his undyin' love gave him a scathing look then turned her attention to one of the several boys gathered 'round her. She'd turned her back on ole Ray and I doubted them boys she was now butterin' up to had enough money in their pockets to buy more than one bowl of cream.

"Do I hear nine-fifty for this splendid cake?" Pa asked the crowd.

You could have heard a pin drop, then Pa said, "Goin once," Goin' twice..."

There was a hushed silence as they waited for Pa to say Sold to Pig Lawrence. Every eye was turned on Pig, standin' there by the tree, a small grin on his face, when suddenly blood-curdlin' howls and screams of pain came from the direction of the orchard. Pa jumped off the wagon and started runnin', with a dozen men right behind him, but before they'd gone more that fifty yards, two of Pig's dogs burst from the orchard, yelpin' piteously and pawin' at their faces. The evenin' breeze had changed slightly and was now comin' from that direction, and on it was the most sickenin, stomach churnin' odor you could imagine.

"It's a pole cat, someone yelled; but the congregation already had the message and were scatterin' in ever direction. I can still see that scene in my

13

mind's eye as clear as day. Amelia was up in the wagon that Pa had just left, with the cake cloth spread protectively over her masterpiece. The Reverend was helpin various ladies up on the tables and Inez was just a flash of pink lace and platinum curls as she disappeared toward the cluster of wagons. Most of the men were high-tailin' it across the field to keep their horses from runnin' away. Grandpa Lawrence still stood by his ice cream freezer lookin' intently at the orchard and everbody left in the area was thankin' the good Lord that the dogs had taken off down the hill toward the creek.

Pa and his group had taken temporary refuge behind the barn. I stood on my apple crate and watched the orchard to see if the skunk might amble out toward the house but he must have kept goin' about his business in the other direction. It didn't matter anyway for the smell was unbearable and there was nothin' for it but to leave, which most of the crowd had already done.

I glanced at the tree where Pig and Ray had been standin' and Pig was still there, but Ray was gone. Grandma was standin' quietly by the tub where she'd been mixin' cream, lookin' out over the orchard. Her lips were movin' but I couldn't hear what she was sayin' from where I stood on my apple crate, then ole Pig turned and stared at her intently and I reckoned she must have said somethin' to him. Grandma and Pig stood there for several minutes, then Grandma went on about her business again as though nothin' unusual had happened.

I got off the apple crate and started to go look for Pa when the breeze picked up and on it was the most wonderful smell of roses I'd ever smelled. Amelia took her handkerchief from her nose and sniffed the air cautiously. The Reverend said thank the Lord and began helping the ladies off the tables and Pa and the men came from the barn lookin' strange and shakin' their heads. Grandpa Lawrence dropped his dippin' spoon on the table and ran to meet Pa.

"What happened, Almus?"

"Darned if I know. One minute it's polecat all over the place, the next thing I know the air is clean with roses on it.

"Well, I think it's mighty peculiar," one of the men said.

"That it be," Pa agreed, lookin' 'round as though he'd never been there before.

Grandpa Lawrence stared at the orchard, shakin' his head. "Something odd about this Almus. Skunk smell just don't disappear in a few minutes, you know that well as I do.

"That smell would be around for days," Pa agreed "and it'd cover a wide area, too. Why I've seen it cover a mile or two and last for days at a time." He turned to Grandpa Lawrence. "You got any wild roses growin' 'round here?"

"Nary a one. The only rose bush around here is that one growin' by the front step and as ya know, we didn't smell roses until that skunk come along. Besides, one rose bush couldn't stop a skunk smell." He studied Pa's face. "You got any ideas, Almus, on whats goin' on here?"

"Maybe, maybe not." Pa murmured.

Pig and a Sack of Stray Cats

The crowd gradually drifted back to their places, with everbody talkin' about the strange turn of events. The smell of roses was so heavy on the air you could almost taste them. I gulped that wonderful smell into my lungs 'till I was dizzy. Several people looked at the sky as though the answer might be there; but most of the crowd was huddled together in a big circle, their faces dazed and fearful. Pa climbed back in the wagon and looked for Reverend Moore.

"Pastor, would you come and address this situation and tell us what you think?"

The Pastor crawled into the wagon, his face somber.

"Ladies and gentlemen," he said, "I think we've seen a miracle here tonight."

"Did you pray for a miracle, Pastor?" someone asked.

"No, I was too busy to pray," he said sadly, "but someone here wasn't too busy and I'd give a lot to know who it was."

He looked out at the faces, waiting ," but no one stepped forward. "I'd say that it's fitting for such a prayer to remain private, known only to the person who uttered it" I will say it's the strangest miracle I've ever seen and if the good Lord sends roses to cover a polecat smell, at the request of one of his children, I'd say he's mighty pleased with that child. Since we're gathered here to raise money for the church roof, I believe this is an omen from the Lord. I hope that whoever uttered this prayer is a member of my church for we need such consecrated christians who live the Lords commandments."

About that time Pig's two dogs come runnin' around the house straight toward Pig. People began to scatter again, but ole Pig leaned down to pet them, then he stood up and grinned at everbody. "They smell like roses," he laughed happily.

The Reverend raised his arms upward and began to pray. From his mouth came the most beautiful words of praise and thanksgivin' for God's love I have ever heard. It seemed God's Spirit filled the air along with them roses and several people in the crowd began to pray also. I ran over to Grandma and grabbed her hand, standin' there amazed as the crowd lifted its voice in unified prayer. Those wondrous prayers drifted over the hills, and into the valleys, risin' up to the heavens in a glorious outpourin' of love to the Lord of us all. Grandma's hand tightened on mine and I fancied I could feel a special love runnin' from her hand to mine.

There were tears of joy on the upturned faces and someone started to sing Amazing Grace. No words can describe the sudden revival we had that night, in a field on top of a hill, under a star-studded sky, with a gentle breeze from the apple orchard laden with the scent of roses.

Finally the preacher raised his arms for silence and addressed the gathering. "Friends, there won't ever be an ice cream supper the likes of what we've seen here tonight. Truly we've seen the hand of God touch this humble people that have come together to fellowship and raise money to repair His house of worship. Someone's faith touched the heart of God tonight and He responded to that faith. It's the kind of faith we all should have; indeed Miracles should be as natural as breathing and I'm sure that each and everyone will leave here tonight with a renewed heart and much pondering; but this party isn't over by a long shot for we still have a cake to be awarded to the prettiest girl, so I'll turn this over to Mr. Hundley and let him get on with the auction.

Pa stood there silent for a moment then he spoke. "After what we've been privileged to witness here tonight, a cake don't seem very important; but it is and the good Lord wants his children to enjoy themselves. Now I've got nine dollars on this magnificent cake, and I was about to say Sold to Pig lawrence for the prettiest girl in the world when that polecat got in the act. So, unless I hear a mighty fast bid from one of you gents... then this here cakes sold to Pig Lawrence for the grande sum of nine dollars for the prettiest girl in all the world, Helen Ruth Fitzgerald. The crowd cheered and cheered and I wanted to fall in a hole someplace since ever eye was on me but ole Pig had already made his way to me and had me by the hand. He walked me to the wagon and we stood there while Amelia cut a huge piece of that scrumptious cake for me and pig. We took our cake and sat on two apple crtes under a tree.

"Am I really pretty, Pig," I asked curiously, forkin' up a big bite of Amelias masterpiece with half of one them roses on it.

He looked at me critically for a minute. "Yeah... yer pretty e'nuff."

"Cross your heart and hope to die?"

Cross my heart and hope to die" he replied solemnly.

"Well I'll be switched," I mused, astonished.

"Now look here," he said, his face puckered in a frown, "Don't ya go actin' like a girl on me. We're blood friends to the end but that don't allow fer goofy dresses and big bows in yer hair and settin' in a chair all day pinchin yer cheeks and talkin' silly girl talk."

"Not to worry," I assured him, lettin' ever minute of the past hour run through my mind in joyous triumph. It sure had been a wonderful day, swimmin' in the lake, playin' games, Pig defendin' me to Ray, jillions of bowls of ice cream, not to mention the polecat and now the cake for the prettiest girl in all the world. I sighed happily. It would live in my memory 'till my dyin' day.

"Hurry up with that cake kid," Pig said excitedly, "they're startin' a game of fox and hound

After the Miracle

News of the miracle spread like poison ivy from one end of the county to the other and I reckoned it might get to chicago before too long. Word of mouth soon turned the miracle into an event comparable to Moses partin' the red sea. To my way of thinkin' it ranked right up there with it and I wondered what ole Moses would have done with a polecat cuttin' loose in his back yard.

Reporters from the Vienna Times, the Harrisburg Register and ever newspaper in that end of the state swarmed all over the Lawrence farm lookin' for clues like rose bushes and such. The farm still had a slight rose smell to it and Pig's ole flop-eared houndogs positively reeked with roses. They became stars overnight with folks pattin' them on the head so much Pig feared they'd end up addled in the brain. Hundreds of pictures were made of everthing on the farm, specially the dogs. Grandma Lawrence grumbled she couldn't take her early mornin' coffee on the front porch anymore cause there was a reporter with a camera behind ever tree.

One lady came to the farm and insisted on sniffin' every animal on the place but when she got to the pig pen she allowed as how the Lord had bypassed everthing 'cept the dogs.

Grandpa Lawrence declared that if one more person come lookin' for clues and sniffin his animals, he'd personally show them off his property. Got to where he couldn't open his mouth but what it was in the Vienna Times. Finally he put a "NO TREPASSIN" sign up on the gate down at the end of the road and locked it with a big chain.

Reverend Moore's church was runnin' over with strangers ever Sunday come to stare at him and the faithful. He was beside hisself with joy, givin' long invitations to come forward and surrender their souls to the Lord and a few did, which was cause for much rejoicin'. The Reverend was a happy man. He told Pa he didn't even mind when the strangers would lean close as they shook his hand to see if they could get a whiff of roses. Pa told him he ought to buy a bottle of Rose scent and wash his hands in it and the good Reverend blushed and said that very thought had crossed his mind. The roof was about finished what with all the extra help they got after the miracle. Pa said one day they had more help than shingles and he feared the roof might cave in.

Tunnel Hill, a halfmile down the hill from the church had become a hub of activity. There was so much traffic on the gravel road everybody was chokin' on the dust. People poured in from all over the state, as far away as chicago, takin' pictures, buyin' souviners and sniffin' the air for roses. Uncle Fate's store was doin' a landslide business sellin' everthing from alladin lamps to penny candy. One city slicker bought a plow from Uncle Fate and when Fate asked him where he was gonna use it, he said, "I'm going to exhibit it on a rock in my front yard in chicago with a bronze plate on the rock saying, "From the land of miracles." Uncle Fate swore under his breath and told Aunt Ann he'd never in his life seen such a waste of good equipment. "Wish I had a horse to sell the fool," he muttered.

Aunt Ann admonished him on callin' someone a 'fool'. "You know what the Lord says about that Fate." Aunt Ann was an angel everbody loved and respected and some folks thought she might have just dropped down from heaven one day when nobody was noticin', just to redeem Uncle Fate. Some allowed as how Uncle fate was a terrible cross to bear and only a Godly person like Aunt Ann was up to it.

OK Hodges store, compared to Uncle Fate's jot-em-down store was Sears Roebuck and Montgomery Ward all rolled into one. Hodges couldn't keep anything on the shelves and like The Reverend Moore, Mr. Hodge was an extremely happy man.

One day a man picked his way through the litter of Uncle Fate's store and inquired about a waterin' hole. Uncle Fate told him there was a pump out back if he cared to use it.

"No, No, he finally said in plain English. I'm talking about a saloon or tavern or whatever you call it in these parts.

Fates small eyes, recessed under brows thick enough to braid, regarded the city slicker with scorn then led him to the door. "Tunnel Hill don't have no such places as that. Besides Ann here wouldn't put up with it." Then his eyes twinkled omniously, "but ye can follow this road to its end, 'bout a mile or so down the way there, then take a footpath up into the woods to a shack up there. They'll serve ya all ya can drink. Cheap too."

The man got as far as the road when Uncle Fate called to him. "Almost fergot, son. Better have yer gun loaded and slip in there easy like, 'lessen ya know the pass word; else them Kern's boys 'ull shoot ya first and ask no questions later.

Me and Pig spent a lot of time in the Tunnel watchin' the city folk buy stuff they didn't need, and listenin' to the endless questions they asked everbody.

"Sure wish I knew who prayed for that miracle," I said to Pig one day.

"Guess a lot of folks would like to know that," he said.

"Well, aren't you curious?" I asked.

"I been givin' that a lot of thought," he replied.

"So's half the state from the looks of it," I laughed.

"I've got a nickle," he smiled,"let's go to Hodges and get us a candy bar."

"Let's go to Uncle Fate's instead, we'll buy one and Aunt Ann will give us one."

"Uncle Fate won't make any money that way, kid."

"Not on candy," I laughed, "but he does on other things. Sides, Aunt Ann says storin' up treasure in heaven is a sight more important than puttin' it away down here."

Pig sighed and shook his head. "It's a good thing yer Aunt's not in the store all the time, else he'd have a store with nothin' in it."

Next day me and Pa was up at one of the little hole-in-the-wall stores on the other side of the tracks on that goat path they call a road, accordin' to Grandpa Lawrence. It was so narrow I always scrunched close to Pa's side to keep from seein' the ravine below.

"What can I do fer ya, Almus," asked Mr. Verble, his tall thin body folded over the counter like a wet towel.

"Just a can of prince albert today, Dave."

Pa glanced out the door at the dust hangin' over the railroad tracks . "Sure is busy 'round here these days," he said.

"Yep! It's mighty good fer business but hard on the lungs sometimes. Never seen so many people runnin' about, askin' questions, peepin' in windows and sniffin' the air like hound dogs. Sometimes I laugh 'till my sides ache at the crazy antics goin' on. I'm not complainin', mind ya. Business is good and I already made myself fifteen dollars today and its only three o'clock," he beamed. "They'll start walkin' all over the Tunnel after the sun gets low. I've sure sold a heap of soda pop, it bein' so hot and all. Ya know Almus, one of the nicest things about this is to have so many folks settin' out on the porch again, sippin pop and talkin' to each other."

"I noticed you've put a lot of extra chairs out there," Pa smiled. "Give me and Helen here a pop and we'll try them chairs out fer a spell."

Mr Verble laughed happily. Will ya be havin' yer usual RC Almus? He didn't wait for an answer. Of course, Helen will want her favorite orange crush, he chuckled to himself, elbow deep in the ice water of the big soft drink case "I'll just join ya and we'll watch the slickers go by. Ya know, Almus, what we need around here is a nice miracle ever three years or so. Mebbe have the next one right here in ole Tunnel Hill itself."

"Do ya suppose we could stand the strain?" Pa laughed

A few days later I was settin' on the porch of Nippers store with Aunt Ann when a big shiny car came to a stop and a man in funny black clothes and a peculiar cap got out and opened the back door for a lady dressed in the prettiest dress I'd ever seen. The tall man held her arm carefully as she swept into the store leavin' a trail of lucious perfume in her wake. I almost blacked out from takin' so many deep breaths.

"Do you have that scent in the store?" I whispered to Aunt Ann.

"I'm afraid not child. I imagine you could buy a good horse for what that perfume cost."

"Jeepers!" I gasped.

"Guess I best go in and wait on the lady," Aunt Ann said, her blue eyes twinklin' merrily. "I don't expect shes ever been exposed to anyone like Fate before."

The lady didn't seem to mind the clutter or the boards formin' walks on the dirt floor or the dark corners that always sent shivers down my back. She walked slowly along the cluttered shelves, a rapturous look on her face, her oh's and ah's mixed with chuckles of delight. The tall gentleman hovered close by as she made her selections, whiskin' them off the shelves and back to the counter where Uncle Fate watched in open mouth delight. The counter was soon filled with this and that and the other, as Grandma always said.

"I love these quaint old lamps," the lady mused, referrin' to an alladin lamp.

We were amazed at that since it was the latest thing and anyone who had one was up there, so to speak, and if you owned two, well you were a notch above the average, no two ways 'bout it.

She had a bottle of each scent from the cologne display, several packets of safety pins and needles with a popular red apple pincushion. There were a half dozen straight razors with fancy pearl handles, six shiny razor strops and six of Fates best shavin' mugs that must have cost at least fifty cents a piece. Uncle Fate positively glowed at the stack of growin' items that kept the tall gentleman hoppin' back and forth. She walked around all the shelves at least three times then glanced about longingly and sighed.

"I simply would love to have one of everything in here," she smiled. "This is the most charming store I've ever seen and the whole little community is just enchanting."

Well, she sure had enchanted Fate with that piled up counter. He had pencil and tablet ready to add it all up but he was careful not to hurry the lady in case she'd forgotten anything.

"I do wish I could take some large item back with me for George though," she murmured wistfully. "It's his birthday, you know." Then she laughed like a little child. "I must break this habit of thinking out loud. George is my husband," she explained.

Aunt Ann murmured somethin' appropiate; but Uncle Fate had a lapse of common sense, forgot he was in the presence of gentility, opened his mouth and put both feet in it.

"Ye oughta take one of them miracle horses from the Lawrence farm back with ye," Fate said "Put a sign 'round its neck. This horse don't eat, don't drink, don't sleep, and works hard.".

The lady was incredulous. "Is that a fact?" she asked wonderingly.

"Yep!" said Fate. "Eli ain't got many of 'em left though; but iffen ye hurry..."

Delighted, the lady exclaimed, "Thank you so much, Mr. Nipper. As soon as I'm finished here I'll go right out there."

She circled all the shelves once more then smiled sweetly at Uncle Fate.

"You may talley my purchases, Mr. Nipper and Charles will settle the bill with you."

She walked toward the door, just bustin' with happiness. "George will be so thrilled with a miracle horse," she said, thinkin' out loud again.

Aunt Ann gave Uncle Fate a witherin' look and jerked her head in the direction of the departing lady.

Fate cleared his throat loudly, then spoke reluctantly "Madam!"

The lady turned to him inquiringly.

"I forgot to tell ya one other thing, maam."

"What's that, Mr. Nipper?"

"That miracle horse'll be dead in two weeks less you feed and water it regular."

There was a stunned silence as the lady stared at Uncle Fate in confusion. It was the only time I ever saw Fate at a complete loss for words. Aunt Ann hurried to the lady, her smiling blue eyes tryin' to smoothe everything out.

"My dear, forgive my husband," she said, givin' Uncle Fate a reprovin' look. " He does so love a joke now and then and I'm sure he saw that wonderful sense of humor you have under that elegant appearance." She stared in sincere admiration at the lady's dress. "My, I've never in my life seen such a wonderful frock as that and..." she paused, hands clasped to her bosom in an attitude of rapture, her angelic face glowin'. "And that incomparable matchin' hat." Aunt Ann faked an abject look of envy, which was not altogether fake as she enthused, "Why, from the looks of it I'd say it's a Paris creation."

"How ever did you know?" exclaimed the lady in startled surprise.

Aunt Ann's face fell into sad remembrance. "There was a time, my dear, when I..." her voice trailed sadly away into yesteryear.

The lady clasped Ann's hand in a gesture of sympathy. The haves consoling the have-nots. "I knew you were a lady of quality the instant I laid eyes on you my dear. What a pity you're stuck in... that is to say, you seem to have dedicated your life unselfishly to some cause." She looked around for a worthy cause and seeing only Uncle Fate, she fluttered her hands vaguely in the air and allowed the tall gentleman in the funny clothes to assist her to the porch.

Aunt Ann followed, a bemused smile on her face. They clasped hands lightly, as society ladies do, said Aunt Ann later, then she climbed into the back seat of the biggest car I'd ever seen. It was twice as long as Uncle Bill's Emerald Green Packard and when I asked Ann about that she told me the lady from Chicago was ridin' in a limousine.

"Why, you could get five or six people in that car and not be crowded at all," I said in astonishment.

"Yes, you could, but a limousine is sort of a status symbol as well as transportation."

"What's a status symbol?"

"Well, I guess you could say it's the difference between a throughbred horse and a billy goat," she laughed.

"Jeepers! The man in the funny clothes, who is he?"

He's called a chauffer and he drives the lady and her family wherever they want to go and helps her in and out of the car and just makes life convenient and plesant for her."

"Would you like a limousine and chauffer to make life convenient and plesant for you Aunt Ann?" I asked worriedly, lookin' 'round the shabby, dusty porch and dirt street.

"My child," she said seriously, "I'm the richest lady in the world in all the things that count. I have friends and dear Fate, whom I love very much and I have a precious ray of sunshine. When I looked puzzled, she laughed. "It's you dear child. You're like my own."

I thought on all she'd said for a long time, then looked at her gentle, sweet face which reflected her loving, generous nature, and suddenly I felt rich too.

"That lady sure spoke the truth," I said.

"What truth, dear?"

"You are a lady of quality Aunt Ann and I'm glad yer my kin."

She gathered me in her arms, planted a kiss on the top of my head and suggested we go in and have a candy bar and a bottle of pop on Uncle Fate.

Pig and a Sack of Stray Cats

Me and Pig went to school together, back in the thirties, in a one room school house set back in a clearin' fringed with woods full of Maple, and Ash, and Sassafras, and Hickory, and wonderful ancient Oaks for climbin' and hidin' in; or just for day dreamin' on a friendly old limb twenty foot off the ground where no one in the whole world knew where we were, and even if they did they couldn't get at us. Pig would slouch on his limb which was five foot higher than mine -just to show he was more growed up than me- and we'd talk about everything from Goddard's Cow gettin' stuck in the pond to Choat's chickens bein' killed by a weasel. Pig would allow as how a weasel was a nasty tempered animal.

"Kills for the enjoyment of it," he announced gravely. "A quick bite through the brain and on to the next."

Word pictures raced through my mind in horrifyin' sequence of dozens of dead chickens lyin' in clumps every where, their feathers movin' gently in the breeze, some driftin' aimlessly about the yard as though seeking the lifeless body from which they had been savagely torn. I'd shiver and imagine what it would be like to be a chicken.

To this day, I can still feel the rough bark of that old Oak against my back; feel the warm dopples of sun jiggin' and dancin' through the leaves, flashin' magic dazzles all over our skin and clothes. So, this story and a hundred more just like it, untold, is about me and Pig, and farms and cattle, and clear runnin' creeks to swim and wade in, and it's about sweet years of growin' up in the country where the air was pure and the crystal skies were scrubbed to a blue gloss by mountains of white clouds.

On the banks of the windin' road that led to the Sandburn schoolhouse, there grew honeysuckle so dense and lush you could have burrowed down and hid in it if you'd wanted to. No one ever did though, for its heavy, sweet blossoms drew thousands of bees whose dronin' sounds quivered in the air above the dusty road like curdled cream.

Butterflies were so numerous you could spend hours chasin' them on their erratic flight through green pastures and prairie grasses dressed extravagantly in glorious wild flowers, whose colors were clumps of rainbow dropped from the sky. Pantin' for breath, we would often find ourselves a mile or so from home, but there was always a hundred things to explore, especially the big culvert that ran under the railroad tracks. It always had five or six inches of water in it, and a small pool at each end, which usually had a few fish swimmin' about. We never figured out where they went when the pool dried up around the first of July, or how they would always be back when it filled up again. I don't want anybody out there explainin' it to me either, for some mysteries are best cherished when least understood. Right now I reckon someone is wonderin' what Pig looked like. Well, Pig wasn't much to look at, now that I remember him through eyes that have seen more than sixty-five years of life; but to an unworldly, naive country girl of nine he was Sir Lancelot, Robin Hood, and all the other glamorous heroes rolled into one who rode white horses and performed brave deeds on the landscape of my dreams.

Pig had short, mud color hair, which spiked in every direction like a badly mowed field of hay. It bristled atop a square face held together by a pair of jug-handle ears and a wide, determined mouth that could never quite be serious enough to hide a ready smile. His nose was pug and serviceable. Looking out from this conglomerate package of mismatched parts were two eyes the color of an alpine blue Lake I'd once seen on one of them picture calendars hangin' on the wall behind the glass candy case in Hodges store at Tunnel Hill. So, take an average size boy of twelve, put him in a cotton shirt and faded bib overalls with the knees out and the legs turned up to hide frayed seams, and you have an accurate picture of old Pig. Best of all, me and Pig were friends, had always been friends, and I was sure that in the long life allotted to us, would be friends forever.

We were most always barefoot and at least two toes would have bloody stob marks. Stobs were small bushes that had been cut off four or five inches above the ground; but the area most infested with these lethal weapons were the banks of the country roads. A humongous road-grader, totin' a long sharp blade on its front, would rumble up the hill and every kid within two miles would be gathered at the top, shy grins plastered on eager faces, waitin' for the show to begin. Knowin' that the smallest thing from the outside world was a big happenin' to a country kid, the driver would make a big show of backin' around to position the blade on a perfect forty-five degree angle. He requested assistance from time to time, which pumped-up egos and drew murmurs of approval. When all was ready, the big machine would rev up, a puff of black smoke would roll from the tail pipe, the blade would be lowered into the bank, and the bright yellow steel insect on its wobbly front legs would roll forward, slicin' the bank as clean as a hound's tooth.

For a few days those banks were like glass, and we'd spend every wakin' moment runnin' up, down and sideways, seein' how far we could go without tumblin' to the bottom. Then the stobs would edge upward just a mite taller than the surface and toes would rapidly become raw, bloody casualties.

The game now shifted into high gear. The lucky boy or girl who could run amid the bristlin' stobs all the way to sugar creek a half mile down the hill, was the Champ. The champ would be held in high esteem for at least an hour or two. But woe be to the hapless soul who slipped and rode the bank to the bottom on the seat of his pants. The most excruciating sounds of pain would issue from the victim, and prevalent among these was an energetic suckin' in of breath, accompanied by deep agonizin' groans in the throat. I left enough blood and skin on those banks to transfuse and graft half the world.

Barefoot back then was not only fun, it was a necessity as hardly anyone had two pairs of shoes. Most generally everyone had one and a half pair. When a new pair was bought, they were accorded the tender care one would ordinarily give a baby, and the almost worn out pair of cracked, wrinkled, tongueless, run down at the heel veterans with their short knotted laces, were now called upon to hold these valiant workhorses of drudgery together for yet a little while. The new ones languished in their tissue stuffed boxes until Sunday mornings, although each member of the family had most certainly looked at and caressed the smooth leather a dozen times each day. I can tell you that feet accustomed to the freedom of nothingness do not take kindly to the pain and torture of a leather prison. So, for a space of time torture was endured until that magic broken-in stage was achieved. As strange as it seems to me now, no one appeared to notice that each member of the family walked remarkably like a duck on crutches. All in good time blisters became callouses, toes sprouted ingrowin' nails and an adult would frequently grip the toe of a shoe in one hand, the heel in another, and snap them back and forth in an effort to whip some limber into them.

Stubbed toes - as Pig and I had long known - were vastly more comfortable than the new shoes, that is, until you had to stuff a stubbed toe into a new shoe. There is no pain to equal that; but I'm driftin' a bit so to speak; sorta takin' side trips up the creek of my memory.

The Sack of Stray Cats

Once upon a time, good old Pig whose worst crime up to date -and that one was all on account of a stupid dare from the neighborhood bully - had been an attempt to drown a sack of cats in Bowman's lake. Some of you are wonderin' how an upstandin', courageous pillar of the community such as Pig, could ever be induced to even think of drownin' a cat, much less doin' it. Well, at the time, scrunched down behind a clump of bushes watchin' the drama unfold with disbelievin' eyes, I was wonderin' the same thing.

The bully and his two foul-smellin' henchmen, sat on the bank and watched avidly as Pig waded hip deep into the water holdin' a toesack of squirmin' cats aloft, his eyes glazed with pain and anger. He'd show them he was no coward; no siree, old Pig had enough steel in his backbone to make a whole passel of bullets, which shot the bullys chicken theory all to crap.

"Too bad them CATS ain't packin' some of them bullets," said a little voice.

Pig tried to ignore the voice that was interruptin' his thoughts; that same voice his grandma had solemnly proclaimed to be his conscience.

"Everybody's got one Pig. Its a safety net that will catch a lot of mistakes if we listen, but a lot of folks like listenin' to the other voice better."

"What one is that", he had asked.

Her face set in stern lines of warnin'. "The tempter, Pig. He can take the ugliest sin and put a good face on it. Just you mind not to get fooled by him."

After serious consideration, Pig had named his conscience the Nigglin, and for the most part didn't have much trouble with it. His thoughts were jerked back to the present by terrified yowls and hissin'sounds eminating from the sack, and had he looked up he would have seen the sacks outer mesh bristlin' with cat claws flashin' like miniature scythes in the sun. "I love cats," he mumbled guilitly, but a man's pride is at stake here, and a mans pride is a fierce somethin' not to be messed with.

Pride goeth before a fall," warned the Nigglin.

Didn't he have enough to worry about without his conscience pickin' this minute to spout sayins' from the good book? "Jeeze," he grumbled, you'd think this was just a Sunday walk down the railroad track with nothin' but swimmin' on my mind. Men don't complain, he reminded himself, even when bein' a man is a heap of trouble. It was beginnin' to look like an unlucky day.

"A stitch in time saves nine, Pig."

"Yeah, I know." grumbled Pig. "Look before you leap. Think before you speak."

Pig had stopped bein a kid way back at eight, when he'd punched the lights out of a kid two heads taller than him, for goosin' his sister Jolene. At that time, sproutin' a black eye and bloody nose from what he considered a lucky blow, he figured he was about as growed-up as he was gonna git.

Old prim, proper, starched Jolene, whose every curl was always in place, had shocked the whole school by cuttin' a shine the likes of which they had never before seen. At the moment Jolene's dignity had been violated she had highstepped into the coal bucket by the potbellied stove, absently grabbin the long poker to steady herself. When she was unable to extract her foot from the bucket, she floundered about in panic, wavin' the gaf-hook poker above her head like a windmill. The walls were soon pocked with gouges from the flailin' weapon, and her last effort - just before she fell - struck the stove pipe and brought it crashin' down. From the hole in the wall, a cloud of soot fell in cascades of black velvet on Jolene's hair, defyin' gravity for a brief moment, then the large mound slid toward the floor, down the pink dress that would never in this life ever be clean again. She slumped to the floor in total shock and mortification, not quite clearin' Mr. Taylor's spittoon, which rested discreetly in the corner. From the depths of the overturned spittoon, a thick dark ooze crept across the floor, reachin' hungrily for Jolene's white petticoat which lay in a helpless fan of defeat. A man does what a mans gotta do: So, he had defended Jolene's honor and was her hero for about a week, then he went back to just bein' a creep again.

"Now see Pig," the tempter purred. "It took pride to defend Jolene's honor, so see how useful a little pride can be?"

He agreed with that, mentally listin' a number of things where a little pride was useful. A on his report card, wipein' his feet before walkin' on mom's linoleum, muckin' out the barn.

"Atta boy Pig, you're a fast learner," shouted the tempter.

Pig was so busy feedin' his pride he almost didn't hear the Nigglin.

"You're splittin hairs again Pig. Remember about puttin a good face on wrong?" Then the voice became faint as though the Nigglin wearily closed a door between them. "Kindness pays, haste makes waste. Love Gods' creatures," floated softly through the closed door, and Pig felt a pang of conscience. The water was nearly up to his arm pits now, and he was dimly aware that his toes were headed slightly downhill no matter how hard he dug them into the slimy bottom, which could only mean he was close to the brink of Eternity Gorge. Fear licked through him like a burnin' icicle. It was no place to be with your clothes on, holdin' a sack of cats that were thrashin ever which way, held aloft by arms rapidly turnin' to jelly.

"Hey Pig!" The bully crooned. Felt anything slimy 'round your legs yet?

Pig gave an involuntary start and stopped short, toes diggin precarious foot holds into the precipice of eternity. His arms trembled heavenward in seeming supplication, although there was no Divine hope in the gesture, and only the realization of where he was kept him from leapin' in panic over the edge. The two henchmen laughed loudly, and Pig could imagine them clappin the bully on the back, their eyes full of subservient worship. Them two ain't real no which way you look at em, he thought. Shadows is all they are; no more real than the shadow rabbits and dogs Pa flashes on the walls at nite.

"Well Pig," The Nigglin asked in a sad voice. "Aren't YOU just a shadow of Mr. Pride?"

"Now don't you go lettin' him browbeat you boy, "the Tempter shouted. "Just you stand right up to him, like a man."

"Which one are you, Pig," whispered the Nigglin, "A boy or a man?"

Pig swallowed hard over the lump in his throat and his eyes felt all funny and watery.

"The bully turned to his henchmen, being careful to keep his voice loud enough so Pig wouldn't miss a word. "Fellers, do you remember that drought we had two years ago that sucked up most all the water in the state?" The henchmen allowed as how they did. "Well I knew that poor unfortunate man who walked out in this lake on one of them hot days to cool hisself off... and that's when that terrible thing happened to him. "Yes sir," he rambled on slowly, observin' Pig's delicate balancin' act; "in this very lake; old Bowman's lake with Eternity Gorge settin' square dab right in the middle of it. They say nobody knows for sure how many bodies are down there, sucked under by that old whirl pool; course it don't whirl all the time, and some expert out of Chicago who come all the way down here to study it, said there was a big old cave bout half way down to the bottom- wherever that is- that starts it up from time to time. No one has ever outswum it though, SO FAR"

He paused to let Pig digest this information and from the white, frozen look on Pigs face I could tell he hadn't missed a word.

"But, You're a pretty fair swimmer, Pig. You just might be the first. Why, you'd be famous, and maybe git writ up in one of them big New York newspapers by Walter Winchell and maybe you might even be on the radio with good old Gabriel Heater." Ah, theres good news tonight folks," old Gabriel would tell the world." Southern Illinois country boy successfully outswims deadly whirlpool, known as the infamous Eternity Gorge, which is located in Bowman's lake, a favorite swimming hole in the community. Seems he's the first to ever accomplish such a feat. When asked what motived him,the boy replied solemnly, "I reckon there ain't no motivator to beat the fear of death, sir."

The bully warmed to his subject, eyein Pig with malicious intent.

"I can just picture you Pig, ridin in all them parades in the back seat of a new Chevrolet convertible, lickin' a triple decker ice cream cone, and wavin' at all the purty girls. And maybe," he drawled lazily "they might even put a statue of you right here on the lake."

The henchmen were gigglin like fools, and I -all scrunched down behind the bushes- gritted my teeth, and hung on for dear life to keep my feet from runnin' over to tear their hearts out. About the time I was wonderin' when the big disaster was gonna happen, and maybe Pig might step off into oblivion- and I was gonna go save him even if he killed me for bein' there in the first place- he turned slowly and stared at the bully and his henchmen. There was somethin' 'bout the way he stood there, straight and tall, balancin' that sack above his head. The look on his face was a look I'd never seen before. A look all mixed up with anger and disgust and hurt and resolve. Evidently the bully hadn't ever seen that look before either, for he was all quiet now and I could see him easin' up straighter, his eyes glued on Pig. The henchmen sat with their mouths open, silent as night with nary a giggle to be heard. The bully seemed paralyzed with shock at the sudden turn of events. When he saw Pig turn around and start toward him, the smirkin' arrogance slid off his face like lard off a hot skillet. As Pig got closer, the bully flinched, standin' first on one foot then the other, no doubt wishin' he was swimmin' over Eternity Gorge with that old whirlpool suckin' at his heels instead of facin' this cat-lovin' fury.

Pig advanced on the bully and his henchmen with calm deliberation, and when he stepped out of the water onto solid ground, he set the sack down carefully. The cats seemed to know a change for the better had come about, for all were quiet, and only the smallest movements disturbed the surface as they settled into comfortable positions.

The henchmen now had their toes dug in the dirt, their bodies leanin' unmistakably in the direction they intended to run, and I half expected someone to chant, One for the money, two for the show, three to make ready, and four to go.

Next thing I knew, Pig and the bully were all mixed up on the ground, arms and legs flyin' in ever direction, with clouds of dust swirlin' round their heads. Pigs dedication to the task at hand was, in my opinion, a sight better than his dedication had ever been in school. About that time he must have spied the henchmen about to make their get away, for he suddenly shoved the bully aside and pinned them in the dirt, cuffin' first one than the other. Last time I heard yellin' and screamin' like that was when Grandma threw a pan of scaldin' dishwater out the back door on old Streator, Grandpa's favorite coon dog.

After the skirmish was over and the bully and his henchmen had run off down the road with their tail between their legs, Pig turned back to the sack, carefully untyin' the line cinched around the top. His hand rested briefly on each cats head, as though pronouncin' a benediction on them. A few minutes later I proudly watched old Pig clomp triumphantly out of sight, talkin soft and gentle to them cats that were squirmin' in and out of his legs, purrin' and meowin' and actin' like he was The Lord's own light. I dug my toes out of the dust, pried my stiff hands off that bush and tried to stand up. Walkin' home, I thought on all I'd seen and heard and wondered if Pig would ever tell me what he was doin' there. I shuddered, thinkin' how close old Pig had been to the gorge, and how everyone was afraid of it even if they wouldn't let on.

The grownups would declare that they weren't scared of old Eternity Gorge and on a Sunday swimmin' party, they would line the kids up on shore, then march into the lake all cocky with brave smiles glued on their faces. They'd swim at a leisurely pace until they reached the Gorge, then someone would loudly suggest a race and the water would boil with frenzied activity. Sometimes I feared the whirlpool had suddenly come to life and would make orphans of us all; but it never did and the intrepid group would climb out and sprawl on the far bank, their faces etched with relief.

When I came on the narrow little road meanderin' up through the field to Pig's house, my feet just naturally turned in that direction. Grandma Lawrence answered the door, wipin' flour off her hands on a big dish towel tied 'round her waist, and I just stood there takin' deep breaths of her chicken and dumplins,' and grinnin' like a silly goose.

"Reckon yer lookin' for Pig," she said matter of factly. "

"Yes Ma'am."

"He's on the front porch, and actin' mighty peculiar if you ask me. Keeps huggin' one or tother of them stray cats like he's never seen one before." She gave me a half smile, her thoughts clearly on the front porch with Pig, then, she sighed, as though the whole thing was too weighty to think on. "Run along now little miss and let me git back to my dumplins.' "She half turned her back on me, then paused. "Guess ye've got more important things to do than take a bite of supper with us," she said.

"No Ma'am ,"I smiled, tryin' to contain the exuberant yell chasin' its tail in my throat. "There ain't nothin' in this world more important than your chicken and dumplins'. "Cluckin like a disgruntled hen, she gave her hands a final swipe on the dish towel, then turned toward the kitchen.

"Hi kid!" Pig smiled as I settled on the step beside him. "I hear yer stayin' for supper."

"Can't nobody cook chicken and dumplins' like Grandma Lawrence," I answered, eyein' the sun which was well above the trees across the valley. "I figure by the time the sun slides behind that big oak in the school yard, it'll be about supper time."

"I figure it that way too," Pig smiled.

We sat in comfortable silence, lookin' out over the wooded valleys, green and lazy in the afternoon sun. The Big Four railroad tracks were glistin', silver ribbons windin' their way through the hills and hollers of my grandpa Fitzgerald's land, toward the little community of Sanburn. Across the valley, solid on its hill, the school drowsed in the afternoon quiet, it's sunsplashed windows blazin' with a bright orange flame.

The stray cats stood in paw-raised postures around the edge of the porch, gazin' in timid fascination at the honey bees workin grandma Lawrence's flowerbeds. With necks stretched tensely forward, their little heads bobbin' up and down on nervous springs, they looked like small puppets on an erratic string. One of the kittens crawled into my lap and looked up at me with watery blue eyes. Pig patted it on the head, smiled fondly in my direction and went back to his own thoughts. At long last, the old dinner bell called everyone to supper, its mellow tones ridin' the warm air, and I fancied I could hear the sound hummin' faintly as it floated downward to the valley below. Made me sad, somehow, for I knew I'd never ever hear the bell ring exactly that way again.

Pig's grandpa said a lengthy prayer of thanksgivin', and all that time the rich intoxicatin' steam from Grandma's specialty curled around the table fit to kill us all. His dad coughed loudly; his mom fidgeted, and I could swear I saw Pig's grandma reach out and pinch grandpa on the arm. Course I can't be sure of that since most of my attention was focused through half closed eyes on that big old crock of chicken and dumplins'. Nothin' hardly was said until second helpins' were passed; then the men talked crops and the women talked gardens. Me and Pig ate silently, each one runnin' his own thoughts.

Pig's dad carefully slathered another hot biscuit with butter as though he was creatin' a great work of art, then he smiled at me.

"Where'd you two go today, little miss?"

Mrs.Lawrence regarded me kindly as everyone waited politely for my reply, while I pretended to swallow, tryin' desperately to think of a suitable answer.

"Well, first off, I came by here hopin' me and Pig might go swimmin; but Pig wasn't here, so..." Pig shot a wary look at me, his mouth grim. "so I went to the Tunnel and just roamed around town," I finished quickly. The relief that passed over old Pig's face was downright pitiful.

"Well, roamin' around the Tunnel must have taken all of ten minutes," his dad smiled "

"Land sakes alive son, you'd have to be draggin' your feet some to stretch it out that long," grandma giggled, pokin' grandpa in the ribs.

Grandpa picked the ball up smoothly. "Last time I checked there was nigh on to fifty residents and I reckon that's a real population explosion; leastwise for the Tunnel."

Grandma looked at Grandpa skeptically, "You must be countin them dogs and cats again, Pa." Before grandpa could answer, Pig's dad laughed and slid back into the conversation as though he'd never been interrupted. "Don't know about a population explosion," he said, "but I've never heard tell of anyone gettin' run down by a street car, and it'd hardly be worth a body's time to take a taxi- if there was a taxi- the ten steps between the post office and Nipper's Mercantile."

Pigs mom grabbed the tail of her apron and stuffed it over her mouth to stifle a bout of mirth."Mercantile?" she exclaimed. "Nippers Mercantile? Her and grandma Lawrence tittered over some secret only they seemed privy to, since Mr. Lawrence and grandpa were clearly puzzled.

"Dirt floors, if you can imagine it," she continued, not botherin' to enlighten them. "Boards runnin' here and there as walkways, and cases and shelves so filled with junk, it's worth your life just to step foot in the place."

I didn't remind them that Uncle Fate Nipper is my dad's kin.

"Don't know how dear Ann puts up with it, or him, for that matter," put in Grandma, shakin' her head solemnly; "but, you know," she conceded, "it's kind of an adventure goin' in there and pokin around in all that stuff once in awhile."

I silently agreed with that, for Uncle Fate's store was a wonderland of treasure. A whole dozen jot-em-down stores in one, the likes of which me or no one else will ever see again. I explored in there by the hour, avoidin' those musty, dark places next to the dirt floor where I knew monsters lived, just waitin' to pull me into oblivion. Anything you wanted Uncle Fate had it or could get it. Horse collars in rich leather-which always made my neck ache- harness and trace lines that smelled like grandma's home made lye soap. There were currycombs, horse brushes and saddle soap and blinders for skittish horses whose nerves couldn't stand the strain of seein' anywhere except straight down the road. Nuts and bolts and nails and staples as big as horseshoes, nestled menacingly in wooden barrels and big silver water buckets. Saymon's liniment, bees wax and Cloverine salve was scattered here and there among the canned goods. I peddled a thousand boxes of Cloverine salve in my time. No small job when you consider neighbors lived a halfmile or more apart. Cloverine salve didn't put much money in my pocket, but it gave me a taste of free enterprise; It also taught me independence and gave me a self-esteem that money can't buy.

One whole shelf was filled with kerosene lamps and lanterns and that new fangled marvel, the Alladin Lamp with its cobweb mantle that would shatter in a million pieces if you breathed on it.

I never saw a man or a boy able to pass Uncle Fate's shavin' display. Straight razors with fancy pearl handles, some with beautiful inlaid designs on them. Others had ivory handles with wonderful animals and majestic mountains scratched on them from far-off mysterious places none of us ever hoped to see. The big, calloused, sun-burned hands of hard workin' farmers would gently trace the beautiful scenes, their eyes on distant unattainable dreams, their feet firmly rooted in land passed down from generation to generation. Dozens of strops hung conveniently below the razors, temptin' kids to run their hands through the gleaming leather panels. Strops served a double purpose in those days: It kept razors sharp and kids on the straight and narrow. My dads strop elevated my appreciation for law and order on more than one occassion and I can't think of a single instance when I hadn't earned such a reward many times over.

Aunt Ann had a pretty-yourself-up shelf jammed with powder and rouge and shockin', violent colored lipsticks, which always made my grandma sniff with disapproval. At the end of the shelf, settin' in grand aloofness on white

Pig and a Sack of Stray Cats

lace doilies, were sparklin' bottles of scent in Lilac, Honeysuckle, Rose and Peach blossom and that all time favorite, Gardenia. Their illusive fragrance would hold me spellbound and impatient to grow up.

Big glass jars held horehound candy and licorice and peppermint sticks and red hots that sizzled your tongue. Our mouths watered over the candy bars lined up in the glass case and Three Muskoteers came in three pieces then, each one a different flavor. Now its just a candy bar like the rest and they ought to simply call it One Muskoteer. Purina chicken feed came in hundred pound sacks of brightly patterned cotton from which most of our clothes were made.

Purina's slogan (Full of Pep) stamped on the front of the sack, was a waste of good material as far as my grandma was concerned since one had to cut the pattern pieces around it.

An exceedingly overweight lady who lived out on the hardroad made all her underwear from those sacks. One morning my mom and I walked the five miles of dirt road from our farm to the hardroad to hitch a ride to Vienna. A fine gentleman in a fine car picked us up and as we drove by the ladys house, her underwear was hangin' the entire length of the clothes line. Across each seat was the (Full Of Pep) Purina slogan. When we arrived in town, the man let us out and just before mother closed the door, he smiled and said, "Lady, I don't know about you but when I get out of sight I'm going to pull off the road and laugh until I'm sick. Mom and I sat down on the curb and she howled for five minutes. I mostly worried about what the town folks would think of us sittin' on that dusty curb laughin' at an empty street.

Uncle Fate's store was complete and if that store was here today it would be one of the wonder's of the world; but I'm digressin' so lets go back to Grandma Lawrence's last remark.

"Don't know how dear Ann puts up with it or him for that matter; but you know it's kind of an adventure goin' in there and pokin' 'round in all that stuff once in awhile."

"Well, I could do with less mouse droppins' in my adventurin," Pigs mom replied.

Grandpa's fork paused half way to his mouth, burdened down with dumplins. "I hear tell them mice packed up and left Nippers, bag and baggage," he announced casually, as though he was talkin' about a neighbor down the road instead of a bunch of mice. Me and Pig giggled, which just spurred him on. He grinned mischievously at grandma and winked. "Someone saw them cross the tracks and head toward the Baptist church on the hill."

"Well," grandma opined, "Bingo's about the only excitement the poor things will ever get up there. They'd be a sight better off with that Holy-Roller bunch down there in the holler. Accordin' to what people say, it's pretty lively most of the time, with folks runnin' up and down the aisles, shoutin and singin.' Praisin' the Lord is a glorious thing, mind you; but I

33

reckon the Lord likes a quieter praise just as much as an enegetic praise." She sighed, wipin' imaginary sweat from her brow. " It'd only take one service to wear me right down to a nub," she said tiredly.

Everbody roared at that, 'specially grandpa, who always pounded the table with his knife handle when he heard somethin' specially funny.

Still grinnin', he fixed me with a stare. "I suppose YOU, little miss, also crossed the tracks, and visited that bustlin' metropolis clingin' for dear life to the banks of that goat trail they call a road."

"Reckon I didn't miss a thing," I answered innocently.

Smackin his lips with satisfaction, he continued. "And supposin a little further: I suppose you smelled ma's chicken and dumplins all the way to the Tunnel, eh?"

"Stop teasin, Eli," grandma scolded. "Still..." she mused, studyin' me as though she'd never seen me before, "I can't remember a time when dumplins was on the stove that the little miss here hasn't shown up on our porch like a starved puppy. No offense, child," she said, briefly claspin' a bony hand over mine.

"None taken, Ma'am," I smiled, forkin' up another mouthful of dumplins.

She eyed me speculatively, then, addressed the family as though I wasn't there. "Maybe she'll be a preacher," she murmured. Then her mouth curled in denial of a female ever attainin' such a lofty position. "Naw," she declared positively. " A politician! One of them durn fool politicians."

Everyone at the long table laughed: Pig, most of all.

Ink Well Caper

Sanburn Grade School typified all the elements of Academic excellence and Spiritual values that molded the character of its students and prepared them to take their place in the world.

God was the foundation on which we built our lives and shaped the future and that foundation was there waiting for us long before we were born There were thousands of such schools all over America. These one-room, country schools turned out great men such as Washington, Lincoln, Jefferson and the hard working farmers who grew the food to feed their families and a rapidly growing country.

In the thirties I was privileged to attend a number of them; but my dearest memories are the golden years spent sitting at an old-fashioned desk in the one room school of Sanburn, Illinois, located in the county of Johnson, about three miles from Tunnel Hill if you walked the railroad track.

It was the school where good ole Pig, my dear friend attended. As I look back now I see what a magic time it was. I wrote about Pig in an earlier chapter and I've many more stories of him to tell so he's likely to pop up many times. Those years are a cherished portion of my life. A silver thread stitching the days together in a crazy quilt pattern of memories that mellow and grow more beautiful with the passage of time.

I remember one day when Pig dipped Inez Shaffer's platinum braid in the inkwell and wrote all over his books with it, then carried away with artistic inspiration he drew abstract patterns on the back of her white blouse. She was used to him playing with the braid so paid scant attention until the ink started trickling down her back. Reaching backward she grabbed the braid and pulled it up front for inspection. The two foot long silvery strand was tipped with five inches of Indigo blue that continued to creep inexorably upward like a stalking serpent. Her horrified screech still lives in my memory.

Eight rows of faces turned in electrified silence, staring at the blue braid then all eyes shifted as one unit to the stern forbidding face of our teacher, Elbert Taylor.

Pig's face had changed from deep plum to white so fast I thought he had suddenly died but his eyes were still blinking despite the glaze of sick comprehension spreading across his face.

Mr. Taylor didn't raise his voice nor did he move from his position at the blackboard where he'd been writing out test questions for the sixth grade; but his barbed wire eyebrows beetled ominously as he studied the ruined braid bein' twisted in a handkerchief by an hysterical Inez.

"Pig!" he intoned as one to the dead. "You go to that stand of bushes down by the boys outhouse and cut the sturdiest switch you can find and bring it to me." There wasn't a student in the room whose mind wasn't filled with memories of their own experience with such a dreaded errand.

Mr. Taylor was never one to temporize or beat around the bush. When a situation needed addressin,' he addressed it with immediate action and few words. One of his stern looks through those bushy brows was worth a thousand words any day.

Dear Pig rose on legs that seemed locked out of joint and slowly made his way out the back door, down the steps and across the playground to the thicket. Anything short of an elephant balanced on the flagpole, would have gone unnoticed as we, spellbound, watched the highlight of the week. Every eye followed poor ole Pig's progress in absolute silence, secretly glad it was him and not them, sheepishly grateful for this exciting diversion.

I knew that thicket well, having cut a few switches for my own habilitation and vowed close scrutiny on his selection to ascertain any possible cheatin.' Having heard many dissertations on the proper molding of character vital to one's future progress down the straight and narrow, I was anxious that good ole Pig, of whom I was very fond, shouldn't for the sake of present pain and sufferin' stint in the least on the riches to be gained from this valuable step down the long road of his life. Course it's easy to wax philosophical when you're waxin' on someone else's dilemma.

Not an eye left Pig's bumblin' figure as he sidled in among the bushes studyin' this one and that, rejectin' the unworthy as he moved deeper and deeper into the thicket. My admiration grew by the minute as he searched for just the right one: however it seemed to me a mite extreme to be so diligent and go so far since all we could now see was the top of Pig's spike hair bobbin' up and down.

"What's he doin'," his sister hissed in my ear.

"He's lookin', silly," I mumbled, not takin' my eye from the patch of hair slidin' erratically up and down through the branches.

"Looks like a fool squirrel leapin' from limb to limb," she snickered.

Suddenly the fool squirrel began to move faster and faster, poppin' up and down through the leaves like a feather duster. Then a collective gasp of disbelief rose toward the ceiling as Pig's ganglin' form broke from the thicket, raced wildly across an open field, down into a gulley out of sight.

Hypnotized, we watched the parting bushes settle back into place then all eyes turned to Mr. Taylor who continued writing on the board as though it was just an ordinary day. At length he put a period to the last sentence and laid the chalk in its well. Turnin' he calmly surveyed the room, glancin' briefly in the direction of the departing figure who could now be seen nearin' the top of a hill.

I made a mental note to inform Pig when next I seen him that his frequent excuse for tardiness due to a trick knee acquired from fallin' out of an apple tree, would no longer hold water since the entire class and especially Mr. Taylor had witnessed an outstandin' demonstration of unimpeded speed.

"The sixth grade," Mr. Taylor was sayin', "will be allowed thirty minutes to answer the questions on the board."

We all turned reluctantly back to our books feigning attention to the matters at hand, our thoughts racin' wistfully after our departed classmate.

For Gawd's Sake

Pig was my best growin' up friend in all the world. I can't remember why or how he came by that name for he was an average lookin' freckle-faced boy, but the name fit him like a glove.

For GAWD'S Sake was a favorite sayin' with me and Pig. There was power and strength and authority and meat in THOSE WORDS. Used in any sentence, they confirmed absolutely whatever the user wanted to convey. No other kid ever questioned us when we used THOSE WORDS for you just didn't contradict the powers that be unless you were unwashed and unsaved. I knew one or two kids so unwashed it would have taken a dozen baptisms just to loosen the real estate on them. Course that confirmed their unsaved state since everyone knew that cleanliness is next to GODLINESS.

Me and Pig reassured ourselves we weren't insultin' the Lord's name in no way, shape or fashion since we only used THOSE WORDS on specific things that were very clearly defined in our minds, with not a hint of disrespect intended. However, a devilish rat began to knaw at my conscience when I noticed that THOSE WORDS were never uttered in the presence of an adult.

"Why do you suppose that is?" Pig asked when I brought the matter to his attention.

"I don't know," I said. "Do you ever say THOSE WORDS in front of your folks?"

"Well...no," he hedged. "Never had no reason to."

By mutual consent we dropped the subject, put a gag in the rats mouth and continued to enjoy the admiration of our contemporaries. However, one day I slipped up, provin' beyond a doubt that 'Be sure your sins will find you out' is pure gospel to be relied upon.

Grandma was stirrin' hot applebutter in the iron kettle she used for cannin' and me and my cousin Lucille were feedin' the fire with chunks of firewood.

Lucille was a skinny girl with stringy, blonde hair, blue eyes, a wide mouth that grinned most of the time and the usual abundance of freckles common to country kids who spend most of their time outdoors. She had spindly legs held firmly together with outlandish knobby knees. Course that description fit us all pretty well with just enough exceptions to tell us apart. Lucille's exception was a stumblebum syndrome. She could run like the wind but for no apparent reason and without any malicious intent, she would take out part of a flowerbed on her way. She tripped and fell on the dogs so many times the minute she came on the premises they all dashed under the porch and stayed there till her departure. She couldn't walk in the barnyard without steppin' in somethin', which necessitated numerous trips to the pond with a bar of Grandma's lye soap. She was sometimes referred to as prune foot. Even her attempts to mount a horse was a study in frustration. Dimple, my gentle sweet-natured mare would stand patiently while Lucille stepped up on a log, grasped a handful of mane and leaped weakly upward tryin' to throw one skinny leg over th' mare's back. Dimple would crane her neck backward to gaze at Lucille with big eyes, her face clearly puzzled over such goins' on.

Lucille never carried stove wood but what one or two sticks would fall on her foot or on the foot of some hapless soul close by. So, I was devastated when Grandma asked her to help me keep the fire goin' under the applebutter. 'Course the inevitable happened. On her second trip, three or four chunks of wood hit the dirt. She fell to her knees tryin' to pick them up, clumsily whippin' up the dust which true to murphy's law drifted obediently toward the open kettle of applebutter.

"For GAWD"S sake Lucille," I bawled, "stop slappin' that stick around in the dirt close to Grandma's applebutter." I was still glarin' at Lucille indignantly when Grandma's long stirrin' spoon come out of that hot applebutter with the speed of light and landed on the seat of my pants. I don't know if I was more shocked with the swiftness of the attack or the hot applebutter bein' pounded into my overalls.

"In this family, young lady," Grandma said between whacks, "we dont take GOD'S name in vain. Ever! "Her dark eyes probed my face."Now ye just git' in the house and think on that fer a spell."

Cousin Lucille had a triumphant smile flutterin' angelically across her mouth when Grandma turned 'round and saw her. Pushin' her bonnet back from her face she looked sternly at Lucille."It's not christian to take pleasure in another's misfortune," she chided, "however well deserved that misfortune may be; so ye best set over there on the well curb for awhile and think on all that pride yer enjoyin'."

So, my dear christian grandmother liberally applied the scriptures to our hearts and just as liberally applied the whackin' stick to the seat of our pants. Thus our character was built on a foundation that would never crumble before the storms of this world.

My Grandpa

I spent a good portion of my growin' years on my Grandparents farm surrounded by aunts and uncles and cousins who all lived within walkin' distance of each other. Pa was a farmer, a school teacher and a disciplinarian in the fairest sense of the word. He dispensed love and justice and discipline impartially, for our good, as he put it and I often heard that old sayin', this hurts me worse than it hurts you. To my way of thinkin' back then, it was the only splinter of ignorance stuck in Grandpa's brain.

"Wait'll I git my hands on you Frankie," he'd say to one of my older cousins whose mission in life seemed to be troublemaker. "I'm gonna' wallop the daylights outa'ye." Dreaded words. The culprit's countenance would instantly freeze in wild panic, accompanied by rapid twitchin' of the feet, whereupon Pa would growl knowingly, "You run and it'll go harder with ye."

I can't count the times my own feet have traitorously stampeded across the field into the woods beyond, with logic hangin' on for dear life tryin' in vain to talk some sense into them.

I've also stood, resistin' the overpowerin' urge to run, my heart thumpin' like a drum, goose bumps of dread coverin' my body with instant rash the second I was seized in the wallopin' grip. On this wallopin' occasion, Frankie had burned down the toilet while smokin' home-rolled Ceeg-a-retts, as he called them. He had almost burned the toilet once before, but the two gallons of milk Pa was carryin' home from milkin' Marcy, saved the day. Pa thought it providential that he was in the right place at the right time. Grandma merely thought it a waste of good milk and Frankie was probably home by then, settin' down to supper, not thinkin' on much of anything.

Grandpa was born to teach. He kept law and order, was respected, always brought enough lunch to feed the poor kids who didn't have any, asking their assistance in disposin' of the surplus food packed by grandma whose eyes, he said, were bigger than his stomach. He turned charity into a favor, solemnly thanking each child for his contribution to the waste not, want not commandment, with nary a suggestion toward the enlightenment and possible correction of grandma's folly. Once in awhile a kid who had plenty would shyly place a sandwich or piece of fruit on the table following Pa's example of love thy neighbor. Pa never let on that he had seen the gesture and no one watched which hand retrieved the offering; but sometime in the afternoon his hand would rest briefly on the Samaritans head and the Samaritan would glow with pleasure.

When I was barely four years old, Pa started taking me to school, carryin' my lunch in a syrup pail just like him, ridin' in his lap, my hands graspin' th' horn of th' saddle while he answered a hundred questions on everything I seen. I was listenin' and learnin' more than even Pa realized and havin' th' time of my life. He was a natural teacher and kids seemed to soak up th' things he taught like a sponge. He never realized he had a special gift but I did.

Grandpa talked country like it was a song; the gentle soothing rhythm of words flowin' from his lips like water over a pebbled stream; but when he stood before his pupils in the one room school house way out in the sticks where proper grammar was about as common as ice bergs in the back yard, he shifted into perfect English.

We could talk all th' country we wanted at recess but when books took up it was back to proper English, no two ways 'bout it.

"Why cain't we jest talk natural, Mr. Hundley?" J.D.Deaton complained one spring day when the air was sweet and beguiling with new blooms full of bees and fresh turned earth. Revved- up birds drunk with spring fever captured our attention, their exhuberant songs piercing the air.

It was our favorite time of the year and the sixth grade was havin' a hard time keepin' its mind on the grammar lesson. The rest of us weren't even tryin' as we gazed longingly at the new green carpet spreading across the field and up the hill north of the schoolhouse. A split rail fence separated the school from this area that was used as a pasture for cows and horses. It was also an extended playground mutually shared by kids and cattle alike.

A number of cows with fiesty new calves had drifted into view and were munching the new green grass while their offspring frolicked clumsily about on unsteady legs, bumping into their mothers and each other, surprise stamped on their faces. They'd look around for a minute then toss their heads and be off again. We were so caught in the joy of them that a collective giggle burst out when two of the youngsters collided head on and staggered around drunkenly trying to stay on their feet.

They finally collapsed in a tangle of legs, their eyes rollin' as their mothers hurried over and nuzzled them anxiously.

Pa and the six grade were laughin' with us and the entire school watched and enjoyed this wonderful scene until the cows drifted past the windows out of sight. I never forgot that mornin' and looked at Pa with new respect for allowin' us to enjoy the play of the baby calves whose behavior was very much like our own. Then Pa let us out for recess.

After recess the old dinner bell beckoned us inside and Pa called the sixth grade upto the long bench in front of his desk where each individual class was taught.

"Lets see now," he murmured, opening the grammar book he held in his hand. "I believe you had a question J.D."

"Yes sir, I do. I jest don't see why we cain't talk natural instead of them proper words thet purely wear my tongue to a frazzle."

Pa's blue eyes, set under bushy eyebrows, studied J.D. with interest. "You already know how to talk natural, as you put it. I'm teaching you proper grammar because most educated folk don't speak country. There is nothing wrong with country, mind you. I happen to love it and intend to spend the rest of my days speaking it except in the classroom. But, when you and your friends get out in the world and start chopping your words off at the knees, you'll stand out as an ignoramus from the sticks who won't fit in because they'll assume you know next to nothing. Even if you were lucky and got a job, its importance very likely would reflect your employers observation of your inability to speak proper English."

"Well, I ain't goin' to the city nohow," J.D. declared, so it don't mean a piddlin' to me what some highfaluten cityslicker thinks about the way I talk."

"I'm not going to the city," Pa corrected.

"Thets right smart of ye Mr Hundley," interrupted Rufus Williams, seein' as how not goin' ta th' city ain't hurt ye none." Rufus was smilin' real big, pleased with hisself.

J.D. joined right in with Rufus, his grin full of crooked teeth all jumbled together like a pile of rocks. "Ain't thet th' truth! Here ye' be way out here in th' sticks teachin' us ignoramuses and makin' a good livin'at it ta' boot."

Pa's eyes twinkled, his lips twitchin' with a smile but he kept a straight face as he regarded the two boys in front of him. He finally opened his mouth to say somethin' but Rufus beat him to it.

"My Pa says yer 'bout th' smartest man he's ever seen," Rufus declared proudly.

"Well, now thank you Rufus, but..."

"Mine too Mr. Hundley," J.D butted in. "My Pa and Ma sets a great store by ye, specially Ma, and as ye well know she ain't no great hand at settin' a store by nobody, includin' th' Preacher.

The class room rocked with laughter and I could see Pa strugglin' ta keep a straight face for everbody knew J.D.'S mother was inclined to tongue lash those, who, to her way of thinkin' wobbled off th' straight and narrow. I had fearful misgivins' 'bout J.D.'s Pa ever goin' thru th' pearly gates since she lashed him more than anybody else and I reckoned he seldom hit the straight and narrow anyhow what with thet still he had hid away.'Course everbody knew 'bout it 'xcept J.D,s mom; but thets another story.

Ever head in the room was noddin' agreement on th' nice things said about Pa for he was greatly esteemed by all who knew him.

"Well, now," Pa smiled, "I sure do appreciate all the nice compliments and I'll try hard to deserve them but its time to get back to our little discussion. When I said, I'm not going to the city I was merely correcting your English, J.D., not declaring an intention. Do you think I just got up one morning and decided I'd like to teach? Absolutely not! I went to school and learned the three R's and how to speak properly, then presented myself to the school board for an interview of my credentials. I love the country as much as you and wouldn't live anywhere else; but you must have an education to get along in this world. Not all of you can be teachers; so you either farm or go somewhere for a job.

"Take your dads farm for instance, J.D. Would it support your dad and mom plus you and your brother if you both had families? I'd guess your mom and dad have to manage pretty well just to support you and your brother and sister."

"Yer right 'bout thet, Mr Hundley," J.D. sighed.

Most of the school was engrossed in the discussion and several heads nodded agreement.

Ole Rufus reckoned thet his Pa had already been talkin' college and his mom sure was keen on th' idea. Several faces turned to study ole Rufus with new interest. Here was one of their own goin' off to better hisself and come up in the world; maybe get rich and build a fancy house on a hill lookin' down on New Burnside and one of them big factories that everbody was always runnin' off ta work in. Pa noted the interest and pressed the point.

"Yes sir," he mused, fixing his gaze on the empty pasture outside the window. "You have a fine opportunity here to learn good English and the three R's. Then get High School under your belt, maybe College and all the time you'll be snickering up your sleeve because you not only speak excellent English but perfect country. Think of that! Two languages. From time to time you can let loose with country, tell some country tales, give them a good ole country belly laugh and I guarantee you'll have them begging for more. There's nothing more charming than a country boy from the sticks talking pure country when everyone knows he speaks perfect English.

"Ye ever done thet,' what ye jest said, Mr. Hundley, 'bout tellin' 'em stories in country after they know ye can speak perfect English?" someone asked.

Pa's eyes crinkled merrily. "More times than I care to say son. It's a pure delight to sit among a group of city slickers and spin yarns in country. Why they eat it up and beg for more, so you become sort of a celebrity simply because you talk like an ignoramus from the sticks."

The school laughed and laughed over that and begged Pa for a story he'd told the slickers and of course it had to be told in country,

And so he gave us an all around proper education. He made learning fun and it stuck to us like biscuits and gravy to the ribs of a Hound.

Ole Satan

When I was a kid in ragged overalls our transportation was a mule or a horse, ridden bareback with varying degrees of comfort dependin' on the anatomy of the vehicle.

The steerin' wheel was a bridle laced over and around the ears, anchored by a bit in the mouth and long leather reins held in the riders hands. Our first mode of transportation was a wagon with iron-rimmed wheels and a straight seat across the front powered by two engines named Dimple and Nell whose top speed was about five miles per hour. A small rail on each end of the seat was the forerunner to seatbelts, giving the outside occupant a somewhat precarious margin of safety plus a guaranteed crop of bruises in assorted shapes of pain.

Turnin' signals were a simple matter of gently pullin' the left or right rein in which case your live transportation with its advanced before its time scientific technological forerunner of the computer, would instantly obey any and all commands.

Not always.

Animals have personalities as varied as people. There are a few horses and an occassional mule who'll bite a sizeable chunk from any part of you thats convenient just to whet their teeth and stave off boredom. Grandpa had such a mule with a nasty habit of bitin' just enough flesh to leave a good lump perched in the middle of a plate size bruise. Grandpa had come by the mule in a most unusual way, which gives me goose bumps to this very day. The mule was a mystery who became famous,and added immeasurably to the richness of our life on th' farm. Pa was a legendary storyteller and our front yard was often filled with fifty or more people come to listen and be thrilled by his tales. The mule added hundreds of true tales to Pa's already burgeonin' supply and soon became famous or infamous dependin' on which side of the fence you were on.

One day a band of Gypsies stopped on the road leadin' up the hill to our farm. I stood on the front porch starin' down at five of the most colorful wagons I'd ever seen, only they were not wagons but houses on wheels. I heard the screen door open as Grandma and Pa came out on the porch.

They stood silently regardin' th' wagons below. Pa puffed softly on his pipe as he studied a dark skinned man with a thick black beard and masses of lustrous curls fallin' down his back. His hair was that shade of blue black which is rarely seen 'cept among indians and other dark-skin people whose pictures I'd seen in books.

Grandma has that color hair with dark brown skin and piercing black eyes. She is Cherokee, and beautiful, not to mention the other jillion attributes that make her outstanding. Suddenly I looked from the Gypsy to her in surprise. They could be blood kin, I thought with a shock. I wondered if she had noticed the similarity, but her face was inscrutable.

The Gypsy sat erect and proud in the lead wagon, on a seat whose surface was carved with animals and flowers and rivers that flowed through wild mountains and thick forests, all painted so beautiful and natural lookin' I imagined I could hear the roarin' waters and feel the cold air as it swept down th' mountains through the forests below.

The entire wagon was hand carved with every scene you could imagine. Birds, flowers, bees, animals, scrolls, circles, strange writings, slashes and streaks that looked like lightenin' to me, and it was all painted from muted shades to the wildest, strongest colors of the rainbow.. I'd never seen such colors and the artwork mesmerized me into an almost hypnotic state of mind.

"Isn't it wonderful?" I murmured.

"It is indeed wonderful, child. We are privileged to see such splendor in our lifetime for this art comes from one who understands th' goodness and wisdom of God's nature. Such a soul is pure and free from the things of this sinful world, a soul that lives within th' purity of its thought." She sighed wistfully. "I would be greatly honored to meet such a one."

"The Gypsy was aware of our scrutiny, his own eyes assessin' us and our farm and I had th' oddest feelin' this man could see everything at once. Only after a long interval did he rise from his seat, momentarily turnin' his back to us as he lowered his foot to a wheel spoke, then dropped gracefully to the ground. His clothing was as black as his hair except for the very wide suspenders he wore. They were embroidered in th' most wonderful colors and I had the feeling they were a beautiful symbol of his authority and honor in the group. He seemed to float up the hill without effort, his legs glidin' over th' ruts and clumps of dirt as though they were smooth glass. As he drew closer I gasped at the perfection of his face for I'd never seen a man as handsome as this one, not even in the catalogs. His black eyes met mine and I knew he had read my mind. A faint smile touched his lips as he made a low bow to Grandma. His eyes returned to Grandma and lingered on her face for a long time and I knew an invisible bond of kinship had passed between them.

Streeter walked right up to him as though he was a long lost friend and wrapped his tongue around his hand. Th' Gypsy knelt on one knee and looked into the dog's eyes for a long time, then stood and extended his hand to Pa in a movement so fluid I hardly believed he had moved. He was a man who moved through time effortlessly, imparting a serene grace to the world around him.

Pa took his hand and smiled, then told me to go get our guest a drink.

"My name is Bali," he said, extending his hand toward the wagons below, "and this is my clan."

Pa puffed his pipe gently and I noticed the Gypsy eyed the curls of smoke with great pleasure. Pa removed the pipe from his mouth and regarded the man in front of him. "What can I do for you, Mr. Bali?"

"The Gypsy seemed to take in the farm at a glance, his eyes shinin' with pleasure. "My people are weary and we seek a place to rest and renew ourselves." he said softly. "The old ones and the babies need to feel solid ground beneath them once more. We've been on the road too long. Our animals are tired, and our wagons need much repair and... " his eyes were soft with hope as he looked at Pa. "I felt a peace in my heart the minute I seen your farm."

Pa studied the man who stood proud and patient in front of him, his pipe hangin' from th' corner of his mouth then raised his arm and pointed to the field where our pear trees grew.

"I ask only one thing of any man," he said quietly. "He must respect my family and my property. You're welcome to stay as long as you wish."

"Well said." the Gypsy smiled. "Respect and honor is a rule my clan has lived by for centuries. Unfortunately, there are those of our heritage who have brought shame to our name, shame that will follow us forever."

'Bout that time I came with a bucket of fresh, cold water. Pa took it and extended a dipper of the sweetest water this side of heaven -as Pa always said- to the man called Bali. He drank slowly although I could tell he was burning with thirst, then smiled at my Grandma and said, "Sweet water from Heaven."

She didn't reply but her eyes had a special glow in them. He bowed once more, handed the dipper to Pa and started back down the hill.

"Wasn't that an odd thing for him to say, Net, about sweet water from Heaven?"

"Yes, quite odd," Grandma murmured.

"Stop by the well and water your people and your stock before you camp," Pa called to the tall figure, and fill your barrels as often as you want." You see, Mr. Bali, this well never runs dry no matter how much is taken from it. There's a good spring runs through th' field yonder, by th' pear trees. It's good for bathing and clothes washin', but th' well is for drinkin'."

The Gypsy turned and bowed his gratitude.

"By the way," Pa laughed, "my name is Almus, my wife is Net and this young'en is called..."but before Pa could finish, Bali interrupted and said, "She is called Sprout."

"Well I never!" I exclaimed. I looked at Grandma and she had a sweet, knowing smile on her face as though it was the most natural thing in the world for a stranger to know my name and him a Gypsy to boot. As I've said before: Grandma knows things beyond what we could ever imagine.

The Gypsies pulled their colorful wagons up the hill, watered their live stock from beautiful painted buckets, then they drank dipper after dipper of our sweet water, exclaiming in a language we couldn't understand, peering into the well for long periods of time, their faces full of wonder. Then at Bali's command they moved across the field toward the pear trees and pulled their wagons into a semi- circle.

That night they sat around a huge bon fire and sang haunting lovely songs in their language, accompanied by fiddles and guitars. Then we heard the soft magical tones of a lute drift'in on the night air like a sooth'in' mist. We sat on th' porch and listened until bedtime and I fell asleep with the lute whisperin' strange things into the night.

It was late March and Pa was busy gettin' crops in the ground, tendin' animals, mendin' harness, spreadin' manure on ground that wouldn't be used 'till next year and plowin' the garden or truck patch -as he called it- so me and Grandma could lay out the long rows of vegetables that would feed us all th' next year. I was watchin' Pa prepare th' truck patch from th' comfort of Grandma's rocker, thinkin' on all that food that would have to be canned for th' comin' winter. It wasn't my favorite time of th' year, nor mom's; still she always took her vacation from her city job so she could help Grandma durin' cannin' season. It was our survival. Money was hard to come by what with the depression and all and while I didn't understand just what depression was, I did know it was a fearsome thing with lots of people goin' hungry cause all the jobs had disappeared. I wondered where they'd gone and if they'd ever come back. Pa and Grandma prayed to th' Lord a lot, remindin' him he'd fed th' children of Israel with manna. I'd sometimes hear him say, "Now all your children are hungry Lord and this world needs th' touch of Yer hand."

Then I began to hear th' name Roosevelt in their conversations. F.D.R. they called him. Some said he'd save th' nation, others said he was just another politician. From what I'd heard, politicians were right next to the devil hisself which caused me a lot of worry. Well, F.D.R. and th' devil would just have to wait, for in a few months we'd be too busy cannin' food to think about 'em anyhow.

Peach time was my favorite and I'd eat until I nearly busted. The fallen fruit was the ripest and best to be canned and I can still see gallon after gallon of golden peach halves gleamin' beautifully as they were lifted from the big iron kettle Grandma used to cold pack them. Sometimes a puff of wind would hit the hot jar as it was lifted from the boilin' water and it would explode, spillin' the golden globes and the hard work it took to process them, to the ground. Grandma would sometimes cry softly over the wasted fruit and it was a day to rejoice when not a single jar was broken.

One day as she and my mom were about to lift the jars from their boilin' bath to boxes where they would cool down, I had an idea. "Hold it a minute," I said, as I ran to the house. Grandma had a box of scraps, which she used to patch clothin' and make quilt pieces and I remembered seein' a worn out quilt at the bottom. I grabbed my prize and raced back to the yard. Mom and Grandma eyed the quilt then stared at me with a puzzled look on their face.

"Now," I said importantly, "Lift a jar slowly from the kettle." As they did so I laid the quilt over the jar before it left the water, thus it was protected from the wind. Only when it was safely in its box did I remove the quilt. After all the hugs and kisses I could stand, they looked at each other and asked why they hadn't thought of that very thing.

"Sometimes we're too set on th' bigger things to think on a simple solution," Pa laughed as he, too, hugged me. "Now Sprout here don't have a fence 'round her cogitatin' apparatus so the solution jest come in natural and unhindered."

"Is that 'cogatatin' apparatus' catchin' Pa?"

"I hope so," mom muttered. "I could use a big dose of it"

The Gypsies had been camped by the pear trees for three days when Pa and Grandma decided to pay them a visit. They didn't walk into their camp, but stood a short distance away waitin' for an invitation. We were surprised to see a wall of tree limbs enclosin' th' entire camp with little bells hangin' from th' branches. Almost immediately, Bali stepped between the wagons and bowed low, his arm extended in welcome. He gestured toward the barrier."Old fears are hard to forget I'm afraid. I hope you don't mind. We took a small portion from each tree so no harm would come to it."

"You have nothin' to fear here," Pa assured him. How're you folks makin' out? Pa asked, grinnin' at several children peerin' 'round a wagon wheel.

Bali looked puzzled, then repeated, "Makin' out?

Grandma smiled shyly. "My husband wants to know if all is well with your clan. Are any sick and do you need some extra vittals?"

"Vittals?

"Food." Grandma smiled. We call food, vittals. I expect you'll understand us shortly, just as we'll understand you. Anyway, we wanted to welcome ye to th' farm with a little gift."

She looked at Pa and he laughed, his baritone fillin' th' evenin' air, causin' th' children to jump behind th' wagon wheel in surprise.

"Don't know what I'd do without Net here to keep me outta trouble," Pa chuckled, winkin' at Grandma.

Pa never met a stranger in his whole life, so he just naturally reached out and laid a friendly arm across Bali's shoulder, as he would have to any neighbor. I saw a flicker of surprise cross th' Gypsy's face, then it was gone. I wondered about that for awhile then I forgot the incident.

"Anyway," Pa was sayin', " we wanted to welcome you to our farm with a little gift. Now Mr. Bali, if ye'll help me with this basket, I'd be obliged."

They carried the basket to the fire then Bali made a great ceremony of seating them on two exquisite hand carved chairs. I flopped on the ground and looked at the strange faces that ringed th' fire. The young ladies were very pretty, dressed in so many bright colors it dazzled my eyes. They were covered in jewelry of turquoise and silver so beautiful it took my breath away.

Some of the very old ones were wrinkled beyond anything I'd ever seen and when they moved I imagined I could hear their skin crackle like old parchment. It resembled tightly crumbled newspapers, yet a strange beauty glowed through the transparent covering. Thin blue veins traced delicate patterns over the skeletal bones of their hands, like rare marble, and I longed to hold them in mine and study their intricate beauty. Their dark eyes were as young and brilliant as the youngest child as they studied me with kindness. I wondered if they could read my mind. The old ones were treated with great respect and dignity, 'specially by the children.

We sat in silence for many minutes, their dark eyes studying us with great interest, 'specially our homemade clothin, but not one eye glanced at the basket, as though it wasn't there. The silence was comfortable as though each one of us was quite alone somewhere in a peaceful place where we could dream and refresh ourselves without the pressure of expected small talk and routine amenities.

Then Bali broke the silence.

"Music," he laughed, clappin' his hands in staccato rythmn as he began to dance around the fire. Bali's feet hardly seemed to touch the ground as he moved gracefully around the leapin' flames; then he stopped in front of Grandma and extended his hand to her, his eyes glowin' like jewels. A murmur of surprise rippled through th' clan and th' faces of th' old ones wore expressions of shock so intense I meant to ask Pa and Grandma about it.

I turned back to Bali and was stunned to see Grandma rise from her chair and take Bali's hand as though it was th' most natural thing in th' world. He did not lead the dance nor did she follow. They seemed to ride th' fiery tongue of flames that pierced th' sky in wondrous colors, wrapped in a magic bubble of perfection. The only sound was th' crackle of burnin' wood thrusting cascades of brilliant sparks into th' darkness. I watched in facination as Grandma's braid came loose, her raven hair slowly fallin' toward th' ground, then gasped as Bali grasped her hands and started to slowly swirl 'round and 'round, faster and faster until they seemed to blur into one.

There was a soft whisper from the clan as Grandma's hair began to wrap itself around them until they were completely enclosed in its beauty. I turned to look at Pa and his face was full of wonder and joy and pride in his Net for I'm sure he'd never seen her dance so beautifully before. She could squaredance with the best, but this was far beyond any country dancin' any of us could even imagine.

It all seemed so unreal, like bein' wrapped in a magic cloud. Suddenly the soft tones of th' lute we'd heard that first night they camped by th' pear trees, began to whisper in th' background. I looked around but couldn't see anyone, nor could I place th' sound. It was in the air we breathed, filling us with sweet peace and happiness and forgetfulness of everything except th' fragrance of each perfect note.

Bali stood like a statue beside Grandma, his head tilted to one side, listening intently to some message that only he seemed to understand, his eyes on th' darkness behind a small, delicately carved wagon. It glowed from within, the glow seeping through the carved exterior like a halo. Suddenly a form came from the darkness, so twisted and grotesque I gasped in dismay as it slowly made its way toward the fire.

The gnarled, misshapen hands held th' lute to its mouth with a grace I hardly believed until my attention focused on the entire being, then the ugly twisted limbs faded away and took on a gentle, spiritual beauty as they moved with royal perfection toward th' flames. Its eyes sparkled like diamonds and a soft glow enclosed its being with light.

Grandma stared at the grotesque body with warmth and love, then she slowly approached him with great respect, never taking her eyes from his. She gracefully lowered herself to the earth and carefully spread her abundant hair before him. It was a priceless gesture worthy of royalty.

The being settled upon the glorious mound, looking into her eyes, then raised th' lute to its lips. Every living creature fell silent as the lute filled th' night with its spell binding music, weavin' a tapestry of spiritual beauty across the sky until every star was singin' heavenly praise to the master of the universe.

I don't know how long it lasted for I awoke th' next morning in my bed as usual, with a happiness I couldn't explain. Grandma hardly spoke a word all day, her thoughts far away, her eyes glowin' like the diamonds I'd seen last night in th' man creatures eyes. Her glance often strayed to the little house across th' field by th' pear trees and I noticed a special gleam illumined her hair.

The Gypsie's stayed all summer, helpin' Pa plant and plow and clean th' barn and a jillion things that have to be done on a farm. They especially loved th' animals, attending to their needs with great care. Never a weed appeared in the truckpatch, which sometimes put Grandma's nose outta joint since she liked workin' in her garden. Pa and Grandma shared our vegetables with them helpin' th' women can large amounts of food.

Bali sometimes asked if maybe they ought to move on; but Pa would laugh and ask him what he would do without all their good help.

"Sides," Pa told him, "Fall is just around th' corner and all them fine fruits will go to waste if ye don'teat them and can enough for th' comin' winter.

Bali would smile and let himself be talked out of leavin'. His people were happy there on the farm and they more than paid for what they got. Grandma kept them in eggs and Pa insisted on th' men goin' to help him milk th' cows so they could help him carry th' milk back home. Our cows seemed to be outdoin' themselves for there was usually four gallons or more than we could use so Pa insisted the Gypsies keep it for th' clan's use..

"Waste not, want not," he'd say. "Sides, them kids need to drink lots of milk to have good bones. Everybody needs milk," he'd lecture as though he was teachin' a class in school. Th' old ones would be settin' in th' sun with a big glass in their hands waitin' for him.He'd hug them all, then pour out a glass of warm milk for each one. Of course they adored him.

"Do ye know what I'd have to do if I took all this milk home?" he'd ask them. Heads would shake solemnly and he'd say, "Why, I'd be churnin' butter from here to next week, thats what. And I purely hate churnin'." They would grin happily and sip the warm liquid.

One day Pa brought one of our crock butter churns to Bali and showed him how to make butter from th' extra milk. Bali laughed and quickly passed th' churn over to th' women. "I don't think I'd like it any better than you Mr. Hundley;" but from then on Pa noticed the children eating bread with thick layers of butter on it.

One mornin' after our first frost, the field by the pear trees was empty. The Gypsies had gone as mysteriously as they had appeared. We felt a terrible sadness for we had grown quite fond of them, 'specially Mr. Bali.

After breakfast Grandma always took her second cup of coffee to the front porch, to her favorite rockin' chair. As I held th' screen door open for her I glanced down at th' rocker. "Grandma there's a beautiful box in your rocking chair," I exclaimed.

She knelt down beside th' seat, a surprised, wondering look on her face as she studied th' exquisitely painted box. For a long time she didn't touch it as though she feared it might disappear. Resting her coffee cup on th' porch railin', she carefully lifted th' box from th' rocker and sat down as though her legs would no longer hold her. Delicate miniature mountains with waterfalls rushing down canyons, framed with trees and flowers we'd never see, filled my heart with a strange yearnin'. She tenderly turned th' box this way and that so we could see its beauty, her face glowin' with a strange happiness. The box itself was a priceless treasure with its delicate golden clasp; but when Grandma carefully raised th' lid we couldn't believe the treasure that lay within.

A silver clasp for Grandma's hair gleamed up at us, its surface covered with flowers and a tiny deer lying almost invisible beneath a small bush. Grandma's eyes were filled with tears as she gazed upon its unbelievable beauty. A tiny lute was lying beside a clump of flowers. It was th' artists signature.

"It's from th' Being," I whispered in awe.

"Yes, child," she said softly, "and that alone makes it special beyond tellin'."

There was another gift wrapped in red silk and tied with red silk tassle's. Her hands trembled as she carefully untied the tassels and released th' covering. She stared at th' gift for a second, then sank against th' back of th' chair, th' gift clasped tightly against her breast. I couldn't see what it was; but I knew it was a thing to be savored in privacy so I slipped through th' front door and left th' house.

Grandpa was in th' barn milkin' th' cows. I settled on a stool beside him and watched his nimble fingers draw milk from th' cow's teats, happy to be in a familiar routine. He seemed to understand my silence, gave me a little smile and went back to his milkin.' I looked around th' room for a package or somethin'; but there were only th' usual things I'd seen all my life. I didn't know if I was happy or sad about that. As though he had read my thoughts, Pa reached behind him and unhooked a green silk sack tied with a string from a nail and handed it to me. I held it in my lap for a long time just lookin' at the brilliant color then slowly opened the drawstring and peered inside. It looked like a rope.

Finally Pa peered at me impatiently. "It won't bite you sprout so pull it out and take a good look." The rope was actually fine white silk cord woven tightly to form a necklace. In th' middle of th' cord was a silver bust of Pa and Streeter. The likeness was incredible and I could almost see ole Streeter smilin' and smell th' smoke comin' from Pa's pipe. "It's super Pa, but what is it?"

"It's called a bolo, sprout, another version of a mans neck tie. They're very popular in th' West."

"Do you like it?" I whispered.

"Do I like it? You bet I like it. It's worth a fortune and too fine for an ole farmer like me."

"Th' one who made it didn't think it was too fine for you Pa, else he wouldn't have done all that fine work just for an ole farmer like you."

"You really think so sprout?"

"They loved you Pa, 'special th' one what made it. Wonder who that was."

"Still, it seems too fine to wear." He mused. His fingers were motionless on Marcia's teat for so long she turned impatiently to see what was holdin' things up.

"It's a work of art sprout and a man's lucky to own somethin' like this in his entire lifetime. I can hardly wait to wear it to Church and show ole Charlie." Finally he slipped it back into the silk bag and turned back to milkin' Marcie.

"I couldn't get over how it looked exactly like Pa and Streeter." "Who do you think made this, Pa?" I whispered. He puffed his pipe and went on milkin' Marcie, his face serene and contemplative. "I'd say th' beautiful being who lived in th' small house did this. You seen how wonderfully his wagon was carved. I expect he is responsible for all the beautiful carvings on all th' other wagons as well. He's special sprout. A gift from God, with a spiritual light shinin' from a twisted body. If he was just an ordinary man, God couldn't use him. I pray we'll see him and Bali and his clan again."

"Me too, Pa. I thought he was glorious. I wanted to touch him so much it hurt, but I was sure no one was allowed to touch him."

"No one except Bali," Pa said. "One night when I couldn't sleep I went out and sat on th' well curb for a long time. Th' moon was bright and I could see th' Gypsy camp as clear as day. Then I seen two figures out in th' pasture where the stream runs. Only one of them was walkin' and that one was Bali. He was carryin' th' being in his arms, showin' him everything, th' trees, rocks, th' stream. For a brief time I heard splashin' and laughter, like two little boys just out of school, swimmin' and havin' th' time of their life."

Pa was quiet for a long time, his fingers automatically drawin' milk from Marcie, then he looked at th' bright light of dawn streaking thru a crack in th' wall.

"I think maybe th' being can't tolerate th' light," he said, "specially th' sun. We've never seen him except that one time and that was night. Remember how his eyes glowed. I can't imagine why that is but there is a good reason and I'm sure it has somethin' to do with th' sun."

When we got back to the house, Grandma was still in th' rocker, Th' gift clasped to her chest.

"Is anythin' wrong Net?" Pa asked anxiously, peerin' at her in alarm.

Her eyes were full of wonder as she pulled th' silk cloth back and laid th' gift in her lap for us to see.

Pa sank to th' porch beside Grandma and studied th' carving of Grandma and Bali dancin'. Her dark hair wrapped them in a delicate web of etheral grace and beauty from which fiery tongues of flame leaped upward. Their eyes glowed like diamonds and I marveled that such wonders could somehow be captured in a mere piece of wood. Th' figures were alive in a way I couldn't explain; but Pa seemed to understand th' reality of such perfection for he kissed Grandma tenderly then laid his hand briefly on her hair.

Neither Pa nor I touched th' dancin' figures for there seemed to be an invisible barrier around them that excluded everyone except Grandma. Their colors seemed to eminate from glowing lights, alive and real like the rainbow and they changed from day to day, growin' more and more beautiful. Grandma kept th' carving on th' corner what-not in her bedroom where she could see it before she went to sleep and when she awoke. She wore th' silver clasp in her hair and it was hard to tell which was th' more beautiful.

"What did you get sprout," Pa asked.

I was so excited over their presents I hadn't given it a thought.

"Well, I'm sure they didn't ferget you, honey, so lets have a look around." We looked everwhere but found nothin'.

Pa puffed his pipe thoughtfully, his thinkin' apparatus goin' ninety to nothin'. "Finally, he slapped his knee and laughed. "Now why didn't I think on that before. It's plain as th' nose on my face. Where do you spend most of yer time, sprout?"

"Well, I guess I spend most every day with Dimple."

"Then thats where ye should look."

I ran to th' barn and looked in Dimple's stall, but didn't see a thing. I even pitched th' hay around, looked in ever nook and cranny but there wasn't a present for me anywhere. Pa and Grandma came to th' barn but one look at my face told th' story.

"Ye jest ain't found th' right place yet sprout," Grandma murmured. They started to help me look when we heard hoofbeats enter th' breezeway and Dimple rushed in to see what all th' commotion was about.

"Too bad Dimple cain't talk Pa."

"Maybe she can," Pa laughed. "Look under her mane. I'd swear I seen a blue ribbon when she ran thru th' breezeway."

I ran my hands under her mane and sure enuff', there was a velvet box tied with a blue ribbon. I carefully removed it, my fingers tremblin' so that

53

I could hardly untie th' ribbon then I gently opened th' velvet lid and stared in wonder at what lay inside. Grandma and Pa were lookin' over my shoulder and I felt Grandma's hand settle gently on my arm.

"Well, I'll be switched," Pa murmured softly.

"It's a treasure, child. No Queen ever had anything finer," Grandma whispered, her voice full of emotion. "Only th' being could create such perfection. May I?" she asked, taking th' box from my hand. She removed a silver bracelet first and slipped it over my wrist. It bore my likeness with delicate flowers entwined in my long hair. We all stared in amazement at such beauty and perfection. Then Grandma lifted a small silk square and there lay a perfect ring to match th' bracelet. A tiny replica of Dimple galloped around its circle with snow covered mountains and streams and blue skies in th' background. She looked so real I could almost see her hoofs kicking up tiny clumps of green grass as she sped through a land of enchantment. Inside th' band of th' ring was a tiny rose with a lute lying beside its petals. "We know for sure now that the being made these treasures for th' lute is his signature. Everyone of th' gifts has a lute on it somewhere."

"What kind of art is this, Grandpa where th' artist scratches pictures on th' silver?"

"It's called Scrimshaw, Sprout. I reckon it's been around since time began."

"Why did he put just my face on th' bracelet and then covered th' tiny ring with a jillion things?"

Pa smiled softly. "I'd say that was a wee bit of ego, Sprout. It takes a superior artist to do such delicate work; but the being is not just an artist. He's a master without equal and since that miraculous gift was bestowed on him by th' master of our Universe, I reckon th' Lord will forgive the innocent pride of artistic perfection he displayed on your ring."

The winter passed slowly. Marcie and several cows were swollen with calves and we expected several colts in th' spring. Th' men started buildin a church beside th' bush arbor we'd used for so long and I felt a terrible lonliness when I looked at the arbor where I'd gone to church every Sunday of my life. Times were changin' and I hated to see it. So did Grandma.

"By th' time you're grown and married, child," she'd tell me, a strange sadness in her face, "There'll be very little left of th' old ways."

"Well, I'm not goin' to change anythin'." I declared. " I love th' bush arbor and if th' preacher wants to preach in that new fangled church when it's finshed, he'll just have to talk loud if he wants me to hear 'im for I'll be settin' in th' arbor. Grandma hugged me to her and I knew she felt the same way.

Th' weather suddenly turned terrible cold and a two foot snow stopped all work on the frame outline of th' new church. Me and Grandma rejoiced and I began to consider ways to hinder th' buildin' of th' new church, or maybe stop it completely, once and for all.

I failed to consider God might have plans for th' new church; but surely, I reasoned, he'd seen how happy we all were in the arbor.

To my disgust, the weather cleared, work resumed on th' new church and God didn't appear overly sentimental about th' arbor. I inspected progress on th' new Church ever day and when they began work on th' roof I almost despaired; but I didn't relinquish all hope of its destruction.

December was too cold to work on th' church and as it turned out January was even colder. Ever time I passed th' new church I rejoiced at th' open walls and th' rough plank floors covered in big drifts of snow.

Down th' road, a stones throw from the new church, th' arbor stood proudly on its flimsy pole supports, its roof of leafless limbs still standin' strong despite th' winds and snow and sleet and rain. I felt a fierce pride for its long years of service, for th' fine sermons given within its flimsy protection, and for th' deer who would stand at th' edge of th' woods listenin' to our songs of praise. Baby rabbits would play in th' grass so close we could reach out and nearly touch them. Sometimes a squirell or two mistook th' roof for home and realizin' their mistake, scolded us loudly before they scuttled down a pole and ran for th' woods.

The Arbor was special. It was God's church where the animals felt free to come and attend. It was th' sounds of nature blendin' with th' singin' and sermons and Amens that rattled th' leaves on th' branches overhead. Farmers and their families filled its open space, settin' on logs sawn in half, with no back rests to lean on, their feet restin' on God's green grass.

Sunburned faces and hands gnarled from years of hard labor, raised in fervent Praise to our Lord and Saviour were th' canvases on which nature painted her pictures. Eyes squinted against a hot sun carved deep seams in their faces with beautiful patterns like old paintings I'd seen in picture books. Sometimes I got so engrossed in studyin' somebody's face I'd forget I was in church, supposed to be listenin' to th' sermon. These sunburned, wrinkled, hard workin', God fearin' folks of our community were th' most beautiful I'd ever seen or ever will see.

Nature had begun to carve a little on Pa's face too and sometimes I could see tiny little lines around Grandma's eyes if th' light was just right.

I knew in my heart the new fangled church would win th' battle in th' long run. Th' bush arbor would eventually fall, never to rise again. Sermons would lose a bit of their fire and brimstone as preachers were made comfortable behind stained glass windows and fancy pulpits, and solid edifices that shut nature out and shut people in. Cardboard fans with 'Jesus Saves' printed on one side and 'Prepare to die printed on th' other side would be replaced with window fans that drowned out th' preacher's voice.

'Course electricity was years away from our neck of th' woods, but it too, would come, then our beautiful oil lamps and th' magical alladin would be banished one by one to an attic or a basement already crowded with useless junk that would one day become priceless treasures; at least those that didn't get dumped in a ditch somewhere to make room for more convenient stuff that wouldn't run th' course, as Grandma was fond of sayin'.

"Progress will proceed, with or without us Sprout, no matter how hard we fight to keep everything th' same," Pa would proclaim in a sad voice.

Grandma said th' peoples hearts would become complacent and their faith weakened when all they had to do was come to a cozy church, sit on soft padded benches and dream about dinner or fall asleep from too much comfort. "There's nothin' like a sudden rain storm with high winds blowin' through th' arbor branches to keep a body awake and alert to th' word of God," Grandma declared.

"And wet," pa added, with a wicked grin. "The days of th' bush arbor are numbered, Net and thets a fact. I love th' arbor as much as you and th' sprout and I'll 'specially miss th' meetin's we have in th' winter at each others house, and th' fellowship we share, not to mention th' good food."

A warm spell covered th' land th' first day of February and everbody wondered if Spring was gonna be early. Grandma began makin' out orders from her seed catalogs and we all got a touch of spring fever. When Pa awoke two mornin's later, he shook down th' ashes in th' stove, put in kindling wood and soon th' kitchen was warm and cozy. Grandma came in and started breakfast as usual. "Seems unusual dark in here Almus. Maybe you'd better light th' Alladin lamp."

Pa looked at th' window and smiled. "Do ye suppose we got up an hour too soon, Net? It's pitch black out there."

Grandma checked th' clock on top of th' pie safe, then checked th' one in th' bedroom. "Both got th' same time, so I reckon it ta be th' right time."

Pa opened th' kitchen door and stepped onto th' back porch his face turned toward th' sky. "Dear Lord Jesus," he exclaimed." Net! Come quick!"

I'd been listenin' to their talk so had dressed quickly and was right behind Grandma when she stepped thru th' back door.

Th' sky was black and blue, with lots of gray rollin' around like fog and jillions of other colors streakin' in ever direction. I suddenly realized the colors was lightenin' knifin'' through th' sky like spider webs filled with blood. Sometimes I'd see a small puff of smoke when one of them struck th' ground, paintin' the clouds with a blindin' brilliance that hurt my eyes. Long dark tendrils began to slowly drop from the blackness to the earth, skimmin' over th' ground like a sheet of rain, swirling and writheing in agony, pulling the blackness lower and lower until it seemed to almost touch th' ground.

Pa and Grandma had watched for just a minute yet it felt like we'd been on th' porch for hours. I thought I heard a small roar, more like a moan and turned to ask Pa what it was when he began to shout orders.

"Sprout, pour a bucket of water on the fire in th' cook stove, then open the storm cellar door and start carryin' quilts and food and water down there. I'll put th' livestock in their shelter with food and water and with Streeter's help I ought to finish in a few minutes. Thank God they are all still in their stalls."

"Net, ye know what to do 'bout lockin' th' house up tight and...." He glanced at th' sky just as a slender funnel dropped from th' sky twistin' and turnin' like an angry snake. When it hit th' ground it sucked up everthin' in its path, growin' to monster size in seconds.

We've got maybe five minutes," he yelled, "maybe not. Grab what you can now and run for th' cellar and thets an order," he said, lookin' straight at me.

Grandma ran in th' house and filled my arms full, drew a bucket of water from th' well and helped me to th' storm cellar. "Stay put," she said, then she was gone. I knew she would be helpin' Pa lock th' animals in their own storm cellar. Th' neighbors had laughed when Pa started diggin' a room out of th' hillside behind th' barn. It had a stall for each animal, with food and water and while it wasn't real big it was adequate to protect them.

"I guess thar'll always be a Noah," some said, but it mattered not to Pa. Once he was fixed on an idea there was no use tryin' to talk him out of it. Ole Charlie had watched Pa for awhile then gone home and done th' same thing. Pa had urged our neighbors to build their own storm shelters for their animals as well as themselves, but they scoffed at th' idea. "Ain't never seen a tornado come close to my place," one said. "Besides I've got a root cellar."

"I've lived here nigh on to fifty years," said another, "ain't never had no need for a storm shelter."

As I sat thinkin' on things I realized me and Grandma had forgotten somethin' very important. I ran up th' shelter steps and looked at th' sky. I judged th' funnel cloud was a couple miles away, then I peered at th' barn. Pa nor Grandma were in sight and I knew they were in th' animal shelter. For a second I fought th' idea of disobeyin' Grandma, then I was up and runnin' to th' house. It didn't take a minute to find what I was lookin' for and when I ran back to th' storm cellar it was still empty. I heaved a sigh of relief then began to worry 'bout Pa and Grandma and ole Streeter. I was about to run to th' barn when ole Streeter ran down th' steps with Pa and Grandma right behind him. Pa secured th' door at th' top of th' steps, then another one at th' bottom.

We wrapped ourselves in quilts and curled up on th' bales of hay Pa had laid on th' floor. He had even stacked them up th' walls to th' ceiling so we were snug and comfortable.

Th' roar of th' tornado grew louder, soundin' like a hundred trains and I knew it was nearly on us. Th' outside door rattled and screeched as th' funnel tried to tear it from th' nails and hinges that held it fast.

We strained our ears for sounds from th' house as it slammed full strength against th' storm cellar. It seemed to sit right on top of th' door for what seemed like an eternity, then we heard lumber being splintered and ripped from its foundation. My heart froze in horror as the shrill high scree of metal grindin' against metal filled my ears and I visualized Grandma's warm morning cook stove filled with her fine iron skillets and cookwear being smashed into pieces by th' giant monster as it sucked th' treasured necessities of our lives into oblivion.

Grandma's face was pale, her lips movin' in silent prayer as she looked at Pa's stricken face. They were sure they had just heard th' house bein' torn

57

from its foundation by th' merciless monster outside. I longed to do somethin' to erase the pain from their faces. Then I remembered what I'd gone back to th' house to save. I took th' pillow case from beside me in th' hay and laid it in Grandms'a apron. "I'm sorry I disobeyed you Grandma by going back to th' house but I had to cause it was so important."

She studied my face, then slowly opened th' pillow case, starin' in disbelief and joy. "What a brave thing to do," she murmured, tears fillin' her eyes. Pa was lookin' at Grandma and th' case as she poured its contents into her lap. There were all th' beautiful treasures th' gypsy being had made for us, shinin' like silver stars in th' dim light of Pa's lantern.

Streeter whined low in his throat, then growled a threat at whatever was out there just as th' outside door was ripped off. A rush of wind came down th' steps shakin' and pullin' at th inner door, lashin' th' boards with rocks and dirt and I thought it too would go any minute.

"Cover your face with th' quilts," Grandma yelled, "and hold on to each other."

Then I heard Pa's deep voice start singin' 'Amazing Grace.' Grandma joined in and I lay there with Streeter wrapped tightly in my arms and listened to them sing song after song of Praise to th' Lord. Th' noise seemed to grow more intense as though th storm didn't want to hear songs 'bout th' Lord; but their voices never wavered. Then it was so quiet I could hear Streeter breathe and I knew it was all over. No one said a word for a long time, just lay quiet and grateful that we were alive and together.

Pa finally opened th' inner door and looked outside, then he began to clear th' limbs and rocks and dirt off th' steps so we could get outta th' cellar. I didn't want to go out and see what might not be there anymore so I held onto Streeter and hunkered up in a corner with th' quilt wrapped tightly around us. "I might stay here forever," I told Streeter.

Pa and Grandma walked hand in hand from th' dim cellar toward a sick lookin' sky, their faces pale

with dread. They must have stood silent and disbelievin' for a long time, then I heard Pa give whoop after whoop of joy, all mixed together with Grandma's prayers of thanksgiving. I ran out with Streeter right behind me and stood lookin' at th' house with disbelief. It was untouched, not even a shingle misiing from th' roof. Grandma was crying with joy as she ran toward th' back porch. Pa was right behind her but he was lookin' toward th' barn.

It was gone!

Not even a board remained to attest that it ever existed. Pa's face was grim as he walked toward th' feed lot, th' fence still standing around an empty space, then he started runnin' toward th' storm cellar he'd built for th' animals. Meand Grandma were right behind him when he opened th' door and looked inside. A dozen pair of eyes looked at Pa in bewilderment, their faces concerned and confused; but not one of them moved an inch from his stall. Pa examined each one carefully, huggin' and croonin' endearments to them. They seemed to be listenin' for th' frightful noise to begin

Pig and a Sack of Stray Cats

again, their ears cocked toward th' open door but little by little they responded to Pa's assurances and began to relax.

I ran to th' back of th' room to see Dimple and got th' surprise of my life. Sampson was squeezed in beside Dimple with Ole Charlie settin' in th' saddle with a big smile on his face. He slid to th' floor and gave me a bear hug." Dimple and Nell are fine, honey and I do believe th' three of them rather enjoyed th' show." Pa and Grandma couldn't believe their eyes when they seen Charlie.

"Almus, if it hadn't been for this here cellar, me and Sampson would have been goners. I tried to out run th' tornado but when I got ta yer place I knew I'd never make it home. Thank God Norey knows what to do and I'll bless ye th' rest of me days fer talkin' me into buildin' a shelter for th' livestock and me and Norey." He shook Pa's hand solemnly and there were tears in his eyes.

"Thank God yer safe Charlie. We're very fortunate, me and Net, for our house wasn't even touched. Let's hurry to your place and see what's happened there. I expect a lot of folks were hit and we'll have to help them build back and get on their feet again. Time is th' important ingredient. Th' sooner they can get back to some kind of normal living, th' less they'll sorrow over what they've lost."

Pa climbed on Sampson behind Charlie and they raced toward Charlie's house. Grandma yelled that we'd be there as soon as we could..

We left th cattle in th' shelter and went to th' house to prepare for th' Lord only knew what. Lots of families would be hungry and shocked and scared. Grandma always said a little food in th' belly made it easier to face th' impossible.

Two hours later we filled baskets with food and set them on th' porch. "Go fetch Dimple and Nell, child, and be sure to lock th' others in th' shelter 'till Almus comes back." We tied th' baskets to th' saddles and rode toward Charlie and Nora Horn's house, two miles away.

Charlie had lost his barn also and had some minor damage to his house but all in all he was in good shape. He suddenly looked around in panic. "Norey! Where's ole Blue?" He started yellin' for Blue, tears streamin' down his face, then we heard a weak bark and Charlie started runnin' in ever direction lookin' for his beloved hound.

"He's in th' storm cellar, Charlie, with th' rest of th' critters"

Norey turned to me and Grandma as Pa and Charlie headed to the cellar. "Thet silly old man loves thet fool dog more'n he loves me but I'm not one bit jealous cause thet dog can't make biscuits or pies or good coffee or whoopee...and thet man sure does love his whoopee."

She laughed good-naturedly and winked at Grandma. "In about ten years ye can tell this child all about whoopee, Net. Now let's go have a cup of strong coffee and a piece of chocolate pie afore we git on with th' business of puttin' our neighbors back on their feet."

Somethin' in Grandma's face wiped out all th' questions I had intended to ask about Whoopee. Not once in her entire lifetime did I ever mention th' word 'whoopee,' even after I was grown up and knew what Norey had meant on that long ago day.

A lot of homes were damaged but only four were completely destroyed. Six barns were torn to pieces, along with th' cattle. Th' white faces of their owners told th' story of how hard it is to build up a herd of milk cows and enough horses to farm th' land. Pa assured them we'd all pitch in with th' plantin' and most ever one promised a cow or a horse.

Why, we'll have new barns built in no time," Pa said, his arms around a shoulder to comfort.

"Course we'll get th' houses built first; but I expect with th' whole community and some help from outside, we'll have it all back in three weeks, maybe less."

Then J.D. Deaton come ridin' up like th' devil was after him, shoutin' and cryin' at th' same time. "Ya need ta come quick," he sobbed. "Thars a terrible thing over ta Grandma Hanson's place, a terrible thing," he whispered, as he slumped from th' saddle in a dead faint.

Grandma Hanson was a widow who lived in her little farmhouse two miles down th' road from us. She was beloved by th' entire community for anywhere there was trouble or sickness, you would find her quietly tendin' to th' needs of others. Just last week in church she was tellin' us that her daughter and son-in-law were coming from Chicago for a visit with their firstborn.

"Imagine!" she exclaimed. "My first Grandbaby." Her cherubic face glowed as she hugged everbody and told them th' good news.

Th' daughter had brought her mother a special gift, a gift no one in th' whole community ever dreamed of having since they were so dear. It was a new wonder of our world. A radio. Grandma Hanson insisted th' whole community come and listen anytime they wanted and she would put it in an open window while we all sprawled on th' grass in th' yard and listenened to Amos and Andy, Th' Shadow Knows, Fibber Mc Gee and Mollie and countless others. It had been a glorious week and th' eight month old baby girl had been held and crooned over by ever woman in th' community, 'specially Grandma Hanson, who could hardly stand for the baby to be out of her sight.

She must have been playin' th' radio and didn't hear th' tornado, else she'd have taken th' baby and gone to her root cellar. We all reckoned that when she finally did hear th' tornado it was practically on her. Neighbors had found her body slumped over an oblong galvanized tub, her hands locked onto th' handles. A large tree limb was driven through her body. They heard a tiny cry and when they were able to pry Grandma's hands off th' tub, there was th' little Grandaughter inside, wrapped in a heavy quilt, safe and sound.

By th' time we got there they had removed th' limb from her body and th' ladies had dressed her in her prettiest dress. Th' men were buildin' a coffin from th' lumber of her house which was scattered all over th' fields and that seemed fitting to everyone since she and her deceased husband had spent their entire lives in that house.

Everyone thanked th' Lord her daughter, Jenny, and son-in-law hadn't arrived back from Burnside in time to see th' horror of how she had died.

"Imagine," one woman said, "th' terror she must have felt when she heard thet terrible wind bearing down on them. I'm sure she heard th' house bein' sucked up into th' air before thet tree limb pierced her body.and ended her life." Th' woman burst into tears and there was hardly a man or woman who wasn't grievin' over Grandma Hanson's death.

Careful what ye all say," admonished Grandma, as she walked with th' babe toward th' road where th' daughter and her husband were runnin' toward th' house, gaspin' for breath, their faces pale despite th' heat. Grandma handed th' baby to Jenny and held all three of them in her arms for a moment.

Jenny crooned over th' baby, searching for any injury to th' little one, cryin' with joy as she kissed th' little face over and over again. Her husband, Dave, held them both in his arms, weapin' at th' sight of little Diedre's blue eyes starin' up at them.

Suddenly, Jenny started runnin' toward th' crowd searchin' for her mother's face, then she stared at th' empty space where th' house so recently stood. "Where is my mother?" she whispered hoarsly, lookin' at th' faces around her.

Grandma pulled her and th' baby into her arms and gently led her to th' home made casket in which Grandma Hanson's body lay. Her mother's face had a peaceful look, th' lips almost curved in a smile as though she had just seen the Lord.

"She saved your baby, Jenny and gladly gave her life to do so. I know it must be impossible to understand these things and your grief will be seem overwhelming for awhile; but God's Grace will sustain you and your husband and He will heal you and turn your grief into wonderful memories of your dear mother." Everbody loved Grandma Hanson for she lived God's word for all to see and never did she turn her back on anyone in need.

Did God cause this terrible thing?" she asked, her eyes full of horror.

"No, child. God doesn't deliberately hurt his children for he loves us with a love so pure it's beyond our understanding."

Then why did he let my mother die?"

"God created a perfect world, Jenny; then sin changed it into an imperfect world where bad things can happen even to good people. Sometimes these tragic things happen to the finest christians on earth and I can't explain why that is; but I do know that your mother is this moment in Heaven with our Lord and Saviour. Don't doubt God and his love for all his creation, Jenny, and above all, you must have faith, 'specially when it seems impossible to understand the things that happen to us here on earth. Now you and your little family will come live with us for a time, as long as you need, and we'll help you through this tryin' time. God is good, child. Don't ever forget that!"

I looked at th' daughter holdin' th baby tightly in her arms, her face white with shock, not quite believin' her mother was gone and felt a terrible sadness that th' fingers which held th' tub down would never again caress th' face of her Grandchild.

The daughter neither cried nor spoke and I wondered if she heard Grandma's comfortin' words. Her spirit was in a world no one could reach. The father of th' child seemed frozen in a state of disbelief and kept lookin' around at th' debris of th' shattered house scattered over th' fields as though if he looked hard enough he might erase th' nightmare that he found himself in.

Grandma held them both in her arms a moment longer then guided them to th' wagon Pa had brought down and me and Grandma took them home with us. She made strong herbal tea with a sleepin' potion in it and persuaded them to lie down for awhile. Th' daughter wouldn't turn loose of th' baby so Grandma put one of her big goose down pillows between them and snuggled th' wee mite into its softness.

Th' homeless were taken in by neighbors whose houses were untouched. They were fed and comforted and encouraged to take heart that their families were still intact.

Every night Pa visited somewhere and prayed and read th' word of th' Lord to them, remindin' them how fortunate they were to have each other and eventually their Spirits started to lift.

Th' men began to rebuild th' houses first, workin' from first light until they could no longer see. A big bush arbor was put up as a kitchen, tarpaulion stretched over ever side to keep th' cold weather ou for after th' tornado, february returned cold and sunless..Cook stoves were moved to th' site and th' smells comin' from th' stoves seemed ta spur th' carpenters to greater effort. As th' women cooked, they consoled each other and when everyone was on his sleepin' pallet at night, we talked and prayed and cried together and formed bonds of friendship that would never end.

Th' third mornin' after th' tornado, Pa looked out toward th' pear trees and there were three gypsy wagons pulled into their familiar semi-circle. Grabbin' his coat and hat he raced across th' field shoutin' and laughin' with joy and about halfway across there was Bali runnin' with outstretched arms, his beautiful teeth spread in a glad smile. They embraced over and over again, tears spillin' down their face.

"What are you doin' here so early in all this cold weather? Pa exclaimed. "Why, I didn't expect ye afore th' middle of March or April."

"Come to the fire Mr. Hundley and I'll tell you all about it." Bali poured out two great cups of hot cofee, and pulled two chairs close to the roaring fire.

"Is there somethin' wrong? Pa asked in alarm.

"I'd say everything is right Mr.Hundley , except this awful weather, although it seems like summer here compared to the mountainous regions of Hungary in the wintertime." He shuddered and Pa knew some painful tragedy of th' past had crossed his memory.

"No," Bali continued, "a month ago the being told us we must hurry to your farm as fast as we could go. He kept saying there was great trouble coming and you needed help. He wouldn't play the flute, nor eat until we broke camp and started."

"But you only have three wagons. Where are th' others?"

"Th' being stayed behind with th' old ones and several men to drive up here when the weather gets warmer. We brought all the able bodied men and one woman to cook for us. I see your barn is gone; but thank Heaven the house is intact."

Then ye know 'bout th' tornado that struck three days ago."

"The being knew of its coming. He seems to know about everything. He said one person died but that the Hundley family was safe."

"Yes, we lost Grandma Hanson but she saved th' life of her baby granddaughter. Terrible tragedy th' way she died. Her daughter is in a bad way. She won't talk, still in shock, hardly turns th' baby loose for a minute and does nothin' but stare out at th' sky as though watching for another tornado. Net is carin' for her but her mind is off where even Net can't reach."

"Maybe," Bali said, then grew silent.

I waited for him to finish, but he turned from th' fire and gave a strange call. Fifteen strong men came spillin' out, laughin' and shovin' each other good naturedly toward th' fire. "We're ready to go to work, Mr Hundley."

Each one of the men carried a steel chest which I later learned contained ever kind of buildin' tool you could imagine.

"Go where?' I inquired.

"To build houses and barns and furniture, and when its warmer we'll plant crops and gardens and help in the harvest. Time is fleeting old friend so let's begin to right the wrong done here and when the others arrive we will have a fine party by the bon fire, listen to the being play the lute, and have a feast to end all feasts."

"Will ye do me a favor Bali."

"Name it and it's yours." "Call me Almus and forget th' Mr. Hundley stuff."

"Done!" Bali laughed. I'm Bali and you're Almus. Right?"

"Right,"

When those whose houses and barns were destroyed, seen fifteen new helpers they immediately held a prayer of thanksgivin' and praise to th' Lord for his provision in their time of need. There was much time lost while they hugged th' Gypsies over and over again, with many affectionate slaps on th' back. Their gratitude was genuine, forged forever with a bond of brotherly love.

Bali stood to one side, a strange smile on his face, then he spied Grandma standin' in th' door of th' arbor.kitchen. He walked to her and they stood lookin' at each other for a long time then he took her hand, raised it to his lips and kissed it gently.

63

Th' houses went up like magic, th' women cooked wonderful food under th' tarpaulin covered arbor and there was much prayer and thanksgivin' for our new friends and helpers. We were all family now, bonded together with compassion and need. The Gypsies were just neighbors and no one thought of them as being different in any way. The Gypsies found our attitude toward them puzzlin' for awhile but gradually they realized we were sincere and soon you couldn't tell Gypsy from anybody else 'cept for th' dark skin.

I was madly in love with Bali, who seemed to understand, and always made me feel special. "Course I still loved Pig too, but he was, after all, just a kid who could hardly walk without stumblin', much less dance like Bali. When I told him how magical Bali danced, he stared at th' sky in disdain and said, "It don't take much talent to kick yer heels together 'specially with a bon fire scorchin' th' seat of yer britches."

"Yer just jealous. Wait till you see him dance; then you'll change your mind."

"Maybe. Maybe not," he replied sullenly.

By th' second week in March th' houses were finished and th' last barn was about done. Ever barn contained at least one cow and two horses and enough food to last 'till th' comin' fall.

Th' Gypsies were masters at buildin' furniture and no one had ever seen such beautiful tables and chairs and wardrobes. Th' beds were European flavor with a rough carvin' here and there and some were even built like sleighs. 'Course th' children claimed these immediately. Each bedroom had a rockin' chair for a newborn who needed rockin' to sleep. Drawers for storage were built right into th' wall which left much needed space for other things. Grandma thought that was th' best idea she had seen.

The women of th' community gave pots and pans and skillets and dishes and silverware and clothin' and anything else that was needed. Some of th' women said they were much better off after th' tornado than before, then blushed and hoped we'd never have another one. Several men said it was time to start plowin' th' fields and get ready for plantin'.

At this remark, Bali leaped onto a wagon and waved his arms for silence. Ever face turned to him with attention for Bali was a man of few words.

"My friends," he said, his white teeth sparklin' in his brown face. "Let us not speak of plowing and planting now and all the work that we know will have to be accomplished; but at this special time of blessing let us be grateful to our Lord and celebrate this great occassion with food and dancing and joy and gratitude for the friends we have become."

He became serious as he studied each face before him.

"The Gypsy has no friends among the whites and few trusted ones among his own kind. He is a wanderer in a land of no opportunities. A liar and a thief. An opportunist who will smile at you as he picks your pockets. In short, a Gypsy can't be trusted. This is true and you should remember it. but there is a rare exception and the clan of Bali is one of those exceptions.

We left Hungary seeking a new life in America. We found a new land but the same old attitude toward Gypsies, and who can blame those who have reason for such suspicion? But it is different here."

"The day I met Almus and Net and the sprout, I knew such a feeling of peace as can't be described. We were given hospitality never before dreamed of and best of all, treated like family. Brown and white skin living close together without prejudice."

"The being said there was such a place to be found and when I seen the Hundley farm I knew we had found that whch we had long sought. None of you have ever seen the being except Mr. Hundley, Mrs. Net and the sprout; but he is so special we care for him as we would a baby. He sent us here a month ago for he knew trouble was coming to you. He and the old ones will be here in March or April and we hope we might live by the pear trees one more summer and be part of the community."

With that he jumped from the wagon and went over to sit under one of the trees.

"Well, as far as I'm concerned Mr. Bali, yer part of th' community and welcome to spend th' rest of yer life here," Mr. Barton said. Iffen ye git tired of Almus's farm, I got plenty of room over ta my place."

"That goes for me too," Charlie grinned; then it seemed every voice spoke in unison to welcome Bali and his clan to our community for as long as they wanted to stay.

Pa jumped on th' wagon and frowned mightly at Charlie and Mr. Burton. "You two whipper snappers best keep yer ideas to yerself, for Bali and his family are welcome at my place forever; In fact I was hoping they would settle down here and make this their home but thats for them to decide."

Then Pa looked over at th' kitchen arbor. "I'm sure th' ladies have outdone themselves on this special day so lets go eat that good food and thank the dear Lord for His goodness to us."

The Being Arrives

Bali's clan arrived the last day of April. There was much huggin' and laughter and back slappin,' and a jillion dippers of th' sweetest water this side of Heaven were consumed with much lip smackin' exclamations over th' miracle well that never ran dry.

Th' animals drank so much they looked ready to pop and after a nice rest under our old oaks th' caravan moved on to th' pear trees where they joined th' other wagons in a perfect semi-circle. Th' being hadn't appeared, but I seen Bali hurrying with a bucket of water to th' little wagon at th' end of th' caravan. He didn't reappear so we knew he was tellin' th' being all th' news and ministerin' to him. I had often wondered how they were related but feared to ask.

A week after th' gypsies were settled in, Grandma and all th' women of th' community got together and cooked enough food for an army with each lady makin' her specialities.

Bali and his clan gathered enough wood to burn half th' county and all th' men put saw-horses together to form long rows of tables to hold th' food.

Grandpa scattered numerous bails of straw for folks to set on and th' gypsies had placed many beautifully carved chairs about for th' elderly and infirm whose worn bodies needed support.

Bali and his men had built a humomgous bon fire and there were numerous pots of coffee settin' on iron rails around th' edge, perkin' their wonderful fragrance into the air.

Th' gypsy women shyly placed their special European dishes among th' country food we were all raised on but Grandma noticed th' anxious look on their faces as they watched wagon after wagon unload its bounty and knew they were afraid we wouldn't like their food. She started walkin' the length of th' tables, lookin' at this and that until she came to their dishes. Th' gypsy women watched as she studied the various dishes; then Grandma walked over to them and smiled, "I can't hardly wait to sample your beautifully prepared food," she whispered conspiratorially. "After eating our country fare all my life it will be a real treat to taste such elegant recipes I've only seen in fancy cookbooks at the store."

Well, I can tell you th' smiles and happy chatter that brightened their faces from then on made me bust with love for my beloved Grandmother. As she bustled about here and there helping th' numerous wagons unload their supplies, a dozen pair of gypsy eyes followed her every move with love and appreciation.

There must have been thirty wagons all in a circle, so th' animals could commune with one another, Pa said, and there was so many kids playin' in th' field, I lost count. The creek was full of splashin' kids, nude as picked jay-birds, their clothes piled in a heap along th' creek bank. I was dyin' ta join them but knew Grandma would frown on my nudity, so I sat and watched until I remembered th' yellow suit she had made for me out of a chicken feed sack. Quick as a wink I dashed ta th' house and changed into th' suit then ran back ta th' creek and jumped in.

One of th' girls said, "Would ya look at miss uppity in her fancy swim suit."

"Not so fancy," said another. "I got a pair of bloomers just like it, same color and all."

"What'uv ya got to hide Miss uppity ?" asked another.

Th' boys looked at the water and pretended not to hear, all except ole Pig who come boilin' up outta th' creek like a streak of lightenin'.

"Look at ya," he said, his eyes rakin' across their faces with contempt." "We all know you two girls that said such hateful things to Helen even though yer about ta drown tryin' ta hide yer guilty faces under th' water. I'm standin' right here until I hear an apology to Helen and I believe I can stand here a whole bunch longer than you mean spirited trouble-makers can stay under water. Besides you weren't too uppity to come to th' party here at Helen's Grandpa's farm and have fun like th' rest of us and unless I hear a sincere sorry from th' two of ye soon then I'm personally gonna escort the both of ye home."

"Everybody here knows how strict Helens Grandma is and if she were caught skinny dippin, well..."

One after th' other come up outta th' creek, sputterin' water and cough-in'. Two red faces mumbled a sorry in my direction, then ole Pig bowed his skinny frame to th' crowd in an elaborate gesture of showmanship and said, "I thank ye ladies. Helen Ruth thanks ye and this creek full of rowdy boys and girls thank ye. Now lets hear a big AMEN?" he yelled, in imitation of Grandpa who was famous for makin' his point with a hearty AMEN.

Amens filled th' air and I noticed several curious grownups lookin' in our direction. Pig grabbed my hand and laughin' and screamin' with joy we jumped back in the creek together. We played games and frolicked for more than an hour before th' old dinner bell called everbody to th' feast.

When everyone had arrived, Pa beat for silence on a pie tin. After they'd all gathered 'round th' long tables of food he lifted his eyes Heavenward to a brilliant blue sky full of rainbow colored clouds edged in silver by th' late afternoon sun.

Grandma stood between me and Pig and clasped our hands in hers. She loved Pig with his pug nose, spike hair and jug-handle ears, and his blue eyes that sparkled with mischief. Most of all she trusted Pig and knew he would always take care of me.

Bali and his clan stood among our neighbors and my heart swelled with happiness as one after th' other reached out to clasp hands in prayer. At first, th' gypsies seemed startled by th' gesture then their faces lit up with joy and th' sure knowledge that they were an accepted part of th' community.

"Dear Lord," Pa began, "we are gathered here to celebrate th' restoration of this community and to thank our new neighbors for their labor and wondrous craftsmanship. Never have we seen such beautiful furniture and houses, with windows so elegant and large, they might have come from a future a thousand years from now. We are overwhelmed with the magic of Bali's clan, their tireless toil in our behalf and I can assure them our gratitude is beyond tellin'; but we are most grateful for their friendship and love for the people of this community."

It seemed to me as I listenend to Pa pray, th' sparks from th' fire grew brighter, th' stars shone more brightly against th' darkening sky, and the many familiar faces we had come to know through th' years glistened with a spiritual radience as they stood reverently before their Lord. Some heads were bowed, others looked heavenword, their lips movin' in silent prayer.

Tears sparkled like diamonds on th' weatherbeaten faces of th' old ones whose feelins' were more tender as each moment swept them closer to Heaven to meet their Saviour.

Only the face of Grandma Hanson's daughter was a blank canvas upon which no emotion was registered. Her husband held her hand tenderly and gazed on the face of their little daughter who would never again know th' loving arms of her Grandmother.

"Dear Lord," Pa continued. "There is a special one of Bali's clan whose Spirit is so wondrous there are no words to describe it. I've seen him once and he is the creator of all these master carvings you see everywhere, and yet I know not his name. My family refers to him as The Being which seemed th' only appropiate name we could think of. He plays the lute like an angel and I can testify that it will cast a heavenly peace on your heart that lasts forever."

"He sent all the young men of the clan on their way to Illinois long before the tornado struck us for he, in his wisdom, saw what was coming and knew we'd need help. So, we ask a special blessin' on this dear soul who has so richly blessed us in out time of need. If we are fortunate and our hearts are filled with gratitude; maybe he will honor us with his presence tonight and his magical lute."

"Thank you Lord for the dear ladies who have cooked so much wonderful food for this joyous ocassion and I'm sure you won't mind if we get started before it gets cold. Amen."

Everone filled his plate and found a comfortable seat on one of th' many bails of hay Pa had scattered around th' bon fire. Th' rich aroma of fresh perked coffee filled th' air as th' ladies filled th' cups of hungry men. I, too, loved coffee, havin' been introduced to it when I had my days and nights mixed up as an infant. Grandma solved th' problem by givin' me coffee in th' mornins' so I would stay awake all day. It worked too for I slept at night like a log, as Grandma put it.

Me and Pig loaded our plates with as much food as we could pile on them and found a bail of hay off to one side so we could see everything and still be private. After I cleaned my plate 'cept for one chicken leg, I set it down and got up.

"You goin' for a cup of coffee? he asked, shakin his head in disbelief.

"Yup," I replied. "No meal is complete without a good cup of coffee with lots of Grandma's good cream in it."

He got wearily to his feet and plunked his plate down aside mine. "Guess I'd better learn to like coffee too if I'm gonna keep up with you," he replied. "I'll come help carry the cups and guess I'll try that cream yer always ravin' 'bout "

"Not to worry," I said. "I can handle two cups of coffee without some silly boys help. Just Keep yer fingers off that last chicken leg while I'm gone."

"Are you kiddin? I bet there's enough chicken legs down there to choke a horse. If yer so worried bout this one, grab up a handful while yer down there cause I'm still mighty hungry. Just don't come back with a wing," he ordered, "I purely hate them wings."

"Well now, Mr.High and mighty Pig. I'm not an octupus with a dozen hands, so you just set yer feet down and high yerself along and git yer own chicken legs. And while yer at it git a couple for me too," I giggled.

When everone was fit to bust and th' tables were empty, th' women cleaned up while th' men sat around th' bon fire and sipped coffee. Soon th' women joined them, visitin' and talkin' endlessly about th' beautiful houses and furniture th' Gypsies had built.

"Do ya suppose they might teach us how to do such things?" Nora Horn asked Grandma.

"Maybe, if we had th' time they have to devote to such things, but we're farmers Nora, we just don't have that kind of time."

"Yer sure right 'bout that, Net. I'm goin from sunrise to sunset and I'm never through," Mrs Hobbs sighed.

"I doubt I could ever work up an interest in learnin' to carve wood," said another; "but the the way they mixed them colors in th' curtains and quilts to look like mountains and rivers is pure magic. Now thet's somethin' I'd purely enjoy tryin' to do."

"Th' Gypsy women sat quietly, smilin' shyly at all the compliments. Grandma asked them if they would share some of their skills with th' other women and they laughed with th' eagerness of children.

There was much banter and joy spoken in their language which none of us could understand as they fetched baskets of Satin and ribbons and lace from their wagons with every color of thread you could imagine. They began to demonstrate their skills on little tables each one had carried with her from her wagon home.

"You mean you do all this by hand?" one woman asked incredulously.

The Gypsy women looked at each other in confusion at such a question.

Grandma then realized they had never seen a sewing machine, much less heard of such a thing, so stichin' by hand was all they knew.

"This is the most beautiful work I've ever seen," Grandma whispered in awe and I've seen some lovely handiwork in my time. Why, I even have a few pieces I've done myself which I'm kinda proud of; but they are nothing compared to this."

She continued to hold the garments carefully in her hands while she stroked them gently and examined the almost invisible stiches.

"Masterpieces." she murmured. "No," she changed her mind. "They are works of art. I make it to our small library in town once in awhile and I looked through an art book once just out of curiosity. Some of th' paintings were very beautiful." Then she smiled apologetically, " but I must confess that most of them I didn't understand." These I understand," she stated emphatically.

She turned to her neighbors. "Let's all meet at my house tomorrow, you all bring yer sewing machines and we'll have our new friends over for a demonstration. As beautiful as these are, these dear souls will be blind as bats afore they're fifty years old. Why it must strain their eyes terrible to make such small stitches."

Several of th' gypsy women rubbed their eyes and said they were already suffering from such close work.

"Why do you continue then?" Grandma asked

"Its tradition." they explained, as though nothin' else was important.

"Nonsense," exclaimed Grandma. "Yer eyes are th' most important thing you have and you simply must not destroy them, even on such beautiful work."

Several of th' younger gypsies vigorously nodded agreement lookin' at th' older women with a I told you so look.

Then Bali leaped to a bail of hay and raised his hands for silence." Everybody have enough to eat?" he asked, his white teeth flashin' in th' light from th' bon fire.

A roar of agreement filled th' air.

"Now that was fine food we had here tonight and I want to congratulat the fine ladies who labored to make this party a sucess. Let's have a big hand for all the beautiful, talented women who keep us in line and make life easier for us.

Th' applause for th' ladies went on and on, and finally Bali held up his hands for quiet. "Now lets not overdo it fellows or we'll never be able to live in peace again. Where's Almus Hundley?" He yelled, searchin' th' crowd.

Pa.stepped from the crowd and joined Bali, a big smile on his face.

"Now here is one of the best friends I've ever had in my life," Bali said softly. He hooked his arm affectionately around Pa's shoulder and looked into Pa's face with the love of a son for his father.

Pa took Bali's hand and held it in a warm clasp as he worked his pipe from one side of his mouth to th' other and stared solemly at the faces around them.

"No greater honor could God have bestowed on me than to bless me with a son like you Bali and I couldn't love ye more if ye were my own blood. Indeed, I'll always feel like a father to ya and there isn't anything I wouldn't do fer ye."

Bali gave Pa a bear hug and said, "Anyone here ever square dance? More important, is there a man who knows how to call a square dance?"

Th' crowd began to laugh and tease Bali for his ignorance. "Why, yer standin' by th' best caller in th' whole country," Charlie Horn yelled. "He's not only th' best school teacher, raises th' finest coon dogs; but they's no other what can call a square dance like Almus."

Bali jumped off th' hay and bowed to Pa and Charlie. "Well, now lets have ourselves a square dance ladies and gentlemen."

Pa looked over th' crowd. "Ok! All you men line up in a row, then all th' women do th' same. Men face th' women, women face th' men.

He studied the two rows for a minute then shook his head sorryfully.

"It's a pity you beautiful ladies have to look at some of them ugly mugs out there, 'specially so soon after dinner, but cheer up fer in square dancin' ye'll hand 'em off to somebody else fore ye can say scat. Bet Mrs Hobbs is happy ta hear thet since she's starin ' ole Charlie straight in th' face."

"Wal I never heered tell thet you won any beauty contests, Almus," Charlie jeered , shakin' his fist at Pa.

Th' crowd laughed and began ta shuffle their feet anxiously.

"Right ye be, Charlie," Pa laughed as he jumped to the top of two bails of hay so he could see everbody and make his voice heard by th' dancers. His eyes twinkled with pleasure and excitement fer nobody loved to dance or call a dance as much as Pa. I watched his feet begin to beat out th' rythmn, then his baritone rose in cadence with th' flames as he began to instruct th' dancers and call th' dance in a harmony so wonderful, no one could ever imitate it. Two gypsies stood beside Pa with fiddles under their chins, their harmony blendin' with Pa's callin'.

Bali stood to one side and listened in awe, his dark eyes glistening with love and admiration fer Pa.

"OK partners, lightly join hands, gents will follow gents 'round th' circle, and ladies will follow ladies 'round th' circle, weavin' in and out with each other and lightly joinin' ever other hand with ever other person, similar to alternately shakin' right and left hands and pullin' by. I can tell yer all old pros at this," he joked. "If any one gets lost just drop out, another will take yer place, then when ye understand th' call, jump right back in again. Here we go!"

Helen Harper

> "Face your honey, all right and left Grand
> Meet ever other one with ever other hand
> Right and left around 'till you meet your maid
> Then join both hands and promenade
> Promenade two and Promenade four
> Keep thet Calico off of th' floor.
> Face partners and Turn with a Right arm Swing
> Turn corners with the Left at the side of the ring
> Now partners right and around you go
> Corners with the left and don't be slow
> Meet your own in a right and left grand
> Meet every other one with every other hand
> Right to left and go around the ring
> Then Promenade home with your own pretty thing.
> Face partners and do'sa'do,' then catch all eight
> Turn your partner right, change to left hand gate
> All the way around and roll Promanade
> Promenade home with your pretty maid.
> Bow to partner and take her right hand
> Go forward now in the right and left grand
> Go forward four, left turn back
> Go right and left back along the track
> Do'sa'do' your own, and Promenade
> Promanade home with your own maid.
> Promanade? that's what I said
> If she don't like biscuits, feed her cornbread.
> Ingo, bingo, six penny high
> A big pig, a litttle pig, root hog or die.
> Honey in a gourd and a gourd on the ground
> When you meet your honey promanade around
> Meet old Sal, meet old Kate
> Meet your promanade eight.
> Meet that gal with a hole in her stocking
> Shoe string flyin', petticoat floppin'.
> Promanade go high and wide
> Promanade on all four sides
> Hand over hand and heel over heel
> The more you dance the better you feel.
> Do the right and then left grand
> Meet every one with every other hand.
> Hurry up cowboy don't be slow
> You won't go to heaven if you don't do so."

Me and Pig danced 'till our feet fell off, then we dropped out and walked toward th' kids playin' games at th' far end of th' camp.

"I'm afraid ta look at my shoes," Pig giggled, " 'cause I'm sure theres nothin' down there but bloody stumps."

"Ain't nothin' more fun than square dancin'." I said, as Pa's voice floated on th' cool nite, strong and beautiful. "Chicken in th' bread pan peckin' out dough."

Pig looked down at me and smiled. "Yer Pa's a special man kid and I know how much ya love 'im."

His hand clasped mine gently as we joined th' games. 'Bout th' time we were fallin' down tired, a strange sound whispered thru th' nite.

"It's th' Master," one of th' gypsy children whispered in awe. "Hurry and you can see him."

We all rushed back to th' circle and found seats on a bail of straw with a birds eye view of th' bon fire and th' congregation.

Bali walked to th' end of th' field where th' little carved wagon sat and lifted somethin' in his arms. Those who had never seen th' Being gasped softly at th' twisted limbs and deformed body; but when Bali came within th' bright light of th' bon fire, th' glowin' eyes and deformed body took on a beauty so wonderful th' crowd fell silent, their faces filled with wonder and awe. A Spiritual love that could only come from The Lord Himself, flowed from th' Being to every man, woman and child. Peace filled th' air with a Heavenly fragrance so wonderful I felt I could rise up and fly if I desired.

Bali walked slowly by everyone, then when he came to Grandma Hanson's daughter, Jenny, he gently lowered th' Being to a blanket at her feet. Th' Being looked up into Jenny's blank face for a long moment, then he raised th' lute to his lips and began to play softly. Th' notes filled th' air with praise and love for th' God of us all.

My heart was beating so hard I was gaspin' for breath. I looked at Pig and could tell he was feelin' th' same thing. I slipped my hand in his and felt his fingers close tightly on mine.

The Being played for five minutes, never takin' his eyes from Jenny's face, then I seen her eyes begin to focus from an unseein' stare to a kind of recognition of somethin' outside of herself.

Jenny's husband was watching her face anxiously, a smile beginnin' to form on his lips as he seen th' tiny change in her. He looked down at th' being, then back to his wife, a look of incredible joy on his face as he watched her slowly turn to th' form at her feet. She stared into th' glowing eyes of th' Being for what seemed an eternity then she gently laid her baby at his feet then lowered herself to th' ground.

Th' Being gazed at th' baby for some time then he fastened those glowing eyes on th' mother, playing a different sound on th' lute, more softly than before. She never took her eyes from his. After what seemed like hours; a slow recognition of memory began to form on her face. Suddenly she burst into tears and moaned her mother's name over and over again. It was so heartbreaking to watch her live the ghastly memory over and over again, her body shaking with grief. Then th' Being did a most peculiar thing. He wrapped his deformed limbs gently round her shoulders and lifted her face to his and his eyes gleamed with a fire so bright I had to look away; but Jenny seemed to lose herself in them for the longest time, then a look of joy glowed on her face so bright it was almost as brilliant as th' eyes of th' Being.

Bali had knelt on th' ground behind th' Being and I was astonished to see tears streaming down his face. I guess there wasn't a dry eye in th' crowd as we witnessed the miracle taking place before us.

God's presence filled th' air as one voice after another was lifted in prayer to our Glorious Master, th' Lord Jesus Christ.

Th' Being removed his limbs from her shoulders and raised them to th' heavens in Reverance to God. After a moment he raised th' lute to his mouth and joyous music filled th' air. Bali lifted him gently in his arms and walked slowly to th' little carved wagon at th' end of th' field.

Jenny held her infant in her arms and turned to her husband, whose arms enfolded them both in a tender embrace. Not a word was spoken as he led them toward Grandma's house. I knew they would have a peaceful night after enduring their tragedy for so long.

Finally, th' crowd began to speak softly, gathering up their belonging's and loading their wagons to go home. No one would ever forget tonight and th' wonderful healing of Grandma Hanson's Jenny.

Pig held my hand as we walked toward his horse, not saying anything, just thinking our own thoughts about th' wonderful events of this day.

"Up ya go," he said as he hoisted me onto Emily's back; then he leaped up behind me, took th' reins and turned Emily toward Grandma's house. "Grandma said yer welcome to th' cot on th' porch. It's all made up and everthing."

"I'm much oblighed to yer Grandma; but I prefer th' hayloft with all that soft hay to snuggle into, not ta mention th' wonderful smell of fresh hay."

"It's up ta you. Breakfast is at seven sharp so don't be late."

"Good grief," Pig exclaimed. "Don't ya ever sleep in?"

"Only if we're sick. 'course you can sleep as long as you want if you'd rather eat oats with Emily than Grandma's good cookin'."

"Never mind," he grumbled, "I'll be there at seven sharp."

"Good decision," I smiled, as I slid off Emily's back onto our front porch. I didn't tell him that Grandma had made a nice bed for him in th' hayloft, with blankets and a pillow and an alarm clock already set for 6:45.

"Goodnight kid," he whispered.

"Goodnight Pig. Sweet dreams." I watched him and Emily walk toward th' barn until they were out of sight in th' breezway.. I looked up at th' vast, star studded sky and breathed a prayer of thanksgiving to God for his goodness and mercy. "I don't know who th' Being really is," I said; "but I know how much he loves you and you must love him a powerful lot ta give him th' power ta heal and play such magic on that Lute."

"I know it ain't none of my business Lord; but how can he be so ugly and yet so beautiful at th' same time?"

The Lord didn't answer, so I went to bed.

Jenny, her husband and baby got on th' Greyhound bus at Burnside two days later and went back to Chicago.

"Your mother's land belongs to you now, Jenny," Pa told her. "Someday when Chicago gets too big fer comfort, maybe you'll come back here where your roots are and live with those who love you."

A Sad Fairwell

That fall Bali told us they wouldn't be back th' next year, maybe not for many years. He told us th' old ones wanted to live their few remaining years in their home land and sleep with their ancestors. "The Being wants to go back to Romania where he was born for he feels his time is near."

We were devastated for th' Gypsies were like our family and Pa asked Bali if he would ever come back and see us or perhaps settle down here.

He was very sad to leave but felt he must honor the request of th' old ones.

"I can understand that," Pa said; "but remember that parcel of land will be yours when you return."

Summer went by so fast we couldn't believe it and Grandma said it was because our friends were leaving and our hearts were hurting.

One mornin' in September th' field by th' Pear trees was empty. We stared at th' empty space for a long time, our hearts filled with unbearable sadness.

Pa wondered how they could leave so early without making any noise; but he knew the ways of th' Gypsy is sometimes magical and with th' Being and his powers, anything was possible.

Grandma ran to th' front porch rocker to see if any gift had been left for her but there was nothing and she returned to th' kitchen to make breakfast. Pa went to feed th' cattle and we knew he would check th' barn for anything they might have left. In a minute he came runnin' to th' house out of breath with a strange look on his face.

"Look at th' corner of th' feed lot," he exclaimed excitedly. We stared at th' corner in disbelief for there stood a mule so ugly and scraggly he resembled a nightmare more than anything from th' animal kingdom. It was beyond our imagination how he came to be there. We ran from th' house to th' feed lot to examine this strange phenomen and found a note pinned to th' rope around his neck.

> *"Dear Almus,*
>
> *We found this mule in a ditch along the road somewhere in the south. He was in bad shape and we felt sorry for him so took him in and doctored him th' best we could. He looked as though he'd been in a fire for his hair was singed and his hide scorched in so many places he hardly resembled a mule. We soon found out how mean tempered he is and will bite you every chance he gets. He trusts no one, not even the Being so we decided if anyone could help him it would be you and Net and this farm where there are other animals to keep him company. At least he will feel more at home on a farm than traveling with a band of Gypsies.*
>
> *We couldn't bear to destroy him and the Being predicted he would find his peace here and would become a valuable worker for you. I have no idea how this will come about but I have faith it will all come right in the long run. Forgive us for leaving a problem with you. We will try to come back here in a few years after the old ones have found their rest with the Lord.*
>
> *The mule's name is Satan, which seems fitting somehow. God bless you and yours and we thank you and the community for the kindness shown to us.*
>
> *My sincere affection forever,*
> *Bali."*

Well, Satan proved to be as mean as predicted and we wondered what in th' world to do with him. He was a good worker and valuable to Pa in that respect, but his misdeeds far outweighed his willingness to work. Like it or not, he was now a part of th' family. I stayed away from him but I still felt sorry for th' hurt and misery I seen in his eyes. He never suspected it showed or he would have been furious. He kept to himself and made it quite clear he would not permit any attempts at friendship.

Satan had a disconcertin' way of lookin' you right in the eye with that devilish light of meaness flashin' in his own eyes, promisin' revenge at the earliest opportunity. He didn't need an excuse to wreak havoc on you either for just the fact that you were there was enough reason for Satan.

Grandma disliked the mule, mutterin' darkly of possesion and predictin' dire consequences if Pa didn't get rid of him. Course you could count on satan to fulfill all dire predictions. That was his lot in life, his mission, his goal, and he embraced such responsibilities with demonic fervor and fury.

A number of careless people had had an experience with Satan, none of which had a happy endin'.

'One Sunday afternoon a visitin' preacher from New Burnside rode out to pass a word or two with folks and let them know he was in town. Pa took the preachers horse to the waterin' trough and grandma poured him out a glass of her famous buttermilk with it's yellow globs of butter floatin' in it. Course one swallow by the thirsty Parson produced the most extravagant compliments you could imagine, which grandma calmly accepted as her due. He was on his second glass when Pa came back and sat down on the steps. Grandma handed Pa a glass of buttermilk then returned to her rocker where she resumed fannin' herself with a church fan emblazoned with the words," Jesus Saves" on one side and "Prepare to die" on the other.

The preacher eyed the fan appreciatively, then smiled at grandma. "Now, whoever thought of spreading the Gospel on ladies fans sure had a fine idea. Profitable too," he observed, "since you hardly ever see a lady without one."

"They're a blessing," she replied, "specially during these hot summer months."

The preacher took another generous swig of grandma's buttermilk, smackin' his lips with satisfaction. A thick, creamy mustache outlined his upper lip.

"Best buttermilk I've ever had," he enthused.

There's none better," Pa agreed, smilin' at the mustache.

The Preacher looked about, admirin' Grandma's hollyhocks and ruby red cannas and her spectacular mornin' glories climbin' thickly on strings from the ground to the porch roof.

"It's a fine place to have coffee in the mornin'," Grandma murmured," when the sun's risin' and the dew is sparklin' on everything like diamonds."

She beamed with pleasure when he 'specially admired the beauty of her snowball bush with it's fat blooms. Many of Grandma's friends coveted that bush. One of the commandments warns against covetin' your neighbor's wife but I don't recollect any mention of covetin' your neighbor's snowball bush. Then the Preacher spied Satan out in the barnyard, lookin' sleek and respectful and muleish as any good, hard-workin', faithful, gentle mule ought to look.

"That's a handsome mule you got there, Mr.Hundley," he said, with a covetin' look in his eyes"

"Well... he's a good worker," Pa said guardedly.

A look of irritation crossed Grandma's face and the tempo of her fan picked up considerable.

"I sure do like mules," the preacher went on, "and if it wasn't for the looks of it, I'd be riding one instead of this horse."

Pa clamped his pipe between his teeth, puffin' clouds of smoke in the air. "The looks of it?" he asked, puzzled.

"Well yes," replied the parson with a sanctimonious air. "The preacher has to maintain some kind of... standard, you see, and a mule just doesn't quite measure up to that standard."

I could tell the preacher had opened his mouth and put at least one foot in it. Pa's teeth were givin' that pipe stem a fit and a hundred years ago the clouds of smoke flyin' round his head would have alerted ever indian in the territory.

"Young fellow," he said with amazing calmness. "Our Lord rode a donkey into Jerusalem and a donkey's a mite lower than a mule; then He walked up the hill of Golgotha carryin' the standard of our redemption and salvation on His shoulders and He allowed himself to be nailed to the cross that we might be saved from our sins and live forever with Him in Glory."

Pa smiled and puffed his pipe as he contemplated the good looks of Satan.

"The looks of a donkey sure don't live up to the looks of a mule by a long shot," he mused, "but that little fact didn't bother Jesus none."

He took the pipe from his mouth, stirrin' the tobacco 'round the bowl with his finger, his eyes still on the mule. "When you understand that part of the Bible sufficiently son," he continued," I reckon you'll be about ready to trade that horse in on a mule."

I took Pa's hand and hugged it hard, I was that proud of him. We had reached the gate to the feed lot when the Preacher turned and studied Pa a minute. "You missed your calling, Mr.Hundley. You might have been a preacher."

Pa swooped his pipe from his mouth and laughed uproariously. "Naw, young fellow. I leave the preachin' to Nettie here for shes mighty fine at it."

Grandma smiled, but just barely.

The Preacher's eyes feasted on Satan. "That's a mule to be proud of alright," he said longingly, "Mind if I look him over?"

"Not a bit as long as you look from this side of the fence," Pa drawled.

"Why this side of the fence?"

"Well, I'll tell you son. Old Satan here has a well deserved reputation for violence. He'd as soon bite ye as look at ye. I expect you'll hear a tale or two about him once you've been here a spell. Some of the tales will be worse than they should be and some won't be as bad as they ought to be."

I heard Grandma mumble somethin' in the background.

"You need not concern yourself for my safety folks," bragged the Preacher. "I have a way with animals. Always have. I believe it's a God given gift," he added solemnly, havin' the grace to blush just a little.

"I've found if we truly love God's creatures, they'll respond to that love."

I could have sworn Grandma's mumble had turned to a giggle. "Oh he'll respond alright," she smiled sweetly. "He's responded to Almus here any number of times."

Pa scowled at Grandma for rubbin' it in, then turned back to the Preacher. "Nevertheless, I must insist you do your lookin' from this side of the fence young man. Can't have the new Preacher gettin' all stove up the first week he's here."

I could see the Parson was one of them young upstarts who had a lot to learn and Satan was just the ticket to get him started. Before Pa could lay a hand on him the Parson slipped through the gate and started toward th' mule with a saintly smile on his face.

I looked at Satan who had been standin' all this time with a benign look on his countenance just like any ordinary mule, all of which was merely a facade he affected from time to time to conceal the ragin' evil stompin' round in that thick hide of his. Now the ragin' evil peered out of Satan's eyes in surprise at this fool advancin' rapidly to most assuredly meet his maker and with a silly grin on his face to boot. Satan could not remember any of his previous victims who had so affably presented themselves for the sacrafice, so, for the barest fraction of a second he studied this unusual phenomenon with astonishment and disbelief.

The Parson was just reachin' out to lay his hand on the mules face when Satan's lips curled back in a fiendish smile to reveal a formidable set of yellow teeth. The Parson instantly realized his mistake and was tryin' to turn around in midair, his feet churnin' ineffectually when Satan nailed him just below the belt.

Pa grabbed a stick of firewood and went for Satan's head, dodgin' the sharp hooves and the Preacher who was flyin' this way and that, held firmly between Satan's teeth. Pa finally landed a hard blow to the mules nose, just missin' the Preacher's backside by the barest margin. Satan dropped the Preacher and staggered backward brayin' in pain and rage.

The hapless Parson lay crumpled in the dust like a pile of loosely stuffed rags, groanin' and tryin' to get to his knees, a posture I considered appropiate, if somewhat late, and I reckoned if he tarried much longer in Satan's domain he'd need all the help the Lord might give him. That old sayin', the Lord helps them that help themselves ran through my mind. Well... he had helped himself to a large piece of Satan's pie despite all warnin' and from personal experience I had grave doubts that the Lord would excuse him from eatin' a fair share of it. I'd been strictly taught, ' Tempt not the Lord Thy God.' I'll never know what grand lessons the Lord might have taught that parson for his good servant, Pa, grabbed the parson and sprinted for the gate before old Satan could recover hisself. I thought the Parson looked to be in pretty fair shape for a man who'd just escaped the clutches of the devil. The back of his coat was in tatters and a fair amount of his trousers was missin' but no one suggested retrievin' the jagged scraps flutterin' limply from Satans mouth.

"Lucky you wore this wide leather belt son," Pa observed as he surveyed the damage, " or Satan might have had your kidney. Peers like you've got a puncture or two from Satan's teeth and a whole mess of bruises but all in all it ain't too bad. The Preacher's face was disbelivin' and full of anguish as he shook his head in wonder " I've never before in my whole life had one of God'a creatures attack me. NEVER!" he declared vehemently.

Settin' in the dirt, leanin' against a fence post lookin' like he'd been drug through a berry patch backward made me feel right sorry for him, but I could see Grandma didn't entertain any such foolish feelins' of undeserved charity.

"Now there lies the rub, preacher," said Grandma, lookin' sternly at him without an ounce of sympathy.

"Satan here ain't one of God's creatures. Ever hair on his ill begotten hide belongs to the devil, so from now on you'd best find out who belongs to who before you go stompin' 'round where Angels fear to tread."

"I expect you have a point there Mrs. Hundley," replied the chastened Parson, moppin' his face with a limp handkerchief. "And now," he groaned, strugglin' to his feet, his exposed backside up against the gate, "If I might just borrow a pair of Mr.Hundley's trousers..." but Grandma was already half way to the house, ahead of everybody as usual.

The mule was strangely subdued as the weeks flew by, standin' around in the barnyard all quiet and mannerly, not once kickin' the fence just to show what he would do to a body if one come close.

"Maybe I've got myself a changed mule," Grandpa speculated one nite at supper.

Grndma's mouth tightened with frustrated anger."What you've got yourself Almus Hundley, is a short memory. That mule's buildin' to somethin,' somethin' bad, like the end of the world in mule reasonin' and he's the one who aims to end it. There's no doubt in my mind but what Satan plans to splatter you all over that feed lot. Justified or not, he'll never forget you took that preacher away from him."

Pa chuckled. "Now Net, you're makin' that mule out to be a whole lot smarter than he really is."

"Well, she replied dryly," he's hoodwinked you into keepin' him for nigh on to three years now, ain't he?"

Then one bitter cold mornin' with the wind hurlin' miniature batterin' rams of sleet against th' house and four foot icicles hangin' off the roof just beggin' to be knocked down, I lay snuggled in bed listenin' to the sounds of breakfast bein' made.

Pa shook down the ashes from the banked coals, piled in fresh wood, opened the damper and soon the cook stove was roarin' away. Grandma's big butcher knife clacked briefly on the cuttin' board as she sliced slabs of ham and layered them in the big iron skillet. Soon I smelled perkin' coffee, and sizzlin' ham addin' its fragrance to the air, then the door of the oven opened and I knew a big pan of biscuits was goin' in. There'd be eggs, milk gravy and honey we took from a tree right out in the woods, and home made jelly the likes of which you'll never find in any store. To this day, breakfast is my favorite meal and what I wouldn't give to step back to that country kitchen of my childhood and have one more breakfast with Pa and Grandma Hundley.

This cold winter mornin,' still half asleep, his mind on a cup of Grandmas good coffee, Pa dashed out to the woodpile next to the feedlot, his eyes squinted tight against the stingin' sleet and bent over to gather up an arm load of wood. Loath to waste the opportunity for which he'd long waited, old Satan seized the upended portion of his anatomy. Pa's screams of pain as he ran erratically toward the house, laced with an amazin' repertoire of non-cuss words brought me and Grandma on the run to see what sounded like a disaster of major proportions.

As he stumbled through the back door clutchin' his crotch it was obvious he had lost his good humor and no tellin' what else, plus a good size portion of the backside of his overalls. I looked out at the feed lot and there stood Satan with his rump to the storm and the jagged piece of Pa's overalls blowin' this way and that from his mouth. I could imagine his countenance contorted in an evil grimace of satisfaction. I was shooed from the kitchen so Grandma could survey the damage and administer first aid, but no one said I couldn't stand by the door and listen, so I did.

"Best git rid of that mule Almus before he really hurts someone," she said for the hundreth time.

"What do you mean before he hurts someone!" Pa shouted indignantly. "He very nearly gave me a voice change, Net. I shudder to think of the consequences if he'd been a few inches lower."

"You keep him around Almus and he'll finish the job next time," she declared grimly. "That mule's unholy and he's declared his own personal war on you."

All the time Grandma was ministerin' to his hurts, Pa argued with himself whether to get rid of Old Satan or keep him.

"Ornery cuss, thats fer sure," he mumbled, rollin' his pipe expertly from one side of his mouth to the other, "but he is a good worker. I could be a lot more careful," he temporized, "watch him closer."

Grandma snorted in disgust then spoke in that tight voice which meant she didn't want to hear no more about it. "You've watched that mule for three years now Almus and he's tore your hide up more times than I care to remember."

I could hear Pa clamp his teeth tighter on his pipe and I knew he was puffin' clouds of smoke in the air as he always did when he was troubled or thinkin' serious on somethin'.

Pa's wounds healed quickly under Grandma's ministrations. Course she could patch up most anything, specially mule bites, having become an expert on that type of injury due to Pa's carlessness over the past three years. His subsconscious had a tendency to forget the fact that Satan wasn't your ordinary mule.

Pa is ordinarily riddled with common sense on most things. People come to him for advice and he can analyze the most difficult situation and bring it to a successful conclusion with his knack for common sense; but about every four months he'll forget Satan's treachery, the door to common sense will slam shut and Satan will nail him again.

Through that long winter we'd hear Pa argueing with himself whether to keep Satan or sell him.

Grandma suggested Pa move the woodpile a safe distance from the fence. His face lit up somethin' wonderful. "Now why didn't I think of that," he asked himself his eyebrows pinched together in puzzlement?"

"I've wondered 'bout that myself," Grandma said.

That afternoon I helped him move the woodpile while Satan stood in his corner watchin' us with great interest.

That evenin' Grandma was cookin' supper and Pa was readin' the Farmers Almanac and sippin' on a cup of coffee. "Looks like you need more wood, Net," he said casually, eyeing the woodbox.

I could see the woodbox plain as day and it was piled high with wood. Grandma said not a word knowin' what Pa was up to.

He strolled out onto the porch, did a little jig down the steps, then walked arrogantly toward the feed lot, not once lookin' at Satan standing in his corner with a look of anticipation on his face.

Me and Grandma were glued to the screen door holding our breath for we knew this was an event worth watching. In a small way the tables were about to be turned on Satan, somethin' he'd never experienced before. We both felt a bit of fear and tremblin', wonderin' what Satan might do with the situation once he realized he'd been foiled. As Grandma always said: He's an unusually intelligent, enterprisin' mule, blessed or cursed (dependin' on ones point of view) with an uncanny, supernatural evil that only the master of hell could bestow.

Pa walked slowly around the woodpile, inspecting each piece with a scrunity that he ordinarily reserved for buying a good team of horses or a prize milk cow. Satan watched this unusual behavior with facination, his neck hangin' over the fence, his nose twitchin' and snortin' as he sniffed the air. Then Pa stopped directly in front of Satan, stooped to pick up wood, his posterior piercing the air temptingly.

Satan's eyes glowed with anticipation as he stretched his neck over the fence to claim the prize. A look of puzzlement crossed his face as he realized the prize was just out of reach. He re-adjusted his position, pushed his chest deep into the fence rail and stretched his neck as far a he could toward Pa's upturned rump.

Then Pa began wrigglin' his rump from side to side, mere inches from Satan's teeth. Suddenly he straightened up and started doin' a jiggin' dance around the wood pile his boomin' voice bouncin' off the barn, fillin' the feed lot and Satan's ears with derisive laughter. He stopped in front of Satan, laughin' in the mule's face, then bent over again, stuck his rump in the air, wrigglin' it back and forth in mockery.

A look of uncontrollable rage crossed Satan's face as he finally realized he'd been duped. His eyes blazed as he stared at the unreachable prize, his teeth snappin' the air in frustration. He stared at Pa's rump for a long time, then to our amazement he turned and slowly walked to his corner of the fence to stare morosely out over the hills.

"Well, I never," I exclaimed.

"Me neither," Grandma murmured and turned back to the stove to finish supper.

A few minutes later Pa strolled into the kitchen puffin' his pipe peacefully, his face filled with satisfaction. He resumed readin' the almanac, sippin' on a fresh cup of coffee and no one mentioned that he hadn't brought one stick of wood from the woodpile for Grandma's cookstove. His truimph over Satan was short lived, for therearfter to Pa's chagrin, Satan ignored his trips to the woodpile, a look of complete indifference on his face.

That night after supper I cleared the dishes away and put them to soak in a pan of soapy water Grandma had on the back of the stove. Then I fetched my tablet and pencil. Pa and Grandma watched with interest, waitin' for me to explain.

"Now," I said, "we all know Satan's bad side but we've never thought he might have some little somethin' about him thats good."

"Harump," Pa snorted, turnin' the tablet around to see my writing. "Look at this, Net," he said, pushin' the tablet over to her.

"Good side," "Bad side," she murmured. She studied the two short statements silently, then handed the tablet back to me.

"Well, what do ya think?" I asked anxiously.

"I think," Pa drawled scarastically, "that ye could fill six tablets on his bad side; but I can't think of one thing on his so-called good side."

Grandma was silent, but I noticed her index finger drew imaginary patterns on the bright red oilcloth covering the old oak table. She did this when she was thinkin' on somethin' special or day dreamin' over her seed catalogs during the long cold winters. Finally, she looked over at Pa. "A few weeks ago, Almus, I heard you tell that visitin' preacher that Satan is a good worker."

Pa puffed his pipe and stared at the flickerin' lamp light dancin' on the ceiling.

"That don't count for nothin' Net. He's a mule and a mule's supposed ta be a good worker."

. "Like a rose is a rose is a rose." she murmured. So a mule is a mule is a mule." She sighed, not lookin' at me or Pa, just drawin' invisible pictures on the oilcloth.

Pa was watching her face now waiting for her to speak her mind.

"I seen many a mule in my time Almus and nary a one of 'em was the same. Some are too lazy to drink for themselves, let alone work. Now, there's Satan and he's ours whether we want 'im or not, and I suspect he's well aware of how we feel toward him." Grandma looked sad. "You know that's bound to have an effect on his behavior. Evil or not. He's got feelings just like the rest of us."

I'd never thought that Satan might have feelings that could be hurt. I just knew he had a lot of mean ways so Grandma's statement startled me; but I meant to investigate the subject further in th' near future.

Pa openend his mouth to speak but Grandma wouldn't give him a chance.

"Oh I know what yer thinkin' Almus. He's just an animal like the rest but Satan's not just an ordinary animal. There ain't a mule in the here or hereafter; that ever was, or is, or ever will be, like Satan." Grandma smiled at the tablecloth. "A mule who wades through fire and brimstone, kicks open the gates of hell and walks out on the devil to vent his spleen on mankind, then works as hard as he does for a man he'd love to stomp through the ground, is nothin' short of a miracle."

Grandma clasped her hands to her bosom and looked reverently toward Heaven. "Forgive me Lord for findin' anything good about one of Satan's own; but I reckon you'd agree he's a fine worker."

Pa puffed furiously on his pipe and gave Grandma an agitated look. She didn't even notice, her finger still tracing patterns on the tablecloth.

"I thought ye didn't like that mule, Net. Now here ye are tryin' to make him seem better than he is."

"It ain't nothin' ta do with likin' or dislikin' Satan. Just tellin' the truth, Almus. I think I know where he come from and it'ud take a miracle th' likes of which Heaven never dreamed of to change that bull-headed mule from what he is to what he oughta be."

I hardly breathed for fear I'd interrupt this facinating conversation, but I'd already written 'outstandin' worker' under Satans good side.

Pa went to the stove and filled his cup, ruminating to hisself as he detoured by the screen door to stare out at the darkening feed lot.

"Alright Net, I'll give 'im that. He's a good worker." Pa slurped the hot coffee noisily, passin' the hot mug from one hand to the other to cool it down."Look at 'im out there still standin' in that corner he thinks he owns. The other animals are in their stalls asleep and he's still outside thinkin' on no tellin' what. Probably eavesdroppin' on us if the truth be known," Pa grumbled, "or worse yet: maybe he's gettin' some personal instructions from the devil hisself on what terrible thing to do to me because I bested him for a change." He puffed his pipe, his eyes narrowed on the smoke as it drifted toward the ceilin' "Remind me ta tell him it was yer idea, Net, to move that woodpile."

Grandma laughed and I ran to the door. Sure enuff, there he stood, lookin' right back at us, his ears thrust forward in a listenin' position. "Can mules hear real good?" I asked Pa.

"I bet that one can hear a knat sneeze a hundred yards off." Pa grimaced, returnin' to the table.

I laid the tablet aside and washed the dishes while Grandma and Pa had their usual chat before bedtime.

At school the next day I could hardly keep my mind on what the teacher was sayin', anxious to get home and get supper over with so we could continue to discuss Satans good and bad side.

That evenin', Pa and me went about the business of milkin', feedin' and curryin' the animals. All the while Satan stood in his corner watchin' in a detached way as though he was just an observer. He always gave the impression he was just visitin' for a short spell and might take hisself off anytime the notion struck 'im or maybe he'd just get bored with us and this part of the country and go to a neighbors farm. Course his reputation had spread far and wide so I doubted anyone would take him in..

"Never seen you in such a hurry sprout," Pa remarked, lookin' at me oddly. Anything wrong?"

"No, but when we finish I want to help Grandma get supper."

"I see," he mused., givin' Nell an affectionate pat on her muzzle. "Well since we're almost finished why don't you run on and help Ma. I'll be in directly. Tell her I'm hungry as a wolf. Don't know what shes cookin' but it smells powerful good."

"I know but I ain't tellin'," I giggled as I ran toward the house. Grandma was makin' her famous, specially seasoned little pork pies in her buttery, light as a cloud special crust that was so wonderful you wanted to run 'round and 'round the house shoutin' at the top of your voice. On such occassions even the mule would sniff the air, a pleasant look on his face instead of the scowl he usually wore.

Supper was a masterpiece, ever bit as delicious as any of the fancy restaurants with their famous chefs, people from Chicago always bragged about. There was a garlic butter sauce bubbling so slightly on the back of the stove you could barely see it move. This would be dribbled over the sizzlin' pies as soon as they came from the oven. When we had pork pies Grandma made sure all the side dishes were on the table, her special lemonade poured and most important of all: everybody was at their places around the big old oak, forks in hand, ready to enjoy. All the plates were on the back of the stove, hot as firecrackers.

Now came the special moment we'd all waited for.

She pulled the pies from the oven, quickly placed two on each plate and poured the hot garlic sauce around each pie. They were rushed to the table, prayers were cut short, then we took our first bite, chewing slowly, savoring the incomparable magnificence of every crumb. It was not a dish to gulp down quickly, no matter how hungry you were and Grandma would have considered it an insult if you had. No one talked. Your entire focus was on the food. When you finished your two pies, Grandma silently pulled the pan from the oven and repeated the process until everyone had their fill. As I recall, I ate four and Pa had six. There were always a dozen or so left over for lunch the next day.

"You're the best cook in the world Net," Pa said solemnly, "and that's gospel".

No one even asked for dessert although I'd seen a pan of apple turnovers on the back of the stove. We sat for a long while sayin' nothin', simply enjoyin' the wonderful food we'd been so lucky to have. I wondered how many children had Grandma's as wonderful and talented as mine. I got up, went around to her chair, wrapped my arms around her neck for a moment, then gathered up the dirty dishes and started washing them. I knew there would never be anyone as wonderful as her and Pa and I silently thanked God for the wonderful grandparents He had given me.

Pa and Grandma sat drinkin' coffee, talkin' bout their day as usual. Streeter was snoring under Pa's chair with his head on Pa's boot and I was nearly finished with the dishes. I collected my tablet and pencil and crouched in my chair so excited I couldn't sit still.

Pa gave the tablet a jaundiced eye. He made an elaborate, time consuming ritual of fillin' his pipe, pretendin' he couldn't find his matches, all to kill time and stall further conversations about Satan's good and bad side.

Me and Grandma said nary a word, which vexed him considerable. Finally, he clamped his teeth on the pipe, rotated it around his mouth several times then stared at the pencil poised between my fingers as though it was a snake.

"Can I ask you some questions, Pa?" I used th' sweetest, most respectful, innocent voice I could manage but it didn't fool Pa fer a minute

"Now don't ye fiddle-faddle around with me sprout. I've got cauliflower ears from questions ye been askin' me since ye could talk and sometimes I reckon that seems like a thousand years ago.'

"Thanks Pa," I smiled politely. He rewarded me with one of his fierce looks which I pretended not to see.

"Now, did Satan ever bite or try ta bite you in the feed lot?"

"Wal... no," he answered gruffly.

"When you harness him to go work, or feed and water him or curry him or do anything for him inside the feed lot, the barn, or out in the fields, does he act mean toward you?"

"Well, not to my recollection," he answered, lookin' just a little interested in spite of hisself.

"And as smart as you are you'd recollect, wouldn't you Pa?"

"I reckon, and ye can stop wastin' yer time on all that false flattery," he said irritably..

Grandma was listenin' attentively, her eyes shinin' like diamonds with the oddest little smile on her lips.

I drew a few stick men on the tablet page tryin' to think on all Pa had said. "So, the only time he tries to hurt you is when you're outside the feed lot and he's inside the feed lot?"

"I guess thats about the size of it" , Pa said grudgingly," but don't forget he went after that Preacher a few weeks ago inside the feed lot."

"Thats true; but he don't go after me or Grandma or the cousins or Aunt Mildred and Uncle Jimmy or mom and dad, nor ole Charlie either. He even seems to like Streeter and ole Blue. Must be a reason for that, don't ye think?"

Grandma could hardly sit still, she was so excited. "Why. Almus, don't ye see what she means?"

"Can't say I do, Net, although I have to admit it's an interesting phenomon which I might think on tomorrow if I have the time."

"Why it's as plain as the nose on yer face," she laughed, ignorin' his remark.

Pa puffed his pipe, looked at the ceiling and yawned." Them pork pies just about put my thinkin' apparatus to sleep, Net," he mumbled, closin' his eyes and lettin' the pipe hang from the corner of his mouth. "Besides, I'm not inclined to waste good energy tryin' ta figure out anything concernin' Satan, specially tonight. My belly's full of good food, and I'm content, or I would be if sprout would stop wavin' that pencil around and askin' so many fool questions."

Ignorin' him again, Grandma, kicked the leg of his chair away from the wall where he was propped up and poured him another cup of coffee.

"It's a sorry thing when a man cain't enjoy his supper in peace and quiet," he grumbled. He propped his chair back against the wall and chewed on the stem of his pipe." I can see there ain't gonna be any solitude around here till you and sprout fill up that tablet with somethin' or other 'bout that consarned mule, so git on with it."

"Well, Almus," Grandma said excitedly, "to Satan's way of thinkin' it's about respect and rules and obeying them, absolutely, no matter what his personal feelings toward you might be. You're the master of the animals, the feed lot, working the fields to grow the food. Satan recognizes that fact and respects it. He also knows his duty is to help plow and plant the fields which produces the food that feeds them all. I believe he even understands his responsibility to do his share in providing food for the family as well."

"Harump." Pa grunted.

"I'm not sure the other animals have the same intelligent grasp on duties as does Satan and that is surely not surprisin' considerin' his origins. He obeys the rules that benefit us all; but he has personal rules of his own, too. I expect they are serious grudges for all the wrongs he feels you've perpetrated against him. Besides, his pride has been mortally wounded. He has boundaries he feels are his alone where you are forbidden to intrude and if you step over them boundaries, then you're fair game. If I were you, I'd respect his rules as he respects your's.

Pa laughed. "You're still convinced he's on furlough from hell aren't ye Net? Well, you're right most of the time, so who's to say. Probably drew up his own leave papers and signed them ta-boot if th' truth be known.. Speakin' of rules, Net. I imagine the devil has rules plastered all over hell, so why didn't the mule obey them?"

"The devil's rules are beneficial only to himself. He don't care for the comfort or welfare of his slaves so why would the mule respect an entity like that? I think, if the mule did come from hell, he hated the devil beyond what we can imagine."

"What do ye mean Net, 'if' he come from hell?"

"I don't rightly know. Maybe we judge him too harshly without knowin' why he feels and thinks as he does."

"I'll bet if he was in hell it was by mistake," I blurted out in sudden support of Satan. Grandma smiled at me and Pa said, "Fat chance."

"Imagine, Pa continued," how mad the devil was to find 'im gone, and them fancy red gates of his kicked ta smitherennes by a trusted employee. Now, even I can admire the mule for that little piece of deviltry. Imagine the look on the devil's face when he seen all them red splinters litterin' hell, his prize mule gone and him short on carpenters not to mention lumber since I'm sure trees won't grow in that climate."

Pa was warmin' to his subject now.

"Ya know, Net, maybe he makes them gates outta the caskets them poor lost souls come in. Not too difficult I should think. He's got plenty of fire to mold the metal ta any shape he desires and the demons can come and go as comfortably in all that fire and brimstone as you and me on a nice spring day."

I was beside myself with excitement. I couldn't imagine anyone more interesting or funny, or wonderful than Pa and Grandma, 'cept ole Charlie, who can make you laugh just by sayin' howdy. I was laughin' so hard at Pa's remarks 'bout th' devil, frantically tryin' to write them all in my tablet before I could forget, that I forgot to look at Grandma. I had assumed she was enjoyin' Pa's remarks as much as myself but evidently she wasn't. Her usually tan face was solemn and pale as she quietly listened ta Pa poke fun at the devil and his domain.

"Have a care, Almus," she warned. "Until the Lord casts the devil into the lake of fire, he roams to and fro on the earth devouring whom he may, and with the Lord's permission. We have free choice. We can ask forgivenes and accept the gift of salvation by the shed blood of Jesus Christ and be protected by that precious blood. Or we can sin as we please and serve Satan. We, who have accepted Christ, the Son of the living God who sent the Holy Spirit or Comforter to help us when He ascended to Heaven, must be careful not to be drawn into realms of danger with careless talkin' and thinkin' lest we be caught off guard spiritually."

"Never!"she warned, "engage the devil in conversation or debate. No mortal can out think, out talk or out wit Satan, and I don't mean that mule by the same name out in the feed lot either. The real Satan was once God's chief angel, dearly beloved, with great powers, until he was so taken with himself he decided to be God and rule all by himself."

Pa looked at Grandma with love and respect. "I won't forget, Net, and when I poke fun at the devil, you can be sure I do so only after wrappin' myself securely in the Lords protection. I'm just a school teacher barely able to keep up with a bunch of average kids but I'm smart enough to know better than to try to best Satan at anything, 'cept ta remind him a thousand times a day that I'm washed in the precious blood of Jesus Christ."

Grandma went to Pa and wrapped her arms around him."You're a good man Almus."

"On that fine note, Net, I'm goin' ta bed. I'm much obliged to ye for that magnificent dinner and I better not hear sprout braggin' on it ta anybody outside this house either for I don't have time to fight all the competition that would try to take ye away from me."

Pa slowed down as he passed the stove and lifted one of the apple turnovers from the pan. "I'm a lucky man and thats a fact." he murmured to hisself. "A fine cook with mighty fine looks and she loves an ugly ignormaous like me.Yep! I'm a lucky man."

Grandma acted like she hadn't heard a word and maybe she hadn't for she had poured herself more coffee, and was looking at my tablet with the biggest smile on her face I'd seen in a long time.

"Pretty silly, huh," I said.

"Not silly at all dear child." She opened her hand and I laid mine inside it. It was all rough with little raspy callouses on it from hard farm work, specially berry pickin'. I can feel those beloved hands to this day scratchin' my back or feeling my face for a temperature.

She read down the list several times, smilin' at some and laughin' out loud at others, then she'd listen for Pa's snorin' and we'd both giggle like school girls.

Satan's good side Satans bad side
1 Works hard.
2 Respects the rules laid down by the master who provides food and shelter.
3 Never hurts family in the feed lot.
4 Left hell without permission.
5 Kicked the devil's prize red gates all over hell.
6 Forged his furlough papers and signed the devil's name to them.
7 Gave no indication he intended to ever return. (Jeepers! What a mule.)

Grandma loved the comments four through seven, readin' them over and over, laughin' till her sides hurt. We sat at the table a long time that night, gigglin' and enjoyin' each other's company. I hid the tablet and pencil under the mattress when I went to bed. I was sure Pa wouldn't approve even though a lot of the things I'd written under Satan's good side were the things he himself had said in jest. But, somewhere in all the discussions we'd had about the mule, both good and bad, my oponion of Satan had begun to change. I was beginnin' ta think he was a mule with a lot of potential. A mule that might just be an ordinary mule someday.

That night I dreamed that Satan was flying above the feed lot lookin' at the animals below. He was smilin' sweetly at each one, noddin' his head in a friendly manner as though he'd never kicked or bitten anyone or anything in his life. However, the most amazing thing of all was the beautiful white wings adorning his shoulders. They were silvery white and shone with a strange light

Then the devil suddenly appeared behind him, his black wings glistening in the early mornin' light. His face wore an evil smile of anticipation and triumph, for in his hand he held a large burning ember. He flew silently behind the mule for sometime as though he were enjoying the show but I knew he had an even better show in mind.

I opened my mouth to scream for the mule to look behind him but no sound came out. The devil gave me a quick smile then reached his arm toward Satan. The arm grew longer and longer 'till the hot ember was against the white wings. One feather curled upward in a gentle puff of smoke, then another and another until the tips of both wings were draggin' small flames behind them.

Panic-stricken, the animals below ran for the barn.

The mule must have thought his act wasn't exciting enough for them for he rose gracefully above the barn and began to do fancy loops, his lips spread wide in a hopeful smile. He looked like a glorious mythical creature from never, never land. The small flames streaming from the tip of each feather sparkled vividly against the blue sky. The mule was so busy watching for his audience to reappear in the feedlot below, he didn't see the devil until his second loop.

The devil's eyes blazed with envy and surprise at the mule's white wings. Then a terrible hatred filled them with fire, which instantly engulfed every feather on the mule's wings. I heard the devil's terrible laughter echoing across the sky like a black thunderstorm as the mule fell blazing toward the feedlot below.

I awoke before he hit the ground, jumped from my bed and raced for the window. It was a few hours before the dawn and I was happy to see Satan's corner of the feed lot empty and knew he was safely locked in his stall until Pa would feed and harness him for the workday ahead.

Spring sneaked over the land one night while we slept and the next morning the countryside was tinged a magical green so delicate we stood on the porch and stared at it in awe.

"I've seen this a thousand times Net and I always feel the Holy Spirit stir my soul in a wondrous way I can't explain."

"It's the same with me," she murmured. "What a perfect God we have and I thank him every day of my life for the beauty he gives us to enjoy."

I gulped big chunks of the fresh, sweet smellin' air 'till I was dizzy. "Look at your snowball bush Grandma, and the lilacs and all the trees are budded out and the dead grass is full of green sprouts and listen to them birds sing."

I was so excited I felt like runnin' 'round and 'round th' house shoutin' for joy and my feet just took off by themselves and me and ole Streeter started runnin' up the path toward the old home place. We passed the pear trees and I waved and shouted to them and Streeter barked joyously, then the sweet breeze carried us down the hill and seemed to lift us upward over the barbed wire fence into the cows pasture. Streeter woofed happily at one of the cows and nipped at her heels as he raced onward, lookin' back from time to time to make sure I was keepin' up. Then Pa's baritone voice called us home to breakfast.

After breakfast we did the milking, fed the livestock, then opened the feed lot gate so they could roam over the hills. Most of the snow had vanished overnight and they needed the exercise, specially the horses. The animals had spring fever also and there was much good-natured nipping and kicking of heels as they crowded through the gate. I watched them trottin' down the hill and suddenly realized Satan wasn't among them. They always let him pass through the gate first for his temper was short and his hooves quick to inflict a nasty wound on those who forgot. I looked in the corner where he always stood and there he was, watching the animals as they ran down the hill to the fields below. His face actually looked sad and he slouched carelessly instead of standing erect as he usually did.

Pa! Somethin' must be wrong with Satan."

Pa came from the barn and looked the mule over. "He seems alright ta me. Did he eat this morning, sprout, or did you check?"

"I'll go look," I said runnin' to the barn. His bag of oats was untouched and his water bucket was full and as I looked around his stall, it seemed he hadn't laid down all night. Pa was feelin' the mules head for fever when I returned and said he felt normal. I had brought a handful of oats back with me and held them under Satan's mouth. He sniffed briefly then turned his head away and looked down the hill at the cattle. "I'll bet a dollop of molasses in these oats would make him hungry," I told Pa as I ran to the house.

Grandma listened to my story, poured some sorgum in a bowl and went with me to the feed lot. As I've said before: Grandma has a way with animals and while she wasn't friendly with Satan she certainly cared for his welfare. As for the mule- he often stared after Grandma when she was doing chores and there would be a grudging respect on his face. She mixed the sorgum in with the oates and offered it to him in her hand. He seemed to appreciate this unusual gesture and raising his head he looked briefly into her eyes but refused the food.. "Well," Grandma sighed, a few days without food won't hurt him but he must drink water."

The second morning when the gate was opened, Satan looked at it longingly, watching the other animals go happily down the hill to scatter over the fields of green. His eyes were dark and hopeless and his condition was worsenin' for he wouldn't eat or drink. He'd stand in his corner and watch the other animals as they roamed over the hills and you could tell his heart was breakin'. Finally, Grandma went to the feedlot and sat on the fence in Satan's corner. He gave her a curious look but didn't try to make her leave. I could hear her talkin' to him but I never tried to get close enough to listen.

The third day Grandma carried a pot of liquid with her and I knew it had to contain a fair amount of her special herbs. She sat on the fence for an hour, not offering Satan even a look in the pot. He glanced sideways once or twice at the container and I saw Grandma smile. She sat awhile longer, then almost as an afterthought she dipped her hand in the pot and gently touched the mule's lips. He stood rigid and I was afraid he might bite her but then his long rough tongue began to lick her hand with delicate care. She wet her hand for him a half dozen times and he licked them dry each time. Then she didn't offer him anymore. Finally, he looked up at her as though asking why she quit. She climbed off the fence and held the pot out to him. He buried his muzzle in the pot and drank every drop. She gave him this formula for two days then she offered him a tiny portion of oats with a liberal helping of sorgum and apple cider vinegar mixed in. She fed him three and four times daily, increasing the portions and he began to get well. He still refused to leave the feed lot and while he often walked over to the gate to gaze down the hill, he never would walk through.

One morning, three weeks later, he was waiting at the gate and when the other animals came running out, he nipped a few backsides, placed a few kicks here and there and when Pa opened the gate he walked regally through it all by hisself as though he owned the world.

"Well, he's back, as mean as ever," Pa told Grandma at breakfast. She smiled and said she preferred that behaviour to the starvation behaviour. "I don't understand that mule, Net. He's as mean as a snake, yet he lets you nurse him back to health. I doubt he showed you a scrap of gratitude either. You even gave him back his courage or whatever it took to get him through that gate. I'll never understand that as long as I live."

"Satan's behaviour was and is a very serious situation, Almus. Animals know things we can't even guess at." Grandma looked grave and I knew she was worried. "I doubt we've seen the end of this matter, whatever it is."

Ever morning, Satan was waiting at the gate and the animals stood back a safe distance from him. He would prance through as though he owned the world and high kick several times on his way down the hill just to show them he was back and still in charge.

On the sixth night Satan didn't come home.

Pa saddled Nell and galloped through the gate and down the hill. Feeding and tending the animals fell to me and Grandma. I watched Pa out of sight, longin' to be ridin' with him.

Long after dark we heard Pa ride in. I ran to the barn with Grandma close behind me, but there was no sign of Satan and Pa looked real worried." Thanks for lighting the lanterns sprout," he said, kissing me on the top of my head. " They sure looked good after ridin' in the dark."

Pa ate supper in silence, his eyes ocassionally driftin' 'round the room as though lookin' for an answer. After he finished I washed his dishes while he and Grandma stood in the door lookin' out at the feedlot. I knew his eyes were on the corner where Satan always stood, but now I knew somethin' else. He loved that mule in spite of everything and so did Grandma. I left them standin' there with their arms around each other and went to bed.

"Well, Lord," I said, starin' at the ceilin'. "You know where he is and if he's ok or not. I believe he has some redeeming qualities although he does a lot of mean things. On th' other hand, if he did break out of hell it must be cause he didn't like it there, so I ask You most humbly to look out for him and bring him back home and forgive him and touch him with Your Spirit. Amen."

Early the next mornin', Pa had the chores done before I woke up and was already gone to search for Satan.. Me and Grandma ate breakfast, each thinkin' our own sorrowful thoughts. 'Bout three in the afternoon we heard someone coming up our hill toward the barn. We ran to the barn and there was Pa and two other neighbors ridin' beside Charlie Horn's wagon. Charlie doffed his hat to me and Grandma, his face 'bout as sorrowful as I ever seen it and said, "Net, I seed ye do miraculous things with yer herbs and other remedies and I have a powerful faith in ye but what I got in th' back of this wagon here is about as bad a situation as I ever seed in a animal."

We looked over the side of the wagon and there was Satan layin' on a big pile of hay. Grandma and me climbed up on a wheel spoke and she looked him over for a long time, not touchin' him anywhere. His dark eyes were half closed with a soft glaze in them and his lips hung slack, his swollen tongue hangin' out of his mouth. He gave no sign of seein' at all and his sides barely moved as he took shallow breaths. I looked at Grandma and her lips were set in a grim line, then she reached over the side and softly carressed Satan's muzzle. His nostrils flared briefly as he recognized her smell. She nodded as though he had asked her a question then she spoke to him quietly. "You're not alone now."

Pa and the men hadn't said a word all this time. Suddenly, Grandma looked up at them, a frown on her face. "Why do ye stand here doin' nothin'? Almus, pile a deep layer of soft hay in Satan's stall and cover the ceiling and walls in tarpualian. We got no time to waste so hurry. Nice of you men ta help like this and we appreciate it," she mumbled, jumpin' off th' spoke to th' ground. "Charlie, will you ride Nell inta Burnside and get me twenty yards of cheesecloth at Shorty's store. Better pick up twenty pounds of onions while yer about it, just in case."

Charlie looked dumbfounded but uttered not a word. Pa and the rest were fixin' Satan's stall as Grandma had directed and Charlie rode off on Nell as though the hounds of hell were after him. Maybe they were after us all in a way since we were determined to help Satan and after the dream I'd had where the devil set Satan on fire and sent him crashing to the ground, hounds from hell seemed as normal as sunshine. I looked into Grandmas eyes with my question and she smiled and said, "Pray, child as ye've never prayed before," then she ran to the house.

Satan was carefully lifted from the wagon in the sling that Charlie and the men used to get him out of the ravine he had fallen into and we made him as comfortable as possible. He didn't move the whole time, not even so much as a hoof, which meant he was close to being unconscious. Grandma was back with the pot of herbal mixture she'd used on Satan before. She cautioned them to hold his body as still as possible and when they lowered his body down on the hay, she balanced the sling with her hands and eased him slowly into the sweet smellin hay. She sat down beside his head and talked in low soothing tones as she dipped her fingers inta the brew and held it under his nose. At first he gave no sign of anything, then she ventured further and touched her finger to his dry tongue. She coated the tongue with a thick film of the brew and finally after what seemed like ages, he slowly drew his tongue back in his mouth. She repeated this 'till the brew was almost gone, then she gently rubbed his face and ears and told him he was a good mule. I thought I seen his nostrils quiver but I could have imagined it..

We all sat still as church mice while Pa told us the story of how he'd found Satan..

"This mornin' I found a gulley under the fence where Satan had left our farm. I tracked 'im as far as I could then his trail disappeared toward

Charlie's place. I was on my way there when I met Charlie, Ray and Foster here, headin' this way with Satan in the wagon. Lucky for the mule that Charlie was out lookin' for a stray calf and found 'im at the bottom of a ravine.

Charlie said he wasn't movin' at all. Charlie thinks he's broken up pretty bad inside for there's rocks in the ravine and it's pretty deep ta boot. He thinks Satan might even have a punctured lung or two from broken ribs. Lord only knows he's in a bad way.

"There'll be no more talk on how bad it might be," Grandma told them sternly. He hears ever word ye say and I tell ye he's gonna be right as rain. Right, Satan? " She ran her hand gently down his neck and he stuck his tongue out again.

"Why, I believe he wants some more of yer brew Net," Pa chuckled happily. He reached out and stroked the mule's ears, his face creased in a big smile. Our neighbors, Ray and Foster looked at each other, nodding their heads in agreement. "Bout that time Charlie rode in with a big bundle tied to the saddle horn. He come runnnin' in th' barn and stood lookin' at Satan and Grandma spreadin' brew all over his tongue.

"I'd say he looks some better'n he did, Almus"

"He's got a little liquid in 'im now and that should help a lot; but he's got a long way ta go yet." Pa murmured. "I think I'll ride over and fetch Doc Glass, Net. Won't hurt ta have him take a look, specially since the nearest vet's in Marion and he might be out somewhere and there'd I'd be waitin' no tellin' how long."

Grandma took the cheesecloth and onions from Charlie and put them on a shelf. "Now," she sighed, "let's hope we don't need them."

Grandpa rode out ta fetch Doc Glass. Grandma thanked Ray and Foster for their help and they went home to their families. She sat down again beside the mule and Charlie eased his boney frame into a corner of th' stall and watched Satan, not sayin' a word. I could tell his presence was a comfort to Grandma. She continued to spread brew on the mules tongue and he accepted the liquid six times then he gave a little shudder and closed his eyes. His breathin' improved a little and he didn't move a bit when Grandma spread a thick blanket over him.

"Nights git cold," Charlie whispered, "and he shore don't need a cold on top of everthin' else." We sat silently for three hours before we heard the familiar jangle of Doc's horse and buggy pull inta the barn. He squeezed his large bulk through the stall door, nodded to Grandma and Charlie, then kneeled beside th' mule. He carefully examined ever inch of Satan for broken bones while we held our breath waitin' for his diagnosis.

"Can't find anything broken on the outside," he said, "but unfortunately I can't see on the inside. Wish I had one of them machines they use in th' big hospitals to take pictures of th' innards. They'er real expensive though and I expect it'll be awhile before doctors like me can afford one. Just imagine, Net, If I could see inside this mules body."

There was a look of wonder on Grandma's face as she listened to Doc.

"Pretty soon old fossiles like me, with our limited knowledge of medicine, will be obsolete," he observed sadly, while easin' hisself onto a milkin' stool Pa had fetched from th' harness room. "Yet," he reasoned, "we serve our fellow man as best we can with what we know. Think how it must have been when families crossed prairies, rivers and mountains to settle in a land so primitive each day was a challenge just to stay alive. They practiced their own medicine in the only way possible, just by doing what they could for each other and trusting God to help them perservere. Imagine th' faith and courage it took just to get through each day."

Then Doc laughed his belly rumblin' laugh and winked a t Grandma.

"If I had lived back then with what I know today, limited as it is, I would have been considered a genius and with your knowledge of herbs Net, you would have saved many a life. Today it's an X-ray machine. Tomorrow, one can only wonder. Progress goes on dear friends but it comes with a high price which folks like you and me can't afford. I predict the future will be blessed with miraculous cures discovered by mans genius, but a lot of people and animals will suffer and die by th' time it trickles down ta folks like us. You know what frightens me most?" he asked, turnin' to Grandma. "I'm afraid the cost will be more than the average family can afford, so a lot of them won't be any better off than they are right now, depending on an old fossil like me."

"Me and you Net, have long dreamed of a clinic where the poor could come for free treatment and I know that one day it will happen all over this great land. Of course we'll have to keep the politicians out of it or they'll stuff their pockets and forget the poor."

He turned back to the mule, pressin' his hands lightly into Satan's body, listenin' through his stesthscope. The mule winced a time or two and Doc's listenin' device lingered on those spots for long minutes before he moved on. It took him over an hour to finish. Perspiration dripped off his face and he was gasping for breath. "It's cool outside, Net," he panted, "so why in tarnation is it so hot in here?"

"I had the men seal the stall with tarpauline so the mule wouldn't take cold or worse still pneumonia. How does his lungs sound?"

"They have some rattle but nothin' too serious. You know that could change though, so lets just hope and pray his resistance is strong enough to hang on. Right now he needs all the water and herbal brew you can get down him, with as much nourishment as you can add and still keep it fairly liquid. Don't want to take a chance on 'im chokin'."

He laid his hand lightly on Grandma's shoulder. "If anybody can help him, Net, it's you. I've done all I can, which is nothin' except assure you he don't have any bones broken outside. It's a miracle he didn't break at least a leg or two." Doc looked down at Satan for a long minute, then snapped his black bag shut.

Grandpa had gone outside to fetch Doc's horse from the feed room and lead him out to the breezeway. Doc reached down and shook Charlie's hand then squeezed his bulk through the stall door. He turned to Grandma from the long hall that divided the stalls, the sweet smell of cows and horses and hay mingling on the soft breeze and smiled apologetically."I haven't done him an ounce of good, Net, but if you want me to look at him again in a few days, just send Almus and I'll be here."

Grandma slipped her arm through Doc's and walked him to his buggy. "Alonzo, yer th' most humble man I ever knowed and what ye just said is a bunch of nonsense. Ye not only done Satan good by seein' his legs ain't broken but ye done me a world of good just comin' and lookin' him over. "She reached into a wagon settin' outside the barn doors and pulled a package off the seat. "Here's a ham fer yer trouble. You and the fine lady that puts up with you enjoy it and I thank ye again."

Doc tried to return th' ham but Grandma wouldn't hear of it. "Net," he complained, " you've helped me deliver more babies than I can count, a lot of 'im by yerself and here ye pay me for doin' somethin' for you."

"Almus would hate to tote that ham back ta th' smoke house Alonzo and I don't intend to so I reckon ye don't have any choice."

He regarded Grandma affectionately. They were old friends who understood each other perfectly.

"I'll even th' score dear lady and when the time comes, I won't tolerate no back talk from you either."

With a wave of his hand he picked up Jessie's reins and gently swished them across her shoulder but she was already halfway out the gate headed for home. Doc had slipped a bag in my hand as I handed him Jessie's reins and thanked me for the drink of water and the bag of oats she had eaten while he was there. I watched them halfway down th' hill then ran back to Satan's stall. Grandma was settin' beside the mule on a stool just watchin' him. I emptied the sack inta Grandmas lap. It was full of Three muscoteers, some milky ways and a bag of horehound candy fer Pa. Three muscoteers is my very favorite candy in all th' world and I wished I could give Doc a big hug. Next time, I promised myself.

"We'll have these for dessert Grandma and while you watch Satan I'm goin' to make ham and eggs and I believe I'll just show you what I've learned watchin' you make biscuits." She looked surprised but I didn't give her time to reply as I ran to the house.

Five days crawled by on molasses feet, as Grandma put it; but Satan had gained a lot in those five days. His eyes were open and he regarded us all with a kind of tolerance, poppin' his teeth once in awhile to show he would brook no nonsense even when sick. He allowed us to tend his needs, but was 'specially pleased when Grandma was there. His eyes would follow her with a look of pure love which he thought didn't show and no one gave any indication that he was other than the same cantankerous mule, temporarily down on his luck.

Grandma had sent Pa and Charlie to th' swamp for several wagon loads of mud during those five days. She heated th' mud and covered th' mule's body with it then wrapped him in yards and yards of oilcloth to keep th' heat in. This, she did over and over and the properties of th' mud gradually took the soreness from Satan and healed his internal wounds. She even treated his legs and he was so comical lookin' all trussed up in mud and oilcloth we nearly busted ever time we looked at 'im. No one dared laugh though 'till they were in th' house so Satan never knew how funny he looked..

Then one day Charlie nearly spoiled the whole thing. He hadn't seen Satan in his mud and oilcloth trappins', and when he opened the stall door and seen th' mule, his face split inta a big grin, he opened his mouth to whoop and Grandma, who was standin by th' door with a bucket of mud, grabbed a handful and stuffed it inta Charlie's mouth.

Charlie's eyes flew wide in disbelief as he turned and seen Grandma with her hand full of mud. Horrified, he sucked in his breath, swallowed th' wad of tobacco in his mouth, stumbled out the door choakin' and wheezin', with Pa beatin' 'im on th' back, then me and Grandma heard him gag as he emptied his stomach.

I looked at Satan and I swear there was a big grin on his face. Grandma saw it too. "Our secret, child," she said to me, grinnin' down at th' mule. "I hope Charlie will forgive my rashness but at this stage we have to keep a certain party calm." She had her bucket of gruel and knelt down to feed Satan. He looked into her eyes, th' grin still on his face and his long rough tongue reached out and licked Grandmas hands for th' longest time even though there wasn't a drop of brew on them. She laid her hand on his head, strokin' his ears fondly. "How about some dinner?" she asked him.

Satan was doing so well Pa figured th' mule might sleep safely without him or Grandma sitting up ever night. So, on the eighth day of Satan's recovery, we all slept in our own bed satisfied he was warm and comfortable. I heard the wind blowing durin' th' night but thought nothin' of it since th' barn is sturdy and warm.

Next mornin' I found an empty, cold kitchen and knew somethin' terrible must be wrong. I ran to the barn and heard th' mule wheezin' long before I reached th' stall. Grandma and Pa were bent over his shiverin' body tryin' to take the cold oilcloth off him. I felt a stir of air and looked up to see a large hole in th' roof directly over where Satan was lying. Grandma was pulling the cold mud from him and wrapping quilts around the cleared areas. Meanwhile Pa had gone to th' smokehouse for a small stove we used for curin' meat. He got a big fire goin' and soon it was heating th' stall and th' mule. He was watchin' Grandma and th' mule anxiously, puffin' his pipe as he rotated it 'round and 'round his mouth.

"It's my fault Net for leavin' him."

"Nonsense, Almus. How on earth could you know it would storm and blow a piece of th' barn roof away directly over Satan.? It's a setback and I fear he's got pneumonia but we're goin' ta pull him through if we have ta drag 'im ever foot of th' way. You hear that ye onery mule? Git yer dander up and lets see some fight out of that bad tempered, ill begotten hide of yers. Ye've bitten and kicked dozens of poor wretches fer no reason atall; Now, if I don't see some real stuff outta ye then I'm gonna do some kickin' myself."

I thought I saw Satan's eyes roll up toward Grandma but I can't be sure. Pa patched the barn roof and I went in ta start a fire in th' kitchen and cook breakfast. Neither Pa nor Grandma had thought of anythin' 'cept ole Satan and I was proud of them and proud that I could do somethin' ta help. An hour later I called them in and was they surprised ta see a table full of good food. There wasn't any time wasted as they washed their hands and said prayers and hugged me 'bout a jillion times in between bites.

"Why, these biscuits are as good as yers Net," Pa exclaimed in surprise.

I hung my head in embarassment and fear that Grandma might git her feelin's hurt, but she hugged me real hard and said, "They're better than mine Almus and I do believe this child has a knack fer makin' biscuits and cakes and pies."

"Never tasted her cake and pie but I believe ye."

"Well, them apple pies ye made disappear last Sunday was made by th' sprout here," she declared.

"Pawn my word," he laughed, poppin' another biscuit in his mouth. "Wait till I tell Charlie 'bout this."

"We're gonna need help Almus fer what has ta be done."

"Look no further dear lady," said a familiar voice. "Help is here fer as long as ye need it. Now what is wrong and where do I fit in," said Charlie, his face puzzled.

"It's Satan. The roof blew off in that storm last night and it leaked through a crack in the tarp. Of course it was smack dab right in th' middle of Satan's bed. What I feared most has happened. He's got pneumonia."

Charlie peered in at Satan, then squatted beside the mule. "Ye ain't no stranger ta tough times fella, whats more ye've dished out a few tough times yerself, here and there. Member thet bite ye give me on me...well, never mind whar- cause I know ye ain't fergot it. Anyhow, now ye gotta show yer stuff er by dam I'm gonna bite ye on yer ornery arse so deep ye'll have ta crawl th' rest of yer days." Charlie opened his mouth and got down in Satan's face. "See these here teeth, pilgrim? They be strong as steel and ye don't want to mess with 'im. I reckon pneumonia be lots easier to git over than one of me bites."

The mule openend one glazed eye and stared belligerently at Charlie. His lip curled with contempt and his teeth popped angrily.

I was watchin' Satan and Charlie and I swear when Charlie left the stall, Satan was smilin'.

Grandma's plan was beyond belief." I want you and Charlie to raise Satan off the ground and secure his sling from them rafters up there. Then I want a hole 'bout six inches deep dug all around where he lays. Charlie, build me a big fire outside with lots of rock to support all them branch rocks I been gatherin' fer my flower garden.

Gotta do this quick Almus.

Sprout you start carryin' them rocks over to where Charlie builds th' fire."

Pa took over like always and soon the mule was hangin' from the rafters while Charlie and Pa quickly dug out the dirt. Charlie left to start a fire while Pa finished and me and Charlie began to lay the branch rock in the flames.

Grandma laid a double thick tarp in the cavity, then a layer of smoothe stones. "Them rocks outta be hot by now," she mumbled, reachin' up ta slap Satan's rump.

He rolled his eyes but never flinched.

"Hot enuff ta cook a hog," I opined, lookin' Satan in the eye. "Charlie keeps scratchin' his head and wonderin' if ye intend to roast ole Satan; but If I was you I wouldn't worry too much," I told the suspended mule. "Most folks don't like roasted mule anyhow."

"Quit teasin' that mule, sprout and tell Almus and Charlie ta get a move on."

Charlie and Pa loaded the wheel barrow and come runnin' like th' devil was after them. They spread the hot rocks, put another layer of small stones, another tarp with lots of hay on it then lowered Satan gently onto his new bed. "Keep that fire heaped with rock Charlie, we're gonna need a lot of heat under this mule."

Meanwhile she had a pan of water boilin' on th' little heatin' stove. When the mule was covered heavily with quilts and a tarp, Grandma spooned out a big glob of Vicks salve in th' boilin' water and soon th' little room was a steam bath full of Vicks. "That ought to last five hours or so she said, walkin' 'round the mule to inspect it all."

Pa and Charlie squatted in a corner, tryin' to get their breath, while Grandma sat beside Satan and felt his muzzle. She had a hollow seven inch piece of sugar cane which she filled with water and dribbled in Satan's mouth. He took it without complaint and as the hot bed heated him up he wanted even more, which was what Grandma wanted.

Changing the cool rocks for hot ones was really very simple with Grandmas method. The mule was raised a few feet off the ground, the tarp was rolled back, cool rocks removed and hot ones inserted in their place, then the tarp and hay was placed over that. Satan was lowered onto the bed again as easy as pie.We took turns watchin' him and he seemed to be holdin' his own.

On my watch two nights later he began to wheeze and shake, his eyes rolled back in his head and I ran to fetch Grandma. She examined him, her lips tight with worry. "I'll be back as soon as I can sprout," she muttered, runnin' to the house. Fifteen minutes later she came in carryin a mess of stuff in the dishpan. I watched in amazement as she poured hot fried onions in cheesecloth and secured it to Satans chest with a piece of oil cloth. As soon as one batch cooled, she'd replace it with a fresh hot one. She did this all night and the next day, pourin' water in his mouth as fast as he could take it. The Vicks water on the little stove never stopped boilin', the rocks were kept hot and the next night the mule was breathin' more normal.

"I'd like Doc to come take another look at him, Almus, if ye don't mind the long ride."

Pa was on his way almost before she finished.

Three hours later Doc heaved his vast bulk through the stall door and stood lookin' at the mule a long time, not sayin' a word, then he sat on the milk stool and put his stescope to the mules chest. "Wal, from what Almus has been tellin' me, ye ought to have a dead mule here instead of one I think just might pull through." He smiled at Grandma. "I see yer usin' th' onion remedy, Net. At our medical conventions I've told many a doctor 'bout it and how you saved a lot of folk during that bad flu epidemic in 1919 that killed thousands. Course they don't believe me. I'd like ye to come with me sometime Net and talk to our proud, medical association."

Doc sighed and studied the quiet animal lying comfortably on the warm hay. "You're one lucky mule," he told Satan. "This fine lady here saved your life and you owe her a very large debt of gratitude. Net! If I ever come down with pneumonia, I'll send for you."

As they walked from th' barn, Grandma handed Doc a side of bacon as payment but he waved her aside and crawled up into his buggy. "This is on the house, Net, as all my visits are from now on. We're partners. Remember?. We birth babies together and when I'm not around then you birth them for me. Don't know what I'd have done sometimes without your help. Course, I might accept a gift now and then of your wonderful sausage or some such," he grinned.

I watched the buggy start down th' hill then walked back to the barn. I hated to admit how much I'd hoped Doc would bring another sack of candy. Five minutes later we heard the jingle of harness and there was Doc's buggy back in the driveway. He leaned over th' side and yelled my name. I very nearly forgot your little present, Sprout," he said. handin' out a large brown sack to me.

"Jeepers, Dr. Glass, this sack weighs a ton."

"Well, not quite," he smiled.

He clucked at Jessie and I watched the buggy start down the hill. "Thanks Dr. Glass," I yelled. His hand waved from the window and his, "You're welcome, sprout," came softly through Jessie's hoofbeats and the soft swishing of the buggy's wheels on th' dusty road. I stood and listened for a long time to the faint jingle of metal as night fell softly on the farm. I could imagine Doc grabbin' a few winks as faithful Jessie took him home to a warm bed.

I ran to the barn with my prize and dumped it's contents into Grandma's apron and stood lookin' at the most candy I'd ever seen at one time 'cept at the store. "Isn't it grand?" I laughed. "Look Pa, there is ev horehound for you and lots of it too. I danced a jig in the straw and Satan cast a jaundiced eye in my direction; but I detected a sparkle of humor in them too as he watched us. I couldn't beleive my eyes as I scooped them around Grandma's apron. Milkyways, muscoteers, BabyRuths, Hunks and hunks of milk chocolate, peppermint sticks as thick as my arm and six bottles of orange crush pop. "Jeepers, no wonder it was so heavy," I exclaimed. "Ain't Doc grand? Imagine how much all this cost." I opened a muscoteer and slid one of the three squares in my mouth. "Here, Pa. Try your horehound. Grandma you love chocolate so take tour pick. Golly, we'll have candy runnin' out our ears," I giggled. Grandma put it all back in the sac and handed it to me. "We'll put the pop down in the well to get cold," she said to me, "then you'll have a treat for six days honey."

"Absolutely not!" I protested. "We share and share alike right down to the last pop and candy bar. I'll put it all in that pretty fruit bowl Aunt Bess gave you for christmas last year." I ran to the house huggin' the prize to me, so happy I could bust. Satan was gonna get well, we had all the candy we could eat and my favorite pop to wash it down. It sure felt grand to be rich, I thought, as I lowered the six bottles of orange crush into the cold well water.

"That was a nice thing Doc did for the sprout, Net."

"Even nicer for her to want to share it all with us," Grandma murmured.

Company's Comin'

One nite we were gathered 'round the oak table in the kitchen havin' supper when Grandma carefully took an envelope from her apron and laid it beside Grandpa's plate.

"What's that?" he asked, scannin' the return address in the corner. "Thats a letter from my sister Bess," she replied quietly. There was a happy light on her face and her voice had just the least bit of tremor in it.

"The family alright?" he asked, not touchin' the letter.

"Everbody's fine. They're comin for a visit next week," she said in a voice that couldn't quite believe such a miraculous thing."

"Is that a fact?" Grandpa said plesantly.

"Bess thought it high time for a visit. It's been five years now you know."

"That's a long time Net," he said, taking her hand in his.

"Imagine drivin' all that way down here from Chicago," she murmured wistfully.

"Who all's comin,'" Pa wanted to know.

"Just her and Bill and their daughter Victoria."

VICTORIA!

I'd been quietly listenin' to the news, tinglin' with excitement when lightenin' struck. The big windy, mob infested city of Chicago with its trains that run on tracks up in the air, of all things, was electrifyin' enough; but the name Victoria transported me into another world. Now there was a city name, chock full of style and gracious livin' and gentility.

I rolled it experimentally over my tongue. There wasn't a rough edge on it no matter which way I slid it round my mouth. Yep! That was a genuine city name alright; no two ways about it.

Not an ordinary country name like Helen Ruth which nobody ever called me anyhow, cause somebody was always hangin' a nickname round my neck like Tooter, from my dad, Yellow Britches fron Pa and Child from Grandma.

The name yellow britches come from the time I was wearin' my favorite pair of britches Grandma had made from a brightly flowered feed sack. They were scandulous loud but I purely loved them pants.

One evenin' Pa and me walked to the home place to milk when a couple of the guard dogs run out and barked at me. I was pretty surprised since I'd known them dogs forever.

Pa hoisted me quick as a wink onto his shoulder and I said, "They ain't barkin' at me Pa, they're barkin' at my britches." That was his favorite story and I was his favorite person in all the world which seemed natural enough since him and Grandma had a lot of years invested in my upbringin'.

"How old is Victoria?" I asked, holdin' my breath.

"She'd be about thirteen now," Grandma answered absently, her mind obviously busy with more important things.

Thirteen! My heart sank. Here she is, I thought, livin' in a big city with her fancy skyscraper apartment scrapin' the bottom off the clouds; a glorious, glamorous name like Victoria and on top of all that, she's thirteen.

Any notion I had of a pal was already stirrin' up a cloud of dust down the road a piece.

Next day began what I can only describe as moon fever. When dogs got it they'd howl at the moon. Some folks would sometimes get it right out of the blue, except I never heard tell of anybody howlin'.

Me and Pa and Streator (his favorite coon dog) got home for supper that nite and every stick of furniture from the kitchen, except the cook stove, was settin' out on the back porch.

"What in conscience name is goin' on Nettie," Pa asked as Grandma come flyin' out the kitchen door with a bucket of cleanin' water in her hand.

"I'm cleanin' this filthy place up, Almus. Why, I've never in my life seen such a mess," she fumed to herself.

Old Streator flopped on the grass and stared in amazement at the porch.

Pa set down on the steps and sighed heavily. "Nettie, this place ain't never been a mess since the day I built it, and what kind of visit you and Bess gonna' have anyway if yer' wore right down to the bone?"

Grandma sniffed and hurled the water off the porch.

Old Streator jumped up from the grass, no doubt rememberin' the scaldin' dish water that got him last year and moved up on the step beside Pa; but before he could get hisself in a settin' position, Grandma cast a wary eye on him.

"Don't you step foot in this clean house dog or I'll skin yer hide."

Old Streator's shocked face slid right down to his knees and he gave a little yelp as he fell off the steps and sprawled in embarrassment at Pa's feet.

"Now there's no call for that, Net," Pa admonished, helpin' Streator right hisself. "That dog wouldn't step foot past the door unless you asked him. You know that well as I do. Why, yer already dead tired else ye wouldn't talk ta Streator like that."

Grandma suddenly looked miserable, like she'd been in a bad dream or somethin' as she came down the steps and sat beside Pa. She reached down and cupped Streator's fine head in her hands, tuggin' his ears affectionately.

She didn't say a word but Streator understood it perfectly. A wide grin split his face and his long tongue curled round her hand like a pink ribbon.

We were up early on the mornin' of the big reunion. Chores were done hurriedly and even the animals sensed the excitement for the cows wouldn't give down their milk and kept bawlin' plaintively and lookin' back at Pa settin' on his milk stool.

In early afternoon, from my perch in the top of a tree, I sighted a cloud of dust boilin' up on the road by the home place, a mile and a half as the crow flies and three miles as the road goes. I started yellin' and Grandma come rushin' out smoothin' her hair and lookin' anxious.

"See the dust?" I laughed excitedly. "That's got to be them."

Pa strolled out, his teeth clenched on the old briar that seldom left his mouth and watched the cloud billowin' up one hill and down the other, then it suddenly stopped.

Grandma stared hard at the spot, her hands clenched.

"Nothin' to worry over, Net," Pa assured her. Bill likely didn't like the look of that bridge over the creek. He'll see it's sturdy enough," and sure as anythin' the dust swirled up again bigger than before and Grandma knew Bess was urgin' Bill to go faster.

There's no way I can convey the sweet agony and excitement of those next few moments as the years of distance closed between the sisters. The dust cloud rolled closer and closer as we held our breath in excitement and counted off the seconds until it was almost to our road.

Then we all stood transfixed as a brand new emerald green packard sedan pulled majestically up our little hill and rolled to a stop, temporarily engulfin' us all in a cloud of dust.

"For Gawd's sake," Pa whispered in wonder. "Would you look at that."

I swiveled round to look at Grandma. She hadn't heard the Lord's name taken in vain because sobs were shakin' her shoulders and her eyes were fastened on a small, neat woman rushin' toward her with outstretched arms.

Then Uncle Bill crawled out from the drivers side and I couldn't believe my eyes.

To think I ever marveled over Victoria and her hifaultin' name and her trains runnin' in the air and an apartment wedged between the clouds.

Uncle Bill was an honest to goodness, so help me Hannah, a real-life Humpty Dumpty with a lopsided grin and sky blue eyes bubblin' with good humor. In a courtly manner he tipped his hat to me which reminded me of Peter Rabbit- then reached for Pa's outstretched hand.

"Welcome to the farm, Bill," Pa smiled, and I could see a genuine likin' in his eyes for this man. "We've been anxious for you to get here."

All this time Pa's eyes were devourin' that car and I vowed when I growed-up I'd buy Pa and Grandma an emerald green Packard sedan for their very own.

While Uncle Bill and Pa were talkin', I was surreptitiously studyin' the image in the back of the sedan, but all I could make out was a face shadowed by a big hat.

"My word," Uncle Bill suddenly exclaimed, "I'm forgetting my manners."

Givin' me a little bow and supportin' my arm gracefully he led me to the back of the sedan. I felt like Cinderella goin' to the ball and on my feet were beautiful glass slippers bein' swept by a white satin gown. He opened the door with a flourish and presented me to Victoria.

Victoria's nose was stuck so far in the air it was an hour before I saw her face, but what I could see was beyond anything I'd ever seen before. Long black hair topped with a delicate lace hat, skin that seldom felt the sun and a slender form extravagantly wrapped in green silk.

My good cotton dress looked like toe-sackin' next to her silk and I felt a twinge of embarrassment as I stared at her white skin knowin' mine was nut brown in contrast.

My long red hair hung in profusion 'round my shoulders while hers was carefully brushed, with a fancy clip holdin' it in place.

Her green eyes took me in at a glance and dismissed me, just like that.

Only Grandma's good Bible teachin' kept my tongue silent, but my thoughts were speedin' down the road of sin so fast, I'd need a road map to find my way back. In my mind, right then and there, I sarcastically dubbed Victoria, 'The Queen.'

As Uncle Bill helped her from the car I watched in shock as she stepped daintily into the dust wearin' the most beautiful pair of white suede pumps I'd ever seen outside the Sears & Roebuck catalog. I tried not to notice the small puffs of dust settlin' on their pristine surface with every step she took and by the time we reached the porch her shoes were a tattle-tale grey.

Grandma ran out to throw her arms about Victoria, extendin' a proper hand to Uncle Bill who leaned over it as though he was admirin' a rare jewel, then he kissed her finger tips. What manner of city custom that was I couldn't imagine, but seein' Grandma's face soften with pleasure, I allowed as how it had some merit.

Grandma had a fit over the dust on the Queen's shoes and when they were removed from the Queen's feet she slapped the soles together and like magic the dust fell away and they were new again.

"Child," she said to me," take these pretty shoes and put them on a shelf in the closet."

"Vickie she addressed The Queen, "you must have brought an old pair of shoes with you; or perhaps you'd rather go barefoot."

Did she say Vickie?

I looked at Grandma with new eyes. Addressin' The Queen in such a common manner was tantamount to social treason, and I couldn't imagine what her royal highness would do with such an insult.

Go barefoot!

I waited for the guillotine to fall, but Her Highness didn' seem a' tall put out, givin' Grandma a sweet smile.

After lunch everyone sat on the front porch drinkin' coffee, all talkin' at once, their joyous laughter tremblin' the delicate petals of Grandmas mornin' glories.

Finally Uncle Bill turned his warm smile on me as though I was the most important person in the world.

"Would you show Vicki around the farm, dear child," he asked, his blue eyes full of understandin' and amusement.

I reluctantly allowed as how I would. It was hard to refuse someone as gracious and gallant as Uncle Bill. I was to realize on that visit and subsequent visits just how special Uncle Bill was. He had integrity and dignity and great charm. He treated ladies with the greatest respect and consideration, from those two years of age to those a hundred and two years of age.

When you first met this Humpty Dumpty man you were surprised by his caricature appearance; but shortly after, the substance of his goodness and love for people and life shone so brightly, all you saw was an amazin' man who had the ability to lift people above the grosser elements of their lives.

In preparation for her tour around the farm The Queen had foolishly changed into a pair of white string sandals that showed off to perfection, ten red laquered toe nails. After a few steps I noted with some satisfaction that our good country dust was already makin' sport with them white string shoes.

Serves her right I thought for bein' too uppity to go barefoot.

She seemed overwhelmed and totally out of place on the farm as she trailed regally beside me around the house, her eyes dartin' here and there tryin' to take in our primitive way of life.

"How do you bathe?" she asked suddenly.

I pointed to a galvanized tub hangin' on a long nail on the back of the house. "In that."

I could tell she was furiously mullin' this over in her mind as she studied the tub.

"But where?" she continued, a look of shock on her face.

"Well, in the winter it's most generally the kitchen, but in summer it's in the yard or on the back porch."

She gasped. "In front of God and everybody?"

Grandma keeps a weather eye out for visitors," I said matter of factly. "As for God: Grandma says God has better things to do than lolly-gag over a bunch of naked sinners."

"I'll never take a bath in that... contraption," she spat.

"Suit yourself," I replied, entertainin' plesant visions of a dirty queen glidin' about the farm.

As we neared the pig pen she clapped her hands over her nose, starin' in revulsion at the fat, mud covered bodies pressin' against the fence, their inquirin' snouts twistin' and snortin' as they took in the scent of this stranger. She drew back from their curious stares and I've no doubt they were quite amused at this odd smellin', fancy lookin' female. You may not know this but animals are as curious and facinated with people as people are with them.

Our cows had spied the queen and were congregated in congenial curiosity with their heads hangin' over the fence for a better look.

The Queen seemed pleased with them, rubbin' their faces and ears timidly. She marveled at their big, glossy, gentle eyes and spent a good deal of time starin' into their friendly faces.

Dimple, my mare, was standin' in a corner of the fence waitin' her turn, her eyes bright and curious, ears twitchin' in anticipation as she stared at the approchin', brightly colored figure.

The other horses were hangin' back just watchin', not as bold and friendly as Dimple. Dimple's twin, Nell, ventured only as far as Dimple's rump, her chin anchored to the mare's back, ears up, eyes glued on the queen.

Then Dimple and Victoria were face to face and a magical transformation came over the queen as she gazed into the sweet, gentle face of the mare. I'd heard of love at first sight and held my breath as I watched the response of the animal to our guest. You could feel the vibrations in the air as Dimple whinnied' and snuffled The Queen's face and hair.

The Queen had climbed up on the fence and was now holdin' the mare's head in her lap as you would hold the head of a favorite dog, her hands caressin' the velvet nose, cooin' soft little noises that put a raptured look on Dimple's face. I've seen bonds of love between animals and people before, but this was an instant melding of spirit and heart that is rarely seen.

Well, I thought, the chickens and ducks and geese would have to wait as neither horse nor girl stopped communicatin' with one another. I reckoned there must be some little somethin' nice in The Queen for Dimple to take to her so fast.

"Do you think I might ride her?" the Queen asked.

"Sure, why not, cept Pa will have to saddle her. I always ride bareback myself," I bragged.

"I too, will ride bareback," she announced casually.

As I fetched a bridal from the barn I was secretly hoping for a ruined silk dress.

She took the bridal from me and slid it expertly over Dimple's head, tied the skirt of the green silk into a knot between her legs, gracefully mounted, then touched her knee to the mare's side.

"Well I'll be switched," I said to Nell who was watchin' Dimple and the queen trot down the hill.

I almost fell off the fence as a voice said, "She rides pretty well, doesn't she?"

"She's terrific!" I exclaimed, turnin' to Uncle Bill. "Where'd she learn to ride like that?"

"Let's see," he mused. "We joined the Chicago riding club when she was about five and she's been riding ever since. Seems to have a special way with horses."

"Well," I replied breathlessly, watchin' horse and rider climb a distant hill. "I'd say it's a touch of magic. Never seen anything to beat it."

Humpty Dumpty climbed up on the fence beside me and we sat in mutual silence watchin' the Queen and Dimple climb the ridge and disappear into a tract of timber.

I glanced at Uncle Bill and smiled to myself as the Humpty Dumpty poem ran through my mind.

"How are you and Victoria getting on? "He asked conversationally.

"About as well as could be expected," I answered, tryin' not to show any irritation.

"As bad as all that?" he laughed.

Surprised, I said nothin'.

"You can be forthright with me child for I understand perfectly. Vicki is a wonderful girl, if a bit of a snob," he chuckled. "She's a city girl you see, not accustomed to farm living and she doesn't quite know how to cope, if you get my meaning."

"I get it alright," I replied. In fact I got it the minute she stepped them white suede pumps into the dust, her nose so high in the air she almost missed the ground."

Humpty Dumpty grasped the fence rail, laughin' so hard I feared he'd fall off the fence and hurt hisself.

"Dear child," he laughed, pattin' me on the hand. "You're the most honest, refreshing person I've run across in a long time and I'd say Victoria is a lucky girl to have kin like you."

"Is that your mare she's riding?"

Yes."

"Mighty generous of you to let her ride your very own mare."

"I don't mind, special since Dimple liked her a lot. Funny thing. Dimple never took to anybody like that before."

"How do you feel about the mare liking Victoria?"

"Well, I think its rather nice and I'm not jealous, if thats what you mean."

"Does it change the way you feel about Victoria ?"

Some," I replied.

"Good girl," he smiled, lookin' at me with admiration.

That night at supper a lifetime of memories were taken from secret chambers, dusted off and joyfully released where they hovered over the old oak table just waitin' their turn to be told.

There was laughter and tears and hugs of affection to assure themselves it wasn't all a dream and that they really could reach out and touch a loved one whom they hadn't seen in years.

I'd never seen Grandma look more beautiful, with her black eyes sparklin' like mornin' dew, her dark skin draped satiny smoothe over high cheek bones. The wealth of black hair that framed her fine face was restrained in a thick braid down her back.

Aunt Bess reminded me of a little wren, all warm and sweet and dignified.

The Queen was silent and seemed enchanted with all the wonderful stories and I knew part of her thoughts were on Dimple and the lovely afternoon spent ridin'.

As for me: I was in heaven, soakin' up every word and gesture. The kerosene lamp in the middle of the old oak table bathed each face in a warm glow, castin' their shadows against the walls, paintin' pictures of love and carin' and laughter on my mind that would never fade. I stamped those wonderful faces in my memory, not realizin' that sixty years later they would still be as vibrant and young as that magic night, settin' on the floor of a country kitchen in a clapboard farm house under a star-studded sky with jillions of frogs givin' a concert in the pond down by the barn.

A large platter of fried chicken had disappeared along with corn on the cob, green beans and new little potatoes right out of our garden, and of course Grandmas incomparable biscuits snuggled under mounds of her wonderful milk gravy. The sideboard was loaded with blackberry cobbler, rhubarb pie and Grandma'a speciality, fried apple pies.

Everyone agreed dessert would have to wait and Uncle Bill said a few stories from Pa would just about make the day perfect. Grandma filled everyone's coffee cup then set a fresh pot to perk on the back of the stove. She knew from long experience that Pa's yarns were like the begats in Genesis. They went on begatin' till all hours of the night.

Shiftin' his lean frame in a comfortable position, Pa scraped his chair back from the table and lit his pipe, his face contemplative, his eyes half closed and I knew he was goin' through the endless story file in his mind searchin' for just the right one.

Facinated as always, I watched as the smoke from his beloved pipe drifted out of his mouth like spectral serpents, twistin' and turnin' this way and that in the lamplight.

I noticed the Queens eyes followed them with great interest and I also noticed the Queen had put away her fair share of Grandma's good cookin'.

I put my arm around old Streator who was lyin' just inside the door as mannerly as you could want. He too enjoyed the stories, sometimes watchin' Pa with a sly smile on his face and when his name was mentioned he'd thump his tail on the linoleum floor in pleased acknowledgement.

As you know," Pa began, "me and Net here were blessed with three daughters, but since the Lord knew I longed for a son to hunt with he made one of em' a tomboy."

He smiled broadly, rememberin'.

"Nellie Ruth was our middle girl and she could out do any boy in the county and a fair number of men if she set her mind to it. She once shot the eye from a sparrow fifty yards away and I never saw anyone else that could do that. She had a shooters eye and an uncanny instinct which made her might nigh unbeatable.

The Queen's face was horrified, her skin blanched out more pale than before if that was possible.

"Don't fret Victoria," Pa soothed. She only did that once and I don't believe she thought she could really hit that bird. Anyway, when it fell to the ground, Ruth cried over it all afternoon. She had a big funeral and buried it out back in a match box and put a stick cross on its grave."

He worked his pipe from one side of his mouth to the other, his eyes closed and I knew he was back in the past attendin' a funeral for a sparrow with my mom when she was eleven years old.

"Yep," he mused, "she was a tomboy alright but with a tender heart and..." his eyes rested affectionately on my face, "peers' like this one's gonna' be just like her."

Uncle Bill chuckled. "Ruth was the spunkiest little mite I ever saw alright, no doubt of that. I gather this yarns about her then," he smiled, his eyes followin' the smoke patterns driftin' toward the ceilin'.

Well she was certainly the principle player in this one alright, but then if you took that girl anywhere she was likely to stir up somethin', good or otherwise. It didn't matter to Ruth none what it was. She just liked life to keep on movin', goin' somewhere, anywhere as long as it was excitin'. I always said she should have been born to a circus family for ordinary life was just too dull for Ruth. I once caught her hoppin' on and off a freight train goin' through Parker and had it been goin' full speed no tellin' what might have happened."

Aunt Bess gasped. "Gracious sakes alive, I simply would have fainted right away if Victoria ever did such a thing."

I didn't think she'd ever have to worry about The Queen hoppin' freights in her silk dress and white suede pumps. I couldn't even begin to imagine The Queen in a pair of overalls. The picture of such a thing was too much and I started gigglin'. All eyes focused on me so I straightened up and scolded old Streator for runnin' his cold nose on my neck. He gave me a scornful look, got up and moved to Pa's side and laid down with his head on Pa's shoe.

Grandpa laid his hand on Streator's head, then looked at me, and I could tell by the glint in his eyes that he knew I'd used old Streator as a scape goat. Tiltin' his chair back against the wall on two legs he closed his eyes, his pipe hangin' from the corner of his mouth and resumed the story.

"It was a Saturday mornin' in May," he said nostalgically. "I even remember the weather. Sunny... with just a whisper of coolness in the air; you know the kind of day that fills you with indescribable joy and makes you feel like a kid again.

Me and Ruth were ridin' Dimple and Nell into town for supplies, singin' at the top of our lungs, intoxicated with the beautiful day.

"Dimple kept tryin' to break into a run and finally Ruth gave her her head and they flew down the road leavin' me and Nell in a cloud of dust. Course Nell was strainin' at the bit, snortin' and stompin' the ground in frustration to run with Dimple and it seemed even the animals had spring fever."

When me and Nell galloped up to the hitchin' post at Shorty McCormicks grocery store Dimple was eagerly waitin' for us and Ruth was already on the porch chewin' the fat with the farmers who usually loafed a few hours before buyin' their supplies. She liked nothin' better than listenin' to their stories about huntin' and guns, especially guns. That girl purely loved guns, spendin' hours porin' over the Sears and Roebuck catalog."

"The men accepted her company, respected her ability to handle a gun and more or less treated her as one of them. She had a way about her that defied understandin'. I guess them movie people might call it presence or some such word."

An affectionate smile touched his lips.

"She could already play the fiddle and guitar -taught herself-and played the sweetest hoedowns you ever heard. She practiced all over the farm, settin here and there, on fences, in the hay loft, anywhere. Even seen her settin on a salt lick one day, slap dab in the middle of the barnyard with the cows and horses gathered round her like a real audience. Strangest thing I ever seen."

"Later on she'd pick up that old guitar, start pickin' and singin' wherever she happened to be and people just ate it up. She was fifteen at that time, already a beauty, and could charm the birds right out of the trees if she was a mind to."

"The boys were crazy about her an' while I'm sure the men noticed her good looks, they never let on."

"The ocassional stranger would step out of line but they never got anywhere. Those blue eyes would harden, the jaw set stubbornly and her quick wit would make the wise guy wish for a hole to crawl in. Sides," Pa chuckled, "she always had a rifle with her and I guess would have used it if necessary."

"My old friend, Charlie Horn was settin' on the porch when I rode up and everbody was laughin,' so I knew he'd been spinnin' one of his outlandish tales. "Come join us Almus," he said, pattin' the bench beside him. "Ever see'd a day to beat this'un?" he asked, not expectin' a reply. "Norey is so full of beans today she's tearin' the house apart spring cleanin'. No fit place for a man to be so me and old Blue here lit out fer town."

"I reached out and fondled the dog's ears.

"He's a fine lookin' dog Charlie, a dog to be proud of."

Yep, he'll do to take along," Charlie replied. "Where's old Streator? Don't look right not to see him lopin' along 'side ye."

"I called him but he was off somewhere on business of his own. When he comes home he'll track the horses a mile or so then go back home. He's never been at ease in town where theres a lot of commotion and sometimes

I think the rascal knows when I'm goin' and takes hisself off somewhere. When I get back he'll go through his mock fight with me for leavin' him behind and that will be the end of the matter."

"He's a fine dog," Charlie mused," and I reckon we'd all be proud to own'im."

"Now don't you go gettin' jealous Blue," he smiled, pattin' the hound at his feet; but Old Blue was snorin' so loud he hadn't heard a word and his feet were twitchin' wildly as he chased some critter in his dreams.

Ten year old Yancy Newbold shyly sat down beside Ruth, tryin' to hide his adoration behind a friendly smile.

"You goin' to the carnival at Stonefort?" he asked hopefully.

"Carnival!" Ruth exclaimed, castin' an accusin' look at me.

"First I knowed about it," I said, ignorin' her.

"Just got here last night,"one of the farmers said. "Hear tell they've got a real elephant and a couple of lions."

He rared back in his chair importantly, relishin' his new found audience.

"I heer'ed tell the Stonefort town council didn't want to let them lions in town even though they's likely old and toothless".

"I don't know bout' that Jeb," Charlie laughed. "Yer' old and toothless and they let you in Stonefort all the time."

Everyone hooted and howled over the joke, slappin' old Jeb on the back good naturedly, winkin' slyly at Charlie.

Ruth's eyes were flashin with excitement and I knew we were gonna' go to Stonefort to see the carnival. Truth to tell,I was dyin' to see it myself. We don't see much of that sort of thing round' here and its a welcome break to folks who work from sun-up to sun-down."

It took us an hour to get there. Our excitement was almost unbearable as we got close enough to hear the carney music and the hawkers spiel.

Dimple and Nell were chompin' at their bits, ears flickin' in nervous excitement as they pranced skittishly all over the road.

People were ridin' in from all directions on horses, in wagons, even a buggy or two, though most generally only a doctor could afford a buggy.

We tethered the horses and walked to an admission booth that was all lit up with dozens of colored, blinkin' bulbs even though it was a sunny day. A gypsy woman whose great bulk oozed into every corner of the booth, eyed Ruth's slender figure with envy and collected our money as though she was doin' us a favor."

"How much was the admission?" Uncle Bill asked.

"Adults ten cents and children five," Pa answered. "Some families stood off to the side countin' their money, others knew it was beyond them, so contented themselves to watchin' the garrish activity inside."

He sighed sadly.

"I reckon I'd never be successful at runnin' a carnival cause I'd let the poor come in free, specially the kids with dreams in their eyes and nothin' in their pockets."

Grandma smiled fondly at Pa, absently smoothin' an imaginary wrinkle from her starched apron.

Pa sniffed the air and licked his lips, a dreamy look on his face.

"I always loved the smells of a carnival," he continued. "Clouds of smoke boilin' up from grills where hamburgers and hot dogs sizzled, fillin' the air with overpowerin' smells that made you faint with hunger. Don't know how they do it but you'll never eat a hamburger as good as them that come out of a crowded cubbyhole at a fair, covered with onions and pickles and mustard, all packed inside a greasy bun."

Pa licked his chops hungrily.

"I'll be ready for that cobbler, Net, when this story's told," he laughed.

"I'd earmarked a quarter for the hamburger stand," he continued " when I saw two of my students standin' over by a tree. Their father and mother were strugglin' just to feed em' and the kids often came to school without any lunch."

I watched the pain of rememberin' on Pa's face and blessed Grandma for the extra food she always packed in his lunch bucket for just such a need.

Ruth saw them too and without a word collected the two ragged little boys and walked them through the gate with us. Our hamburger money was diminished considerable but the rapt look on them little faces was worth every penny. We walked slowly through the midway, bombarded on both sides by sharp-faced men promisin' big prizes to be won on the various games of chance. The boys clung tightly to Ruth's hand, fear and amazement on their faces and I knew they'd never seen anything like this before."

Pa stared at the kerosene lamp for a long moment, his face full of sadness.

"At that moment," he sighed, "the world seemed a cruel place, where decent, hard-workin' folks didn't even have the bare necessities of life; and some, like these boys parents, were beyond that, hangin' on to an existance that barely kept body and soul together. For that matter, me and Net didn't have hardly anything ourselves, but we always had plenty to eat and such as we had, we shared."

He gave Grandma a tender look and went on.

"Net used to hitch up the wagon and carry boxes of food to needy families in the dead of winter and never once did they think on it as charity. Net has a way with words," he grinned. "I expect a lot of folks made it through to spring because of her deliveries. Beans and potatoes, a slab of bacon and a ham thrown in once in awhile is food that sticks to the ribs and pulls a body through.

Shorty McCormick would add an extra sack of flour and sugar sometimes cause' he knew Net was buyin' out of pocket for others."

Grandma spoke quietly to Pa, her face flushed with embarassment. "Get on with the story, Almus."

"Well now, Net," he smiled, "that is part of the story. Them boys clingin' to Ruth's hand, dressed in worn out overalls and dirty feet, had their bellies filled many a time by yer carin' nature. Anyway," he said, leanin' over to tug fondly at Grandma's thick braid, "there we were standin' in front of a platform occupied by an overweight jovial lookin' man who was smilin' directly at Ruth and the boys. There was a tenderness in his eyes as he noted her youth and beauty and the boys clingin' to her hand; but most of all a pity that her youth was over before it had begun, for I could see that he thought the boys belonged to her. I expect he'd seen many such things as he traveled over the country."

"Step right up ladies and gentlemen, "his voice boomed through a megaphone, "and see the lizard man kill and devour his live prey before your very eyes."

"There were no shockin' pictures of a lizard man anywhere, such as you always see at them freak shows, and I had to admire the fat man's strategy, for the word pictures he painted filled our imaginations and made us want to see the lizard man for ourselves. By this time a large crowd had gathered, hangin' on every word the fat man said, tryin' to hide their morbid curiosity."

"How many lizard men you ever seen in your life,?" he asked slyly, lookin' out over the serious faces, "cept your Uncle Hiram, of course."

"The crowd tittered nervously over the joke, dyin' to go inside, but afraid a neighbor or friend might catch them in such an unseemly place."

"He waved toward the large tent behind the platform, all the while firin' our imagination with gruesome, thrillin' pictures of what waited inside and soon the outrageous price of ten cents charged for this blunder of nature overpowered common sense and the suckers began to straggle into the dark interior."

Pa slapped his thigh and laughed, his rich baritone fillin' the kitchen.

"As you might have guessed, me and Ruth and the boys were among the suckers."

"The lights were dim inside but I could make out a barred cage in the center of the floor settin' on an enclosed platform about four and a half foot off the ground. The cage was round, about the size of this kitchen and it too, was completely enclosed; even the top had heavy bars."

"My word!" Uncle Bill exclaimed.

"Exactly," Pa agreed. "I remember wonderin' at the time if that was a scare tactic to thrill and frighten the crowd- which were now gathered 'round the cage- or if perhaps there was a real danger that had to be contained inside.

I reckon we stood there about five minutes before the fat man came in carryin' a toe sack with somethin' movin' 'round inside it. Course by then the suspense had reached fever pitch and I could sense a ripple of fear spreadin' through the crowd.

The fat man made his way to the cage and like a real showman, he paused to heighten the suspense. Then he reached inside the sack and pulled a fine lookin' rooster from it. Mind you, it wasn't just an ordinary rooster either," Pa said appreciatively, "but an animal specially bred for its fine looks and fightin' ability.

It's plumage was dazzlin' with rust and yellow gold flowin' like brilliant spikes down its neck. The body was a mixture of rust, yellow and electric blue all magically blended in a wondrous kaleidoscope of brilliance. There was an unusual snowy white star pattern adornin' the base of the tail. Its satiny black and blue tail feathers, tinged with subtle slashes of white and blue, curled gracefully out from this star and billowed upward in a wondrous swirl that fell gracefully to the ground.

That rooster was the most beautiful bird I've ever seen. I've seen pictures of them bein' pitted against each other in the "fightin' rings" of Mexico, fightin' to the death. It's a gruesome, shameful business," he said, his mouth tight with anger, "and I don't understand such cruelty.

"What breed was the rooster, Almus?"

"Well, I finally found a picture of it in the library at Vienna. It was an Old English black-breasted red game rooster. Splendid animal, Bill.

"My word."

"Anyway," Pa continued, "the fat man held the fowl high in the air for everyone to see before he thrust it through an openin' in the cage that was obviously built for that purpose. The rooster's brillant plumage glistened in the light as it flapped to the floor of the cage and stood perfectly still, its neck jerkin in every direction as it looked cautiously about. It

stood that way for a long moment, then took a tentative step forward, the feathers on its neck bristlin' as it waited for a danger it couldn't see, but knew instinctively was nearly upon it.

The attitude of the bird- who was now frozen in a statue like appearance-gripped the crowd with an unbearable tension as they too, stood silently alert waitin', for the Lord only knew what horror was comin'.

Then a trap door in the center of the cage rose slowly upward and a scaled head flowed silently through the openin', followed by a long neck grotesquely mounted on a remarkably human like body covered with green scales; but the tail and feet were without a doubt those of a lizard. The beast was about six foot long and I wondered what unholy alliance and freak atrocity of nature had brought forth such a monster.

The crowd gasped as the beast came to a halt and stood with its head facin' the rooster, who must have at that instant, known it was in for the fight of its life.

The lizard moved in a casual, unhurried way. It was obviously a familiar routine to him, the outcome certain as he performed for his food. The black pupils of the lizard were elliptical, like the pupils of a cat or reptile, and they glittered omniously in the spot lights that the fat man had suddenly turned on for effect.

For a moment the two animals faced each other; the one powerful, the other small and ineffectual, and though I knew the bird didn't stand a chance, I was still rootin' for it all the way.

Suddenly the lizard man streaked across the room, his jaws open wide, confident he would claim the prize as he had no doubt done countless times before; but the terrorized rooster rose straight into the air and flew to the opposite side of the cage. Every feather stood out, its wings fanned downward in a fighting stance as it watched the lizard intently.

Salivia was drippin' from the lizard man's jaws as he turned to face the rooster but this time he restrained himself from a direct attack and began to move slowly 'round the outer perimeter of the cage. Closer and closer he edged toward the rooster who hadn't moved an inch, its eyes riveted on the lizard man's every move. When the lizard was a dozen feet from it, the rooster summoned all its resources and with a loud screech, rose gracefully to the top of the cage and locked its talons around the bars. It clung desperately to the uncertain perch, its beak hooked over a bar, its wings beatin' desperately against the bars as it thrust its neck through the openin', tryin' to propel itself through the narrow space.

The crowd went wild, cheerin' and yellin for the fat man to save the rooster before it was too late.

The lizard man strained upward, his eyes intent on the strugglin' bird, a steady stream of salivia runnin' from his mouth as he waited for the rooster to fall.

After what seemed an eternity of shouting voices screaming for th' roosters reprieve, the fat man quickly stepped inside the cage, pulled the trap door open and gave a strange, eerie whistle.

The lizard looked hungrily at the rooster clingin' to the roof, then reluctantly made his way across the floor to the man, and without any resistance, he flowed silently out of sight

The fat man closed the door and locked it just as the exhausted rooster dropped to the floor. He picked the bird up and again held it aloft; this time the victor instead of the victim.

"This is an unusual animal," he said with admiration, " and has earned his bid to live".

The crowd roared its approval.

At length, the fat man raised his arms for silence and with the rooster still held above his head he slowly scanned the faces around the cage. When his eyes found Ruth's face, he walked slowly across the cage to her, and smiled gently.

Ruth's blue eyes, hard with anger, raked the fat man with scorn but he stood his ground, determined to end the show on a light note.

"Ladies and Gentlemen," he shouted, "I'm presenting this magnificent rooster to this young lady who I'm sure will give it a good home. Thank you all for coming," he said, dismissing them."

Ruth reached out and took the rooster in her arms and it seemed to realize it was through with the cage and all it's horrors forever, for it settled down with it's head tucked under her arm.

She thrust the boys toward me and turned back to the fat man.

"Thats the most disgustin' thing I've ever seen," she said with a catch in her voice."To pit a small animal against a large one to satisfy the morbid curiosity of a crowd and put money in your pocket is a cruel and inhuman act."

"We all have to make a living, little lady," he said quietly, "even the lizard man. I take care of him and he takes care of me. It may seem cruel to you, but every living thing must eat to survive, even you and your family."

"Doesn't the farmer feed and care for his stock all year, then butcher some of them in the fall to sustain himself and his family through the long winter?

"He does for a fact," she replied in a tight voice," but he don't terrorize them with a fight to the death, especailly with the unfair odds we seen here today."

"Would you have come to my show just to watch the lizard man eat a piece of raw meat?" he asked pointedly. "I doubt it. Besides, the lizard man will not feed on anything that isn't alive."

"I'm this young lady's father," I said, steppin' up to the cage, "and I'd like to ask you a question."

"Ask what you will," he said wearily.

"Where did you find that poor creature?" His eyes got a far-away look in them as he recalled a time that was obviously a sad memory.

"I used to work on a freighter," he began," roaming all over the world from port to port and for the most part it was a good life. One day we were unloading cargo at a tough little town in Borneo, and there on the dock was the lizard man in an unspeakably filthy cage, being abused by a greasy looking man who charged a hefty price for people to watch him beat the lizard man into a murderous rage. For this cruel entertainment the lizard was rewarded with a live animal which he devoured instantly and I guessed that he was being deliberately starved to provoke such ferocious attacks; and… people being what they are, they'll just naturally pay money to watch such cruelty." He sighed sadly, scuffin' his shoe on the floor of the cage. "Life is cheap in those countries and cruelty is too often a way of life. The lizard man clearly hated his tormentor, with a hatred that meant to kill at the first opportunity. The man knew it too and took great pains to stay clear of him. My blood boiled at the cruelty being inflicted on the reptile and before I even had time to think on it, I found myself asking him how much he would sell the animal for. His cunning, greedy look told me I was about to be fleeced, but I didn't care as long as that poor miserable creature was out of his hands." He smiled ruefully. "Cost me two months pay, plus a new cage and many months of patient kindness to win the lizard's trust; but I did it and gradually we became friends, if one can say that about such a creature. I spend a lot of time in the cage talking to him while tending to his needs, and when I sit down he will lie beside me like a pet dog. So, you see" he finished, lookin' Ruth in the eye, "We take care of each other and he's content."

I felt a tremendous respect for this carnival man with his big body and even bigger heart; but one thing still puzzled me. "I have one more question," I told him.

"Well, we've come this far," he smiled.

"You're obviously an educated man, so why have you spent the best years of your life with a carnival, showin' a lizard all over the country when you could have done just about anything you set your mind to?"

He stood for a long time starin into space then looked at me broodingly.

"I'm not sure I can answer that question," he replied, "at least not in a way that might satisfy you. A man makes certain plans for his life and it all seems rather simple to him when he's young. The pieces of the puzzle are all there, he's only to fit them into the proper slots and with a minimum amount of maintenance he can just sit back and let life happen. At least that's the way I figured it at the time," he grinned. "To make a very long story short, fate seemed to be always scattering to the wind the carefully fitted pieces of my puzzle, and I never dreamed a lizard would be the piece that would change my life forever."

"I know what you're thinking," he said. "Why not a zoo for the lizard, or release him into the jungle from whence he came? Those are all simple solutions if one doesn't have to deal with his emotions, but I've found that the ingredients that make up a man are beyond comprehending, and they will ultimately weave him into the pattern of his destiny regardless of how hard he may resist. So, I take care of the lizard man," he said, answering my question, "because I want to. He's my friend and I'm the only thing that stands between him and death for he could never survive in any other environment."

He turned and looked at the trap door from which the lizard had made his spectular entrance into the cage only a short while before. There was a faint scratchin sound comin' from the interior and I shuddered to think of the creature that lurked there.

The fat man extended his hand and I was proud to take it for this man had made a profound impression on me.

"I expect he's very hungry," he said matter of factly.

Suddenly Ruth extended her hand also to the fat man, who held it carefully. "I think I understand part of it now," she said, "but I don't understand cruelty in any form, no matter the reason. It was a decent thing you did, rescuin' the lizard, but thats the only good I can say about it."

"That's good enough," he smiled, his eyes tender as he watched her walk away with the two boys clingin' to her hand and the rooster nestled safely beneath her arm.

I realized that in some strange, inexplicable way, Ruth's good will had been very important to him. I wondered why.

"My word," Uncle Bill exclaimed." What an extraordinary story."

Aunt Bess shivered even though the nite was warm, and hugged close to Grandma.

The Queen was hardly breathin' as she stared through the screen door at the darkness outside.

"Do you suppose the lizard man is still alive Uncle Almus?" she asked in a small voice.

"Not a chance Vicki. That was many years ago and no lizard lives that long."

"But he was part man," she worried. "Wouldn't that make him live longer, and maybe he escaped the cage and is running about loose somewhere?" She shuddered. "He could even be in Chicago."

"Why, old Streator would tear him to pieces if he ever come round here," I bragged. "And I bet he'd never step foot in Chicago with all that noise and commotion goin' on all the time."

Old Streator woke up and raised an eyebrow in my direction, then thumped his tail on the floor as Pa's hand rested on his head.

"That's right Vicki," Pa soothed, "I expect old Streator here can take care of just about anything that comes 'round. Besides that, honey, part of him resembled a man; but I doubt he could have been part man so you needn't worry about that. Now I think it's time for some of that blackberry cobbler and maybe one of Net's fried apple pies."

"My word," Uncle Bill laughed," I almost forgot about dessert. I always look forward to your stories, Almus and I wager if you came to Chicago you could charge good money for telling them."

Grandma waggled her pie cuttin' knife at Uncle Bill. "Now don't go puttin' any ideas in his head Bill, or he just might pack us all up and move to Chicago."

"Nothing would make us any happier than that, sis," Aunt Bess said, huggin' Grandma with her eyes all full of love. "Its gotten to where families are scattered all over the country anymore. I liked it better when we all lived in the same neighborhood."

She sighed wistfully.

"I guess I didn't appreciate that kind of life until it was gone and I can tell you I've considered moving back more than once. There's a peace down here that you can't find in the city."

"Well now, Bessie," Pa laughed, "look on the practical side of it. "In the city you don't have to milk the cows or feed the chickens or weed the garden and all the million other things that have to be done on a farm.

Milk is delivered right to yer door and you go to the store and get all the rest, so it isn't too bad. I can tell you there are times when I'd trade with you, 'specially when it's blazin' hot and I'm plowin' ground that hasn't seen a drop of rain in weeks."

"You're just trying to make me feel better, Almus, but I refuse to be comforted," sniffed Aunt Bess. "I miss my family, and it's not like I'm a stranger to hard work either. After all I was raised on a farm you know."

She smiled wickedly at Pa.

"In fact I happened to be there on that very farm the day you rode brashly up to the house, showing off and highstepping your horse all over the yard, to ask Net for a date. Hadn't even been properly introduced either and I can tell you that mama didn't rightly cotton to you one bit."

At the mention of moving to the sticks-as she referred to it- the Queen looked alarmed and I knew she'd wither right on the vine if she ever got stuck on a farm and didn't have the conveniences of the big city.

"Well, who knows what the future holds," Uncle Bill smiled.

Pa gave Aunt Bess a warm hug.

"I reckon until we know what that future does hold Bessie, you'll just have to come on down here more often for long visits. We love havin' you and as you can see it does Net a world of good. Besides, I've got all these stories rattlin' around in my head just beggin' to get told."

He looked at Uncle Bill with a twinkle in his eyes.

"Remind me to tell you the other story of me and Ruth at the carnival, Bill. I daresay you'll be about as shocked as Net was when I told her what happened."

Of course Uncle Bill was beside hisself with excitement and wanted to know when Pa would tell the new tale.

"Tomorrow night for sure," Pa said.

"What's the name of it, Almus?" Uncle Bill persisted.

"He'll give you no rest Almus, until tomorrow night," Aunt Bess smiled.

Grandma gave Pa a mildly disapprovin' look.

"That's just what he wants, Bess. He don't enjoy it unless his audience is whipped into a fever of excitement. He's still a kid at heart and I reckon he'll never grow up."

"Now you two women quit picking on him," Uncle Bill laughed. "I'll furnish all the excitement he can stand and then some. Why these stories are the highlight of my visit," he declared, "and your good cooking Net is right up there with them; but you still haven't said what it's about, Almus and I can't wait another minute."

"Well, I call it " The Shooter" and that's all I'll say till tomorrow night," he grinned, puffin' a cloud of smoke into the air.

I couldn't hardly wait till then myself but as Grandma had told me many times before, the sweet pain of waitin' for somethin' instead of rushin' impatiently through life gobblin' up big chunks at a time-warms the heart and waters the soul.

"This is a tale I purely love to tell," Pa mused, clampin' his pipe affectionately; but I doubt I could live through it again. No, siree. Don't know if this old ticker could stand the strain of such goins' on today, but as I said before, Bill, it's the prize story of my life and one I'll remember for as long as the Lord lets me live"

He took his pipe from his mouth, knocked the dead ashes into the coal bucket, then filled it from a white draw-stringed tobacco sack in his pocket. He struck a kitchen match on the bottom of his chair, then held it to the surface of the bowl.

I watched the yellow flame suck downward into the tobacco as he vigorously drew air through the stem. Soon the contents of the bowl glowed red as he puffed away, his lips smackin' softly in the silent kitchen.

In the stillness of my heart I can still hear that beloved sound today.

As on the nite before, we all watched the spectral smoke serpents coil and slither from Pa's mouth, slide over his face and up through his hair toward the ceiling.

"As a matter of fact Bill," he went on, his blue eyes sparklin', "I like this story so much I might even set down by the pearly gates and tell it to St. Peter before I go in." He chuckled, givin' Grandma a mischievous look.

"What scandulous talk, Almus," said Grandma reprovingly. "St. Peter just might let you cool your heels at that gate a spell before he lets you in; IF he does let you in."

Pa thought that was hilarious and we all had a good laugh at Pa's expense.

"You can see that I'm married to a sharp tongued woman, Bill, and I expect you've felt the same sting since Bessie's off the same tree."

Uncle Bill allowed as how he had, ignorin' Aunt Bessie's friendly frown. I could see he wasn't interested in sharp tongues and family trees as he moved impatiently around in his chair, gettin' just the right degree of comfort before settlin' in for the long awaited thrill of the yarn he knew would be the best he'd ever heard.

Supper was over and as usual everyone was stuffed and ready for some entertainment. Grandma and Aunt Bess had outdone themselves, 'specially on dessert. Two gooseberry pies and a rich chocolate cake burdened down with Grandma's special chocolate cream frostin' waited in tantilizin' splendor on the sideboard.

All day ole Streator had spent a lot of time at the back door sniffin' the wondrous smells driftin' out on the porch and I reckoned he'd just about licked his chops raw.

Grandma filled everybody's coffee cup and set a fresh pot to perk on the back of the stove. The kitchen was fragrant with brewin' coffee and Pa's pipe, which he was now puffin' thoughtfully as his eyes sought a far off time, same as he always did when about to tell a story.

Finally he tilted his chair back against the wall and closed his eyes, the pipe hangin' out of the corner of his mouth. It was a familiar routine, like old Streator's routine of turnin' 'round and 'round before layin' down.

We all fell silent, eyes glued on Pa's face as he began the story.

Me and Ruth and the boys left the fat man's tent and wandered on down the midway lookin' at the sights and turnin' a deaf ear to the hawkers toutin' their games of chance.

He grinned ruefully.

We stopped at the hamburger stand and I scared up enough change to get us all a hamburger and a Pepsi. The boys were clearly starved, yet they ate with fine manners, as though they had hamburgers ever' day. They stared at their Pepsi with wonder, lettin' it slide slowly down their throat and I wondered if they'd ever had one before. Probably not.

Ruth watched them eat, her heart in her eyes and I noticed she had only taken one bite from her hamburger. Course she was savin' it for them.

Tears were runnin' down the cheeks of Grandma and Aunt Bess, and The Queen even had wet eyes.

"I told Ruth to eat her hamburger," Pa continued, "and laid two nickles on the counter. Two more hamburgers for these fine, hungry boys," I told the counter man." There went my months supply of horehound candy, and Net can tell you how fond I am of horehound candy; but it was the sweetest sacrafice I ever made.

Ruth smiled real big at me then tore into her hamburger with a vengence. We'd about swallowed the last bite when a rifle shot rang out,then another and another at evenly spaced intervals, and I counted ten shots before they stopped. Ruth was instantly electrifed and grabbin' the boys by the hand she took off toward the sound with the boys clutchin' their Pepsi's for dear life, their legs churnin' to keep up. I can tell you it was a funny sight I'll never forget.

He sat quietly for a moment, his eyes on the ceilin' watchin' a scene that we could only imagine.

Them kids didn't spill one drop of that pepsi either, he chuckled. When I caught up with them at the end of the midway I saw a tent with a large banner stretched across the front which said, "BILL DARNELL, GREATEST SHOT IN THE WORLD."

We all stood starin' at the sign and the young man settin' outside the tent holdin' a magnificent lookin' rifle. He was sure dressed for the part too. Cowboy boots with silver toes, fancy western fringed shirt, a white stetson with a silver band and white snug fitting trousers to match the hat.

"Was the silver toes and hat band just color or real silver?" Uncle Bill asked.

"It was real silver," Pa replied, "and I reckon it must have cost a pretty penny too. Why, with what that all must have come to I could have bought several head of cattle and maybe a plowhorse or two."

Grandma frowned at the cowboy's extravagance, no doubt thinkin' how many poor people it would have fed and clothed.

He had a thin, sharp lookin' face, Pa went on, that reminded me of a cadaver and there was a crafty, speculative look in his eyes which were th' color of faded blue ice, cold and dead, without a spark of warmth in em'. His fine clothes hung on a skeletal frame that hardly seemed strong enough to carry him around, yet there was a feelin' of power about him that got your attention.

Pa shook his head at the picture in his mind and I knew the memory of this man still troubled him.

He looked like he'd just ridden out of a nightmare and took a wrong turn somewhere, for he was sure out of place in our neck of the woods. I hate to admit it but I disliked him instantly, knowin' in my soul that evil lurked in that thin face.

"If he's the greatest shot in the world," Ruth said under her breath, "what's he doin' in this two-bit carnival in a one-horse town where money is as scarce as hens teeth?"

Before I could answer that, the shooter stood up with a big smile on his face and I felt certain he'd practiced that smile many times in front of a lookin' glass.

"Would you folks like to do a bit of shooting and maybe win one of them great prizes," he said, motionin to a shelf full of stuffed animals and cheap jewelry.

Ruth gave the shelf a derisive look but the two boys were starin' transfixed, their eyes full of wonder and longin' and I knew that never in their life had they seen such wondrous treasures. Neither one of them uttered a word; just looked, as only a child who has never had anythin' can look; all hungry and hopeless and numb before a world that holds no promise for a better future.

There were tears in Pa's eyes as he remembered. "I was almost sorry we'd brought them in," he said softly.

Then Ruth looked down at them, at the longin' in their eyes, and I saw her jaw set in that stubborn way she has and I mentally counted the remainin' change in my pocket for I knew she'd soon have it.

By then a half dozen men had gathered' round and several families stood off to the side watchin' curiously.

The cowboy noted the crowd and knew that this lovely young girl had attracted them in the first place, and he saw an opportunity to make a few bucks. Nothin' wrong in that, Pa said, but I didn't like the way those cold eyes kept slidin' over Ruth. Lucky for him she hadn't noticed. In fact, I doubt she was even aware of the crowd which seemed to be growin' steadily.

"I might take a crack at it," she said casually. " What are the rules?"

The shooter pointed to a plackard nailed to a post beside the tent. "Ten shots for a dollar, little gal. Two out of three wins a stuffed animal, three out of four wins a piece of jewelry."

Ruth turned to me inquiringly and I dropped a dollars worth of change in her hand.

"Ladies and gentlemen," the cowboy said in his best show voice, bowin low to the crowd. "This little gal here is about to demonstrate her shooting ability and try to win one of these grand prizes; but first lets find out a little about her." He walked over and laid his hand on Ruth's shoulder in a familiar way.

She gave him a defiant look and moved away, all the while unslingin' th' rifle from her back.

I saw his eyes harden as a red flush crept upward over his face, for to be rejected by a country girl and in front of a crowd to boot, was a blow to a man who greatly fancied hisself.

"The swine," exclaimed Uncle Bill angrily.

"I hope she shot him," Aunt Bess put in.

Victoria sat mute, stunned to the core of her gentility.

"Well," Pa drawled. "I wasn't sure whether she might shoot him or not, but I should have known she'd get them stuffed animals for the boys first. I'll say one thing for the cowboy," Pa smiled. "He knew when to back off."

"Now, now little gal," the cowboy soothed. "Nothing to be alarmed about. We just want to know your name."

Ruth looked out at the crowd for the first time, and if she was surprised at the number, she didn't show it. She scanned the faces then replied quietly.

"Some of these good folks are my neighbors and they know me; but for them that don't, my names Ruth Hundley."

For some unaccountable reason, they all burst into applause like she was a star or somethin'.

Pa chuckled with excitement, his eyes sparklin' and I knew he was livin' this story all over again and I suddenly understood why it was his favorite. He was proud that his daughter -a country girl- had defended herself with pride and intelligence against this unprincipled, wordly man who had no moral values, and certainly didn't know how to treat a lady.

Grandma sniffed angrily as her rhiteous indignation was aroused, and Aunt Bess had a scrappin look on her face. As for me, I was hopin my mom had shot im'. oh, not dead, of course, but maybe in the foot or somethin'. I reckoned the Lord might consider that just punishment. Pa puffed a few times on his pipe and went on with the story.

She had effectively excluded the cowboy, recognizin' only those folks who lived in the community. The slight wasn't lost on the cowboy for the jovial smile plastered on his face sure didn't hide the malice in his eyes. I knew from then on he'd make it as uncomfortable for Ruth as he could.

The shooter dropped ten shells in Ruth's hand and pointed to a bulls eye target a hundred and fifty feet away.

"Like the sign says, little gal, two out of three for a stuffed animal, three out of four for a piece of jewelry."

Ruth looked at the shells for a minute, took a step or two toward the target then stumbled over somethin' I couldn't see and dropped the shells in the grass. The boys ran to help her find them while the shooter stepped inside the tent, I supposed to get more shells. Between her and the boys there was a lot of fumblin' around. Anyway, she finally loaded her rifle just as the shooter came out with a box of shells in his hand.

"We found them," she said, thankin' th' boys and sendin' them back to me.

"Well then, let's get on with it little gal," he drawled, winkin' at the crowd.

"I guess that circle in the middle is what I'm aimin' at," Ruth said to herself. She had a way of talkin' to herself; said it helped her concentrate.

The shooter slapped his thigh and laughed, then addressed the crowd. "Ain't this little gal a riot," he chirped. "One of you fellows want to run out there and show this little gal where that ole target is? Better still," he went on, "I'll let her move up ten feet closer for a better look. Do you reckon that would help little gal?"

He was enjoyin' hisself now, gettin' his licks in as we say; but the crowd was sullen and quiet, their faces hostile toward the cowboy, which seemed to goad him even further.

Ruth didn't acknowledge his offer of ten feet nor his taunts. In fact she acted as though he wasn't even there at all as she studied the bull's eye. She walked up to a chalk line the shooter had laid down then stepped off fifty feet backward from the target which placed it at two-hundred feet away instead of the hundred and fifty. A murmur rippled through the crowd and there was a hand clap or two as they watched the shooter. His face was blood red, his lips compressed in an angry grimace as he stood with clenched hands, stripped of his arrogance by this country girl who had done so without utterin' a word.

She raised the winchester repeater to her shoulder, looked down the barrel then squeezed the trigger. In one fluid movement she ejected the spent casing, raised the rifle again and squeezed off another shot. She did this seven times then turned to the shooter. "Little man," she said cooly, I'll take two of them stuffed animals and a piece of that jewelry."

The shooter's face went white when she called him little man but he forced himself to laugh.

"First, little gal, I'll have to check that target and count them holes… if there are any holes," he added. "Rules are rules you know."

"You'll find all seven of em' in the bulls eye," she stated firmly, but he was already runnin' toward the target and about a dozen of the crowd were also sprintin' across the field.

Pa threw back his head and laughed in delight.

They beat the shooter to the target and came runnin' back, proudly holdin' the target up, laughin' and slapin' each other on the back as happy as if they'd done it themselves.

"Slap dab in the middle," one of em' yelled. "Why she even spaced em' out so you can count em'. Now that's shootin' if I ever see'd it."

The shooter examined every hole, a look of disbelief on his face. Ruth was watchin' him closely and when he turned in amazement to stare at her, she gave him a wintry smile.

"I'll just let the boys pick out their animals now," she said takin' them by the hand, "and a nice piece of jewelry for their mom."

The crowd gathered 'round the prize booth, cheerin' and congratulatin' Ruth on her shootin' and several of the ladies offered to help pick out the jewelry. Course they mainly wanted to look at it themselves and every one was havin' a high old time, all that is, except the shooter. He kept starin' at the bulls eye with its neatly placed bullet holes in the center, in hope they might disappear.

Bigger is better as far as kids are concerned and the boys picked the largest animals they could find. The smallest one chose a silky unicorn with pink eyes, huggin' it tightly and the other caressed the fur of a giant black rabbit.

Ruth picked out a delicate gold chain with an enameled blue flower hangin' from it for their mother. I reckoned between the stuffed animals and the jewelry, the shooter had finally gotten the short end of the stick for a change.

The crowd was driftin' back toward the midway with me and Ruth and the young'uns' bringin' up the rear, when the shooters voice suddenly boomed out from a megaphone."

"Ladies and Gentlemen. You've seen some good shooting this afternoon, whither by skill or luck, I don't know," he added slyly; "but I'm willing to find out." He paused to let that sink in. "I'm a pretty fair marksman myself," he said, tryin' to sound modest, "and I challenge that little gal to a contest that will determine who's the best shot."

There were some boos from the crowd who had stopped and were now starin' back at the tall white figure holdin' the megaphone in one hand and that handsome rifle of his in the other. His stance was arrogant and challengin'. Reminded me of Goliath, Pa laughed. Course to dare Ruth to anything is like wavin' a red flag in front of a mad bull.

"Well what do you say little gal. Do you accept my challenge or not?"

Everyone stood silent waitin' to see what she would do. Her eyes bored into the cowboy, her face without expression, then she turned and walked back to the tent with the crowd eagerly followin', jostlin' to be close to Ruth who had become their champion, and they meant to support her. I can still hear the excited voices of folks laughin' and jokin' together, gettin' more than their admission price in excitement and suspense. The crowd had grown and I bet there was more than fifty people there.

"My word," Uncle Bill exclaimed, "What I would have given to be there.

"It was a sight worth seein' alright," Pa mused. The shooter was elated with the crowd and meant to milk it for all it was worth. I knew he intended to try to best Ruth right off, then challenge every farmer to a match. He probably was countin' his profits already.

"Counting your chickens before they hatch can be iffy," said Aunt Bess. Uncle Bill hardly heard her.

"Go on, Go on Almus!" he urged.

"Well, we stood 'round waitin' to see what the cowboy had in mind and I could hear bets bein' made here and there in the crowd. Also spied a couple of carney men runnin' up the midway, stoppin' at every booth and I knew they were spreadin' the news about the shooter's challenge. Probably had seen Ruth drill that bulls eye too and figured she just might give the cowboy a run for his money."

"Then the shooter brought a peculiar lookin' contracption from the tent and set it on the ground. All the men crowded in to have a look, some even tryin' to guess what it might be, but I confess I'd never seen one before. When the shooter saw our ignorance he strutted up and down in front of us like a new rooster in front of a bunch of hens."

"Arrogant jack- ass, wasn't he?" growled Uncle Bill.

"I suspect he might have been far worse than that Bill. No tellin' what that man was capable of and no tellin' what made him that way in the first place."

"Describe the contracption, Almus."

Best I can do is it looked like an arm attached to a box with a slot for somethin' to lay in, with a handle attached to the arm. He pulled the arm back and cocked it, then he put a round disk about an inch thick in the slot, pushed a button and the disk shot high into the air.

"Why thats what they use in skeet shooting and the disk is called a clay pidgeon."

"So we found out later," Pa said wryly.

"Ever shot any clay pidgeons?" the shooter asked Ruth.

"Never have," she answered, studyin' the contracption.

"Well lets try you on a few. The way this works is when you're ready to shoot you say pull and my assistant here will release the clay pidgeon. You then shoot it before it hits the ground. I'll demonstrate".

With that he brought his gun up to a certain level, yelled pull then swung upward and fired. The clay pidgeon shattered and fell to the ground. He picked off a half dozen or so and I had to admire his marksmanship. He was an expert and he knew it. The crowd murmured appreciatively as he stepped back and made a sweepin' bow.

"It's all yours little gal."

Ruth raised her rifle, yelled pull, aimed at the target and fired. It was a clean miss. The crowd moaned in sympathy and the cowboy smiled like a cat does when its got a mouse in its claws. She missed two more straight, lookin' at the sky as though they should still be there and I knew she was playin' the sequence over and over in her mind lookin' for the key.

"Pull!" she commanded again.

The clay pidgeon shot into the air, her rifle followed it upward in a smoothe flow stayin' below it just a fraction. The pidgeon reached its zenith and just as it began to fall she fired. A piece flew off of one side. Not a clean hit but a hit never-the- less. The next one she took out a bigger piece, the third one she shattered cleanly. The crowd roared, clappin' and hollerin', "Atta' girl Ruth. You show em' what you can do."

"That dude don't know who he's tanglin' with," said Charlie Horn who had suddenly appeared beside me.

"Where'd you come from so quick Charlie? Thought I left you in Burnside."

"Got me a lift from one of the boys and reckon I'll thumb me way back. Saints alive! I wouldn't want to miss this."

"Don't underestimate the cowboy Charlie. He picked them clay pidgeons out of the air like they were elephants."

"Oh I'm sure he's good but Ruth's got the best eye I ever see'd and with her nerves, I'm bettin' on 'er."

"Are you talkin' money Charlie?"

Charlie grinned sheepishly. "Yep. Fifteen dollars worth. The egg money and the vittals money for the next two weeks. Fifteen dollars right on the best shot in the country."

Pig and a Sack of Stray Cats

"Norey will have your hide for this Charlie. You know how she hates gamblin'."

"Only if I lose Almus and I dont aim to lose. You'll see," he chuckled. "How many times have I set on me porch watchin' that girl thin all the rabbits out of me fields? Got so I had to come over on your land and poach enuff' rabbits for a stew. Never seen her miss and I reckon me money's as safe as a bank. Sides, I got four to one odds."

I was shocked. "Who's given' them kind of odds?"

"Two carney men. Friends of the shooter I reckon. Anyway they think he's good enuff' to give four to one odds and I'm smart enuff to take it. Ought to git in on some of that money yerself Almus."

I was about to remind him how handy Net is with a butcher knife when the shooter started talkin'.

"Practice time is over little gal. Now it's time to get down to business." He threw what he thought was a charmin' smile at Ruth. "This is going to determine who's the best shot and I figure it would be more interesting if there was a prize to be claimed. So, what do you have to put up?"

"This contest is your idea," she replied cooly, " so you make it interestin' or maybe you'd just like to call it off."

"This little gal drives a hard bargain," he told the crowd. He then appeared to think it over. "But that seems fair enough, so I'll start things off with fifteen dollars of my own money. If I win it's still mine, if you win, then of course it's yours. Nine out of ten shots sound fair, little gal?"

Ruth nodded and the shooter pulled a box of shells from his pocket. "I'll even furnish the shells," he added generously.

"Thanks, but I'll use my own," Ruth said quietly.

The cowboy looked annoyed and Charlie and me couldn't figure why she'd refuse his offer and use her own ammunition. Anyway, she stepped up to the chalk line and quietly said pull. The clay pidgeon sailed upward and Ruth nailed it five times in a row. She stepped back and addressed the cowboy. "Want to take your five shots now and make it excitin' for the crowd?" she asked.

He couldn't resist the chance to show off and strutted up to the line. He took four pidgeons out neat as could be but missed the fifth one. His face was blank as Ruth took out the last five, makin' it a perfect score.

"Ten out of ten sure beats nine out of ten so there's no point in my shooting the next five."

Ruth's eyes bored into his as he handed her the fifteen dollars, his lips twisted in a sly smile.

"Tell you what little gal, I'd like to redeem that missed shot, so I'm going to put up twenty-five more dollars and we'll go for ten out of ten."

The crowd was silent and for once Charlie was too. A funny feelin' had begun worryin' the back of my neck but I couldn't figure what was wrong.

"So this is where the crowds were heading," said a voice beside me. It was the owner of the lizard man.

129

"Just about all of the carnival is down here," he smiled. "The word has spread like wild fire and I even seen several people jump on their horses and ride toward town. Guess pretty soon we might have a real crowd down here. I couldn't believe my eyes when I seen your daughter knocking them clap pidgeons out of the air."

He leaned over closer. "Between you and me, she's dealing with a bad hombre there. Very few of the carney folks like him. He'd cheat his own mother out of a dime and you can be sure he's up to something in this contest that's going to benefit him only."

"I don't know what it could be for he's put up the money for the whole thing."

"How much is he in the pot for?"

"Ruth just won fifteen when he missed a shot so he put up twenty-five more and they're about ready to shoot for that."

"Ladies and Gentlemen," the cowboy said. "I think ten shots out of fifteen is a fair test of skill for this twenty-five dollars and since the little gal went first the last time, I reckon it's my turn. Pull," he commanded and the clay pidgeon shot upward then shattered as he squeezed the trigger.

He was an exceptional shot and the crowd loved it. There wasn't a man who wouldn't have given his eye teeth to shoot like that. I could see Ruth was enjoyin' his exhibition as much as the crowd and thats just what it was. An exhibition. He had what every showman wants; an audience and a stage to show off his talent.

"You say Ruth was enjoying herself?" Uncle Bill asked in wonder.

"She'd enjoy watchin' the devil hisself shoot if he was good at it," Pa laughed.

"You'd think she'd be nervous," said Aunt Bess.

"If she was it didn't show. Anyway the shooter drilled all ten pidgeons, then he really did some grandstandin'".

"I'll just shoot the other five for this fine audience, but you only have to shoot ten little gal to make it a tie."

Course he finished the five without a hitch then it was Ruth's turn. She smiled slightly at the shooter in acknowledgement of his skill and moved into place. The crowd tensed and I could still hear a bet or two bein' made. Charlie was mutterin' under his breath and the lizard man was cussin' the cowboy in a low voice with words I can't utter in front of ladies. Ruth downed the ten pidgeons and thunderous applause and shouts split the air. Why I bet they could hear it a quarter mile away in Stonefort, then she raised her hand for silence and it was like the end of the world had come. You could have heard a feather drop. She remained on her mark, quietly said pull then picked off the remainin' five pidgeons before steppin' back. Amazement and grudgin' admiration played on the cowboy's face as he bowed to Ruth.

"Now thats good shooting as you all can see, but I reckon we're at a dead end since the twenty-five dollars still belongs to me."

"Here it comes," the lizard man said. "He's setting her up for the kill."

"What do you mean by the kill?"

"He's going to have her put up something or the contest is over and he's counting on her pride to keep her in it."

"I don't think Ruth's pride will exceed her ability," I replied confidently.

"My thinkin' exactly," Charlie laughed. "Why I'd put her up agin' Annie Oakley herself if it come to that."

"Well, you ought to know," the lizard man replied doubtfully. If he does her bad I'll break his neck myself. He's had it coming a long time."

I turned to him. "You seem to have an unusual affection for my girl and I don't rightly understand it at all."

"It's a long story Mr. Hundley and I'll make it brief. I had a daughter that would be the age of yours if she'd lived. They could have been twins, even to the mole on her cheek. I can tell you it gave me a turn when I looked down at her this morning in front of my tent. For a minute I thought it was my daughters ghost and it took all I had to keep from running down those steps and taking her in my arms."

Tears were runnin' down his face and Charlie and I both put an arm on his shoulder. Old Charlie's eyes were wet and I had a lump in my throat. He swiped his hand across his eyes and gazed at Ruth standin' there in the sun, slender as a reed, her rifle in her hand, long hair hangin' down her back.

"When I seen them boys with her I felt sad. She's so young and pretty to be tied down so early in life."

"That's no problem," I assured him. "Them boys don't belong to her. They're my pupils and poor as job's turkey so we brought em' in with us. They purely adore Ruth as you can see."

"Well that makes three of us then for I loved her the minute I laid eyes on her. I can almost believe I got my daughter back for a little while and when I gave that rooster to her this morning, I gave a part of me with it. I have a bitter hatred for the shooter for he's responsible for my daughter's death."

Me and Charlie listened in stunned silence as he told his story.

"The shooter was always coming around wanting to date Angel but I wouldn't have it, which led to real bad feelings between us. Angel didn't really like him that much, only admired his shooting and fancy clothes as any young girl would. I finally told him to stay away from her or I'd make him sorry; but nothing matters to a man like that. Somehow he got her interested in shooting. One day his loaded rifle was leaning against a tree when she came for a lesson and she picked it up." He shuddered. "It went off. She died instantly and part of me died with her. Someone ran to get me and when I seen her crumpled body with its ugly wound, I went crazy. They say I tried to kill him and it took six men to hold me down but I don't remember it or the funeral either for that matter. That was two years ago and it's as fresh in my mind today as then. Maybe you can understand now how I hate seeing him with your daughter and knowing what an evil man he is."

"I can't know the sorrow you feel," I told him, "but I can imagine how I'd feel if it was my child. As for Ruth, she can handle herself, specially with that rifle. I guess you were'nt here earlier or you'd have seen her hatred for the cowboy. She put him in his place real quick and I reckon that's eatin' him up alive."

"She's got a fast tongue alright," Charlie chuckled. "Never see'd anyone yet who could best her. As fer the shooter, I reckon if he gets out of line me and Almus here'll just shoot him in the foot or elsewhere." He threw back his head and belly laughed.

"Well, gal," the shooter said again. "We can end this match right here even steven, or we can go for a bigger stake. I still got twenty-five dollars in the pot, now it's your move.

Ruth looked out over the field and woods beyond, lyin' green and peaceful in the sun as though it was the first time she'd seen them, then she said quietly, "I'll put up my mare."

Charlie gasped and I felt my heart drummin' 'gainst my ribs so hard I could barely breathe. Dimple was her prize possession in the world and I couldn't believe she'd bet her no matter what.

"Except," she continued, "you'll have to put up a lot more than twenty-five dollars. Dimple's worth at least a hundred."

"It'd take a mighty fine horse to be worth that kind of money," the shooter said.

"Let me tell you somethin' sonny," ole Charlie yelled out. "That mare's worth five times twenty-five dollars and that fancy rifle of your'n put together."

Several farmers called out to Ruth not to bet Dimple."Why she's one of the family, one old man said, like old Streator is to you Almus."

The whole thing had suddenly become a family conversation with everone pourin' their feelins' out to Ruth.The shooter was amazed at this display of community closeness and seemed at a loss for words as he listened attentively.

Ruth turned to me, her eyes steady."Do you object Pa?"

I was stunned but there was only one answer I could give. "She's your mare Ruth and I reckon that's a decision you'll have to make yerself."

"Can you match it?" she asked the shooter.

"Well now, I'm betting on something I haven't seen," he stalled.

"That can be remedied right now," Charlie yelled and took off to fetch Dimple. Five minutes later he rode up on Dimple with Nell close beside her. "One wouldn't come without tother," he grinned.

Friendly hands reached out to pat the mares as they passed through the crowd. The shooter walked around Dimple admiringly, runnin' his hands along her shoulders and down her legs. As he paused by her head she reached out and nuzzled him in her friendly way. His hard features softened and at that moment he looked almost human.

"I like this mare," he said decisively, "and I'll add seventy-five to the pot to make the hundred this little gal says she's worth. And to show my hearts in the right place I'll put in twenty-five more. Yes sir, I surely do like this mare," he said as he rubbed Dimple's muzzle."

A gasp rose from the crowd at such a sum of money, then they began to cheer wildly, exclaimin' what an excitin' day it'd turned out to be all on account of one of their very own.

Charlie turned and asked me how I thought Ruth would spend the money.

The lizard man sucked in his breath. "Pretty high stakes," he said, "and a surprising thing for the shooter to do. Wonder what he's up to... and you can be sure he's up to something."

At that point I just wished the whole thing was over, not that I didn't have full confidence in Ruth's ability; but it just seemed to be movin' too fast with too much ridin' on it. Out of the three of us Charlie was the only one who was throughly enjoyin' hisself.

"Gol dang it," he laughed, "Ain't had this much fun in years. That Ruth is a pure wonder. Yes sir, thet girl's one in a million and I allus' told Norey she weren't cut outa' the same cloth as the rest of us."

"My word, Almus," Uncle Bill gasped for the umpteenth time. "I'm a nervous wreck just listening, can't imagine how you stood the strain of such an occassion."

"Well it wasn't easy at the time but I'd shore like to live it over again now."

Dimple and Nell stood side by side, their hides gleamin' in the sun and as usual Nell had her head on Dimple's back, her insecurity intensified by so many people."

"Why, those mares are a matched pair!" exclaimed the lizard man, eyein' them with admiration. "Why would she take a chance on losing one of them?"

Charlie spat a wad of tobacco juice on the ground and laughed gleefully. " 'Cause she don't aim to split em' up and that's a fact. I'd bet my two best cows on that. Might even bet old Blue here and Lord knows how I feel 'bout old Blue." Blue's tail thumped the ground as he nuzzled Charlie's hand with affection.

Pa smiled to himself as we waited breathless and impatient for him to go on. Old Streator snored at his feet, too full of good food to stay awake and listen to stories. At length he shifted his pipe around his mouth and continued.

The shooter stared at Ruth for a second then he raised his arms to the crowd. "Well, Ladies and Gentlemen, it seems we've got a real shooting contest here. What do you say little gal to ten shots out of ten."

"I'm ready," Ruth said.

He was still starin' at her then he laughed. "What about this little gal folks? Why, she's not even nervous, else she's a mighty fine poker player. Look at that face! Not even a flicker."

The lizard man swore out loud. "He's a real piece of slime, that one. He's trying to rattle her and throw her off, then for sure she'll miss."

"No need to worry 'bout that," I told him. "She actually thrives and performs better when things are tense. Too bad the cowboy don't know that."

"Yep, the more he flaps his mouth the better she likes it," Charlie laughed.

"I'll shoot first this time little gal, as soon as I get another box of shells."

"No need for that," Ruth said quietly, "I've got ten extra you can use."

"Now that's mighty generous of you little gal, considering you've been shooting your own ammunition."

He reached out his hand and Ruth dropped the ten shells in it. The shooter looked down at the shells, picked one up to load, then stopped dead as he gazed closely at it. His face turned pale and his lips set in an angry line as he turned and looked into Ruth's eyes. He quickly fingered the other nine then gave a weak smile.

"Well now," he said, "I'll just get me a new box and you can keep these little gal. After all, fair is fair."

"Now you wouldn't turn down country generosity would you?" Ruth asked in a voice everyone could hear, "especially in front of all these good country folks."

Ruth's face was grim, her eyes angry slits as she watched him. I couldn't begin to follow what was goin' on but somethin' clearly was. The air was charged like it is before a storm and Charlie was laughin' low in his throat the way he does when a fight is breakin' out.

"I'll be dammed," exclaimed the lizard man, "if I don't think she's got him on the ropes; but what did she do? What happened between them?"

The crowd was silent, feelin' the change but not knowin' what it was or where it come from. All eyes were intent on Ruth as she stepped back and bowed gracefully to the shooter.

"Your move little man," she said clearly.

The cowboy moved stiffly to the line like a condemned man and gave the command to pull. The pidgeon leaped upward, reached its zenith, then the shooter raised his rifle and fired. It was a clean miss and the crowd gasped in disbelief. This was uncharacteristic for a man who had displayed such amazin' accuracy before.

"I can't believe he missed," the lizard man exclaimed.

"Weren't as great as he thinks he is," Charlie spat.

Pa took his pipe from his mouth, closed his eyes and smiled at the ceilin'. "I wish I could find words to tell the amazin'thing that happened then. The wonder of it is stamped on my mind as vivid today as on that sunny day in May when the birds were singin' joyously to a world renewin' itself, with Dimple standin' in the sun beside Nell waitin' to be claimed by the best marksman."

Uncle Bill was on the edge of his chair holdin' his breath, as we all were, the only sounds in the kitchen comin' from the frogs hollerin' in the darkness outside the screen door. It was as though we'd all been frozen in time.

Pa's eyes were closed as he played it over again in his mind and I wished mightily I could see what he was seein'. Finally when we were about to die of anticipation, he took his pipe from his mouth and continued.

No sooner had the cowboy missed than Ruth raised her Winchester and shot that pidgeon outa' the air. The crowd went wild, yellin' and whistlin' and clappin'. Charlie was doin' a jig around me and the lizard man, with old Blue right on his heels barkin' and whippin' our legs with his tail. I just stood there overwhelmed by the magnitude of what she'd done. I seen it but couldn't hardly believe what I'd seen.

"My word!" Uncle Bill exclaimed over and over. "Then what Almus? I swear you're going to give me a heart attack if you don't get on with it."

Pa smiled fondly at Uncle Bill. Nothin' he liked better than to keep everyone in suspense.

Well, what happened was: ever' time the cowboy shot, he missed and Ruth would shatter that old pidgeon in a thousand pieces before it could hit the ground. That crowd was absolutely silent Bill. There wasn't a sound. Not even a whisper. None of us could understand what was goin' on or how in the world the shooter could miss five shots in a row. They were lookin' at Ruth with awe and disbelief for she'd gone beyond good marksmanship. What she'd just done was borderin' on magic. Pa smiled into the past. "For the first time I didn't begrudge all them boxes of shells she used to hit me up for. Oh, I'd seen her do some amazin' things with a gun but even I didn't dream she was capable of such a feat. I'll say one thing for the shooter, he was game."

Then Ruth did a peculiar thing. She handed the shooter five more shells, watched him eject the remainin' five in his rifle onto the ground, then she scooped them up in her hand and smiled thinly at the shooter who had turned to stare at her. He loaded them, commanded his assistant to pull, swung the rifle upward toward the soarin' pidgeon and fired. It was a clear miss and again Ruth nailed it before it could hit the ground. Shocked, he looked at Ruth again, then calmly told the boy to release the clay pidgeons in rapid succession. The remainin' four were disposed of in a great display of skill and the crowd gave him the acknowledgement such skill deserved.

Uncle Bill was beside hisself with excitement. "What did she do then Almus?"

"Well, Bill, that ought to have been the end of the matter for Ruth had clearly won the match but she had the boy release ten more pidgeons one after the other, which she dispatched like a pro. I can tell you I was surely proud of her. Not just her ability, which was greater than even I had realized; but what I later found to be her fairness and sense of justice.

The shooter seemed to be in a daze, standin' there lookin' at Ruth for the longest time, then he reached into his pocket and pulled out some bills. He slowly counted out one hundred and twenty-five dollars into Ruth's hand. Ruth took the money, gathered up Dimple and Nell's reins and walked away with the boys taggin' along beside her.

The shooter-his face inscrutable- watched Dimple move away from him and I knew at that moment he was sick with sadness at losin' the mare.

I can tell you Bill, me and Charlie and the lizard man were havin' a square dance right there in the field. I've never been so happy or relieved in my life. I ran down and gave Dimple a hug and Charlie kissed her smack-dab on the muzzle, sayin', "I knew ye' weren't in any danger girl, not with that Ruth in yer corner. Why, I've sacraficed many a rabbit and I daresay a few squirrels so that girl could practice and it was worth ever bit of it. Yes sir, I've missed many a rabbit stew on account of that young'un there and lookit' what come of it."

Ruth hugged Charlie and told the lizard man that every word Charlie had said was true.

Then Charlie got a rapturous look on his face and began to jig even faster, slappin' his thigh and yellin' with old Blue workin' hisself into a frenzy.

"Almus!" he laughed, grabbin' Ruth and the lizard man by the arms swingin' them 'round and 'round. "I clean forgot. Why I've made meself a bundle of money on that girl today. Let's see, fifteen dollars at four to one makes..."

"Why that's sixty dollars Charlie! I reckon yer a rich man and that's a fact. Wish I'd had some money on her myself," I said regretfully.

He danced even faster, laughin' so hard he was doubled over, then he slapped me on the back, his eyes as full of devilement as I've ever seen em'.

"You do have money on her Almus and that's a fact. This mornin' Norey gave me ten dollars to buy that calf from Ezra Pritchett and I put it smack-dab on Ruth- in yer name- to win. Let's see. I'll take Norey''s ten out and I reckon yer forty dollars to the good."

"I can't do that Charlie, take money you bet. It Wouldn't be right."

"Gol dang it Almus, iffen it weren't fer yer girl I'd be right whure I was this mornin'. As it stands, I've got all me money back and sixty dollars to boot. Now hush yer mouth and take yer forty dollars or else yer gonna be huntin' by yerself from now on."

"Charlie, you beat anythin' I've ever seen and I guess I'd be proud and happy to have it. Lord knows we can use it."

"Then it's settled and I don't want to hear another thing 'bout it."

He went off to collect the money and me and Ruth and the lizard man walked slowly toward the midway with the little boys skippin' happily around us.

"I've never seen better shooting than that miss and I've seen some mighty fancy shooters in my time."

"Thanks," Ruth said. "Reckon I have to thank Pa for buyin' all that amminition when I was learnin. Better not forget ole Charlie either for sharin' his rabbits and squirrels with me."

"Well, he did mention you'd cleaned him out of about every animal on his land."

Ruth laughed. "He's a wonderful ole rascal but tends to tall tales now and again. Bet he also told you he had to poach rabbits off our land to make rabbit stew," she said fondly.

"He did mention that," smiled the lizard man.

"I remember one day when I was huntin' he come runnin down the hill yellin' and wavin' his arms at me and I knew I was in for a scoldin'."

"Now you lissen here girl," he started in, "I'm gonna ration ye on these here rabbits of mine. Why my rabbits be fairly scart outa thur' wits with ye stompin' 'round and shootin' up the place."

I leaned over and kissed his leathery cheek. "Now how do ya know these are your rabbits, Charlie? They might be our rabbits and maybe they're just crossin' yer land to get back home before dark."

"Jest like yer Pa," he snorted, "always layin' that silver tongue on folks. Well, it won't work with me girl, so ye jest high yerself off' me land and me special rabbit thicket, lessen..." he drawled, fiddlin' with his cob pipe and studyin' the thicket thoughtfully, all the time sneakin' glances at me. "Lessen ye'd like to consider a deal."

He watched me slyly but I didn't show any interest at all which I knew set him on edge. I too, eyed the thicket, even gave it a kick or two but nary a rabbit ran out. Charlie frowned at that for right at that minute he'd have liked a dozen rabbits to flush, just to prove his point. I scowled at the thicket, walkin' slowly 'round it, studyin' the whole thing as though my life depended on it.

"Peers like them rabbits might have moved on, Charlie, and maybe I been wastin' my time huntin' down here...but then maybe they ain't all moved on," I said slowly, kicken' the thicket thoughtfully. Bout that time two rabbits exploded under my feet and took off down the creek.

Charlie's face split in a triumphant grin as he yelled, "Shoot em' girl! When I just stood there lookin', he come runnin' 'round to my side of the thicket. "What're ye waitin' fer," he fumed. "Gol dang it, shoot em.!"

I sat down on a log and studied the sky. "This here thicket ain't mine Charlie and I reckon it'd be hard to tell our rabbits from yer rabbits as fast as they're runnin'."

"Dag blame it girl, you beat all I ever see'd. Hard headed as a stump, jest like yer Pa. Never see'd two people so much alike or so ornery."

"Well, we might as well talk over that deal you mentioned," I said, "Besides, I need a rest." He brightened a little and settled on the log beside me.

"Its simple, girl. Ever two rabbits ye shoot, I git one of 'em and ye can hunt anywhure on my land ye want, which is what ye been doin' since ye were knee high to a pup anyway."

"I don't know bout this deal Charlie, I got to walk all over harrikins deck to find them rabbits and then there's my ammunition to consider, specially if I miss one or two."

He looked at me suspicious. "It's a fair deal and ye know it. Sides, ye ain't missed a shot in years so I reckon somethin' else be stickin' in yer craw."

"Now that ya mention it, Charlie, there is. I think givin' ya one rabbit outa three is a might better deal all around, specially since you can set on your front porch and have the fun of watchin' me hunt, and in a manner of speakin,' deliver yer rabbit stew right to your door."

"Well," said Charlie, puffin his pipe irritably, "in a manner of speakin,' I reckon ye put a whole lot more importance on me watchin' ye hunt me critters than it's worth. Yer no Annie Oakley ye know. Now iff'en ye wus ridin' a horse and shootin' them rabbits on the run then I might consider it worth watchin'."

"So it's entertainin' ya want," I replied huffily. "This winter when I'm wadin' snow up to my elbows, settin' traps, fetchin' rabbits, skinnin' em out and nailin' em to your smoke house while ya set by the stove readin' the farmers almanac, then I reckon that'll entertain ya right enough. For all that I get one measly rabbit to show for it."

He squinted at me for a minute then stared off down the creek. "Reckon all that snow be a might much fer a sprout like ye at that.... so I'll sweeten the deal some. On Sunday's ye get two outa three and thet's as fer as I'm goin' with ye. Why, ye'd skin a pole cat outa his scent jest for the contrairness of it."

"Ya know I don't hunt on the Lord's day, Charlie," I said, castin an accusin eye on him.

"Well, thats a lucky break fer me rabbits," he grumbled, kickin at a stick.

I figured I'd aggravated him enough, so standin' up I slung my rifle over my shoulder then leaned down and kissed the ole codger on top of his bald spot. "Charlie," I said fondly, "your first deal is great with me; peers you forgot how much me and you are alike. We both hate a quick done deal." I loped off up the hill and left him settin' there starin' at the creek. As I neared the top I heard Charlie whistlin'. We'd played the haggle game, each of us satisfied. Course he's pretty much enjoyed the same deal for years cause I very nearly always divided my hunt with him, even off our land. At the top of the hill I turned and waved and Charlie lifted his pipe in salute."

"The lizard man was facinated with Ruth's tale about Charlie and so was I since I'd never heard it before. I wondered what all was in that head of hers that we'd never know or hear about."

I turned to Ruth."What was all that business with the shells and how come the shooter missed five shots in a row; and why on earth did you give him five more shells and keep the ones he ejected from his rifle?"

Ruth laughed slyly. "Cause the ten shells he gave me to shoot the bulls eye target had been tampered with and I probably couldn't have hit a barn door with them. When I saw what he'd done I pretended to drop them in the grass, then I substituted ten of my own shells, droppin' the faulty ones in my pocket. You remember he fetched another box real quick, which I expect were as bad as the ten he thought I'd lost in the grass. He thought I'd found them and was loadin' his shells but I simply exchanged his for mine. I had an idea from then on that he was up to somethin', so I just waited to find out what it was."

"So, you handed him the faulty shells when you were shootin' for Dimple and that's why he missed five shots in a row?"

"Right! When he missed the first five shots, I gave him five good shells and thats when he knew for sure I'd been on to him from the beginnin'."

"He didn't deserve it and that's a fact," the lizard man grated angrily.

"Likely not," Ruth said quietly; "but I didn't want to strip him of all his pride. Besides, I'd made my point and I hope it taught him a lesson on fair play".

The lizard man looked back at the cowboy with hatred and contempt. "I doubt he's capable of anything fair or good; but I admire you young lady for your charitable nature."

"But why did he miss one of the five shots after you gave him the good shells?" I asked her.

"Cause he was very upset and angry that I'd beaten him at his dirty little game. No tellin' how many poor folks he's cheated all over the country with this scheme. Maybe now he knows a little of what they felt."

She reached in her pocket and pulled out the bad shells and dropped them in my hand. "I kept the five he ejected for evidence in case he tried any tricks. I still had Dimple and that's all that really mattered."

"Well, I'll be damned," the lizard man chuckled. "I'm proud of you girl and you're the only one I know of thats ever bested that evil man."

Pa stared at the ceilin' for a long time, puffin his pipe with a faint smile on his lips then he continued.

"I reckoned I'd never tell a tale as good as this one and its been my favorite ever since. Couldn't wait to share it with Net. Course I knew she'd lecture Ruth on the evils of gamblin' and she'd be right too; still it had turned out good and had been the most exciting day of my life."

The lizard man beamed down at Ruth and again there was that tenderness in his eyes.

"Well, young lady, I'm proud to know you and you can't realize how happy I am you beat him

at his own game; but what are you going to do with all that money?"

"If I had as much money as places to put it I reckon I'd be rich indeed," Ruth smiled, " but there are some very real needs that ought to be tended to right away."

"Such as," he queried.

Ruth blushed and hung her head.

"Before we go on with this conversation," I interrupted, "I'd like to know your name. I can't go on thinkin' of you as the lizard man"

He smiled at my reference to the lizard man. "My name is John Lanyard. I was born in Missouri about a hundred years ago it sometimes seems and I'm old enough to look forward to retiring on a little farm somewhere."

"Me and the lizard man could use a few years of rest where it's quiet, with no crowds and carney noise." He sighed. "I long to hear crickets and frogs at night and smell fresh country air washed with rain, and maybe raise a few cattle and hear roosters crowing at dawn."

He stopped in embarassment and I caught Ruth lookin' at him with sympathy in her blue eyes.

"It's a fine thing to look to," I said. "Lord only knows what I'd do without my farm, and while its back breakin' work, specially in the spring, I wouldn't be happy anywhere else."

His face broke into an incredible look of joy.

"You live on a farm?"

"We do for a fact. Born and raised on the farm; don't know anything else 'cept teachin' school and I guess I always wanted to be a teacher as much as a farmer, so, I just did both of 'em. The best of two worlds, you might say."

"I'd say you're a lucky man Mr. Hundley. It sounds like a dream come true to me."

"Well I don't know 'bout dreams but I just had me a fine idee. Why don't you come home with us and have supper and we'll walk over the farm and you can see what yer gonna' get into."

"Well now, I don't know," he said, glancin' uncertainly at Ruth.

Ruth looked at me sharply with disapproval in her eyes, then she watched the lizard man -as I'd come to regard him- to see what he would say. I knew she still felt a little hostile toward him but she hid it well.

"We won't take no for an answer will we honey?" I asked Ruth.

She hesitated a moment then replied, "I think it's a nice idea dad."

"Then it's settled. Do you have a horse John? If you don't you can ride Ruth's Dimple and she can ride with me. Course you'll have to tag them boys on with you. Can't have them young'uns hoofin' all that way home. I expect they're all tuckered out after the day they've had. Think you can handle a couple of dirty little rag-a- muffins?"

"Yes, I'd love to see your farm," he laughed, shakin' my hand enthusiastically, but I won't need the horse: and I won't mind the little boys one bit, but I have a car and if you'll just give me time to make arrangements for the lizard, I'll be ready to go."

"I'd never seen so much happiness on a mans face Bill, over such a simple invite and I could tell it touched Ruth's heart as much as mine."

"No sooner said than done. Make yer arrangements and meet us at Shorty McCormicks store in New Burnside. Take yer time John for we have to pick up supplies and the ride back there will take us about an hour."

Back at Shorty's, Ruth bought the boys a triple decker ice cream cone and settled them on the porch while she shopped.

She began piling things on the counter, hummin' happily to herself. Yards and yards of material came off brightly colored bolts, with thread and needles and a good pair of sissors and I knew how happy the boys mom would be over that.

She picked out overalls and shirts for the boys with sturdy new shoes for school; She bought brightly colored pencils and paper and that luxury every child wants; crayola crayons in the biggest boxes Shorty carried. Course, what's crayons without a color book? She sure was thinkin' of everything.

Shorty watched her in amazement then finally exclaimed. "You rob a bank or somethin' Ruth?"

"Just a bit of luck Mr.Mcormick. I expect you'll hear 'bout it right soon now," she smiled, goin' on with her business."

She bought blankets and soap and groceries' till I was sure she wouldn't have a penny left, then she filled a big paper bag with ever kind of candy Shorty had. It was like christmas in May and my heart burst with pride as I watched the generosity that was so characteristic of this girl of mine.

"Chip off the old block I'd say," Aunt Bess replied.

My word," said Uncle Bill. "Magnificent, magnificent!"

"Yes, I thought the same thing," Pa murmured, suckin' some life back in the old pipe that had been restin' in his hand for what seemed like ages. I later learned that she'd also bought overalls and shirts for their father, dresses for their mother and a bottle of evening in Paris perfume."

Pa slapped his knees in pure delight.

"Can ye imagine such a grand and glorious gesture? Why, perfume is an unheard luxury for poor folks and I'd have given a pretty penny to see that lady's face when she saw that perfume."

Pa again fell into one of his thoughtful, pipe puffin' daydreams of the past, and we sat silent, waitin' for him to come back to us.

"She outdid herself for me and Net too, pickin' out a fine suit for me with a vest and fancy tie to match. Then she carefully selected the most beautiful silk dress you could imagine for Net, and a hat all crusted with delicate flowers to go with it."

"Later on that night I found a hugh bag of horehound candy on my pillow. First time in my life I didn't parcel it out to myself one piece at a time. Sure was a joy to eat a piece of my favorite candy anytime I wanted."

Pa's face took on a shine, almost as shiny as the tears that glistened on his cheeks."

"But I guess the best part of all was the new plow she had Shorty deliver to the boys dad."

"Don't see nothin' here for you Ruth," Shorty observed, carefully foldin' everything in a neat stack.

"Reckon I'll get to that in due time," she chirped happily.

"Well, John arrived about then and offered to haul her booty in his car, along with the boys."

Pa smiled and puffed his pipe, his eyes off again somewhere in a distant memory. "I expect we made a strange lookin' procession to the town folks with John's car stuffed to the gills with parcels and two dirty little boys, followin' Dimple and Nell out of Burnside."

"I still have that hat," Grandma murmured. "Wore the dress to church nearly ever Sunday till the ladies started teasin' me 'bout it. Still have it too; 'cept its worn thread bare now."

Pa studied Grandma for a moment, his face soft with tenderness.

"Never seen Net look more beautiful than when she wore that dress."

The room was silent with everyone thinkin' his own thoughts. Then finally Uncle Bill spoke.

"How did John like the farm, Almus?" .

"Never seen anything to beat it," Pa laughed." He was like a kid turned loose in a candy store. First off, he met Net and it was an instant friendship. She happily plied him with roast pork, corn on the cob, green beans right out of the garden with new little potatoes in them, corn bread and green onions which turned out to be one of his favorite foods."

"What did she have for dessert?" Uncle Bill asked, his face keen with anticipation.

"Might know Almus that Bills big thing is dessert," Aunt Bess teased.

"I got the same weakness, Bessie," said Pa "and Net had one of my favorites. Dewberries were in and she had a humongous dewberry cobbler. Never seen a man eat like that man did. Must have been years since his last home cooked meal and he kept grinnin' at Net and thankin' her over and over again, lookin' at us like we were out of a dream or somethin. He was some happy man and thats a fact."

"Purely made me sad to know how lonely this man was. I suddenly realized that the excitement and the wonders of travelin' with a carnival wasn't all it's cracked up to be, at least not for this man wolfin' down food in our humble kitchen. I knew that from then on I'd not have quite that same longin' I sometimes felt when I seen one drivin' down the road to someplace I'd never see, and to far off places I could only dream about. Grass ain't always greener on tother side and thats a fact of life."

"Amen," said Grandma.

Grandpa sat there for a long minute thinkin' his own thoughts, puffin' contentedly on his pipe, his eyes closed, hands restin' in his lap. A lazy breeze drifted through the back door and the kerosene lamp flickered briefly, then resumed a steady flame, its warm glow reflectin' on the rapt faces 'round the kitchen table. There was a smell of rain in the air; a smell that always wrapped me in a wonderful blanket of serenity and I drew in big breaths of it until I was dizzy. Old Streator smelled it too and lifted his head briefly to sniff the air.

"Bill, you asked how John liked the farm. I reckon he asked me a thousand questions 'bout everything he could think on and some I'd never thought on at all. He inspected ever animal, looked over the machinery, askin' about crop yields and how much I estimated it would take to get a farm started."

"So, he really was serious about settling on a farm?"

"Absolutely."

"It was dark when we finished so Net prevailed on him to stay the night and hear them roosters crowin' in the mornin,' and by golly he surprised me by sayin' yes. Ruth asked about the lizard man and he said he had a helper who tended the lizard when he was away."

"We were all sorry when he had to leave the next mornin' but not before he put away a half dozen eggs, ham and gravy and of course Net's famous biscuits slathered with home made butter and blackberry jelly. There were tears in his eyes as he said goodbye. He looked tenderly at Ruth and I looked forward to tellin' her and Net about what had happened to his daughter and what a shock seein' Ruth had been to him."

"Did you ever see him again, Almus?" Uncle Bill asked eagerly.

"As a matter of fact we did. He wrote during the year and told us all about the places he had been and seen and with his way with words it was the next best thing to bein' there ourselves. The carnival came back to Stonefort ever spring and John spent a good deal of time with us."

"How did Ruth come to feel about him Almus," asked Aunt Bess.

"Ruth felt sorry for him losin' his girl and all, but a bit uncomfortable knowin' she looked like a twin to the dead girl. She didn't hardly know how to treat that and would get on Dimple and ride out for hours at a time."

John, hisself put the matter to rest for her. One day he said, "Ruth you're not my daughter Angel, and you could never be, and thats as it should be. I love you because I like you and because you remind me of a very great treasure I once had and have no more." We were at the dinner table at the time, and John reached over and took Ruth's hand. "So, be yourself, child," he said gently," and be my friend if you can; but if you can't and my presence makes you uncomfortable, then I'll stop coming."

"Well, Ruth burst into tears at that and John took her in his arms as natural as could be, and from that time on a special bond grew between them. I believe he came to look on her as a daughter. Always brought presents from distant places and you can be sure Ruth always got somethin' real special. One year it was tortise shell combs for her hair, then silk scarves which she wore 'round her neck. Sure was a sight to see her ridin' Dimple down the road, dressed in overalls and a cotton shirt with them silk scarves and the dust from Dimple's hooves swirlin' out behind her."

"It was quite an elegant picture," smiled Grandma, "in spite of the contrast it made."

Then Pa dropped a bombshell.

"Would you like to meet the lizard man, Bill," he asked slyly, knowin' full well what a shock that question would be.

"Land sakes alive, Almus," Bill sputtered, "are you kidding me?"

"Not on yer life. In the mornin' we'll ride over there and say hello, maybe bring him over to spin a few yarns of his own. He's quite a storyteller hisself and I can't tell you what a joy it's been to have him in the neighborhood."

"Me and Bess will fix a special dinner, Almus and we'll have us a celebration. John will love that."

I looked at the queen. Her face had turned white as a ghost when she learned that the lizard man lived nearby.

"Oh, Uncle Almus," she whispered fearfully, "that awful lizard will kill us all in our sleep."

Pa laughed uproariously, slappin' his knee with delight. "Not to worry, Victoria. The lizard died years ago. That's when John left the circus for good and moved back here to a little spread he bought a few years after that first visit with us. So, you see you've nothin' to fear and I'm sure you'll love John as much as everone else does."

The queen heaved a tremblin' sigh of relief and leaned weakly against Aunt Bess.

"If you say so, Uncle Almus."

"I say so darlin, just you wait and see."

Pa chuckled happily. "I deliberately waited to tell you that John lives here now, till this story was told. John's been here 'bout eight years now and we're all the richer for it."

"My word," exclaimed Uncle Bill, using his favorite expression. I can hardly wait to meet him. How old is he Almus?"

"Nigh on to seventy, I'd say, though I never asked him his age and he's never volunteered that information. Net bakes him a cake ever year, with no candles on it and we sing happy birthday, and he don't seem to care if she has the right month or not." He smiled affectionately. "I'd say the death of his daughter closed off a few doors that won't ever be opened again; but he seems happy enough, even content, and we don't pry into his private life."

I sat there dumfounded at this revelation about John Lanyard for I'd known him since I could remember and Pa had never told the tale of the lizard man before. I looked at Pa curiously. Why hadn't he told the tale of the lizard before? Well that was his affair and I knew he had a reason for everthing. Sides, I'd long ago given up tryin' to figure out grownups and the peculiar things they sometimes did.

Drought

The summer of 36 was a scorcher.
The sun blazed from a pale sky with a relentless heat so bright you couldn't look at it even for a second.

Heat waves hung in the air, shimmering silver undulations that raked fingers of death through every green thing, burning the road dust so hot a bare foot was soon blistered.

Even the horses high stepped uncomfortably, weaving from one side of the road to the other in an effort to find a cool path. They'd shy sideways, tossing their heads up and down, eyes wild, snortin' and wheezin' th' hot air, their muzzles dripping foam, then plunge into the weeds and bushes along side th' road.

The slightest breeze played an omnious dirge through the cornfields, their dead stalks rattling like skeletal bones.

Creeks dried up, their bottoms cracked and desolate looking.

Paths worn bare by generations of plodding cattle meandered like white dusty serpents through fields covered with a brown carpet of dead grass.

Birds squatted listlessly on limbs with wings hanging loosely at their sides, beaks open as they drew in the hot air.

Cows congregated under trees, reluctant to leave the shade long enough to go to a pond with a meagre supply of muddy water. They refused to forage for the few blades of green grass scattered here and there; so returned to the barn at night ravenously hungry and thirsty. Only when the sun went down would they go to the pond to drink.

When the water in the pond became too hot and muddy to drink, Pa ran a wooden trough from the well to the barn, drew up buckets of water by hand and watered them with the sweetest water this side of heaven. At night before the milkin' was done he carried water from the trough to wash and cool them down and they would regard him with their big luminous eyes full of affection.

Pa took care of the needs of his stock before his own and I never knew him to eat or drink before they had their fill.

He also talked to them. I'd hear him say, "It'll get better soon, just hold on." Pa had a way with his animals just as did Grandma and would admonish me and the cousins that if it wasn't for the animals and their hard work we wouldn't eat and we best learn right now how to care for them properly.

"Why do you talk to them Pa?" I asked one night as he washed them down.

"Cause they love companionship just as we do."

"Do you think they understand what you say?"

" More than we imagine I expect."

"I swear they give more milk after a bath," he told Grandma that night as he sat at the supper table drinkin' coffee.

"Ever creature responds to kindness and comfort," she said as she got supper on the table. She brushed a wisp of damp hair from her face with the back of her hand. "There's times when I'm cookin' in this hot kitchen I'd enjoy a bucket or two of cold water poured on me."

"I'd be happy to oblige that little favor anytime Net," Pa grinned, a wicked look on his face. "Just say ye the word."

Pa loved talkin' to Grandma and after a long day in the fields his favorite place to sit was by th' window in the kitchen, hot or cold, and watch Grandma work her magic on the old warm morning cook stove.

No matter the weather Grandma baked somethin' ever day. The temperature of the oven was determined by knowin' just how much wood to burn in the firebox. A glass enclosed temperature gage was built into the oven door and she'd watch it creep upward to the temperature she wanted then put in a cake or a bunch of pies. I don't reckon she ever baked just one pie in her life since the farmhouse usually had an extra mouth or two at mealtime from somewhere or other.

Charlie Horn was often a drop in and Grandma most generally referred to him (when he wasn't around of course) as drop in Charlie. Course he was welcome and I can't remember them ever sayin' a bad word about Charlie. His sharp wit kept everbody in stitches and he was welcome at whatever door he knocked on. He would peer at the stove and shake his head in wonder at the good food Grandma produced with that old stove.

"Net," he'd drawl, "Ye be touched with a bit of magic or else theres a genie in thet there stove."

Grandma would allow a small smile then go on with her businesss. She had a special likin' for Charlie with his wide smile that crinckled his face and sparkled his brown eyes. I reckon he did more for her morale than the rest of us put together.

"Don't ye ever burn somethin?" he asked one day when she had the top of the stove loaded with pots and pans plus four pies in the oven.

She turned a jaundiced eye on him and Pa. "I've come close when a couple of pests park in my kitchen, gettin' in the way, and stickin' a finger in everthing.

Charlie frowned at Pa and lectured him on the merit of good manners and Grandma dished up a piece of pie and a cup of coffee waggin' a warnin' finger at the two of them as she went back to her cookin', while I settled down in my favorite place by the screen door with ole Streator to watch her cook and listen to Pa and Charlie spin yarns.

She enjoyed listenin' to the yarns and would take care not to make too much noise at the stove, her face intent on ever word. When she took a minute to sit and rest I'd jump up and wash whatever was dirty in the dishpan on the back of the stove. I would feel her eyes on me warm and loving and I often wished I was growed up so I could help her more. Anyway I never knew a cake to fall or a pie to come from the oven of that old stove that wasn't perfect. So, maybe a genie did live in there, I don't know, but I do know Grandma had a magic touch with food.

On this scorchin' day in particular Pa sat over by the open window, his chair tilted against the wall on two legs smokin' his pipe and sippin' on a cold glass of Grandma's famous buttermilk while he watched her get supper ready. His face and arms were a deep brown from the sun except for a pale halo around his forehead where the band of his old straw hat hugged his head.

The setting red globe that was causing so much misery and destruction in the county had cast a crimson tide over the countryside, spilling through the windows and doors into the kitchen, painting Grandma's brown skin a rich burnished gold.

Deep shadows from the furniture writhed like giant dragons across the floor and up th' walls in shimmery reflection.

Outside the window the great white blooms on Grandma's snowball bush were a brilliant crimson against the red globe. The little wren that lived in the bush was flittin' back and forth with tidbits in her mouth for a brood of little ones whose shrill cries shattered the stillness when her head appeared over the rim of the nest.

A slight breeze stirred the leaves of the oaks and the undulating song of the cicadas seemed to pick up a little and didn't seem as halfhearted as before. Grandma wiped her hands on the tail of her apron and peered hopefully out the screen door at the sudden movement in the trees, lifting her face to the soft uncertain swirls of air.

"Sure hope that breeze keeps up. Maybe it'll bring a little rain tonight."

"Be a blessin' to get some rain," Pa agreed.

A pork roast smothered in onions simmered on the back of the stove and a hugh pot of fresh green beans with new little potatoes in them added their fragrance to the wonderful smells of the kitchen.

On the sideboard sat two apple pies all plumped up with juice bubblin' through steam holes in the crust.

A glass full of onions, their long green blades lookin' wonderfully cool in the hot kitchen, towered above a platter of sliced ripe tomatoes in the center of the table.

"Don't know how you do it Net," Pa said appreciatively. "Here it is a hundred degrees out there in the yard even though its five o'clock in the evenin' and you manage to cook fine meals in spite of it." He shook his head in admiration and pride as he watched Grandma's slight figure bustle from the stove to the table, her long apron smudged with flour, the black gloss of her braid hanging heavy down her back.

"Sometimes I don't know how I do it either," she said glancin' at the Big Ben clock tickin' on top of the sideboard. 'Bout time for Charlie to show up," she added. "He can smell roast pork cookin' a mile away not to mention apple pie. Never seen a man so crazy about apple pie as Charlie. Sech foolish goins' on as he comes out with when he smells apple pie bakin' sure does a body good." She smiled to herself as she went to the screen door to peer down the road for a sign of ole Charlie.

"Reckon he'll have to get a move on if he wants to eat." Pa grunted, chompin' on his pipe. I'd just as soon he stayed home tonight with them apple pies lookin' so good; still I can't begrudge him, what with Nora down to her mom's this week. When do ye reckon she's comin' home?"

"I don't rightly know but there's plenty of food to go 'round."

"Reckon ole Streator might disagree with that."

Streator licked his chops and gave Grandma a soulful look.

"That dogs got a hollow leg," she said, smilin' down on ole Streator who was lookin' at Grandma with worshipful eyes. "Got to pick them dewberries down in the bottoms tomorrow," she said, changin' the subject. "Never seen the likes in all my life. Here we are in a terrible drought, everthing up here dyin' and down in them bottoms its a green paradise. I expect the dewberries are all we'll get this year though, less it rains and perks things up a bit. Could use some help pickin' if ye have time." She glanced at Pa and he nodded his head in the affirmative.

"I'm helpin' too Grandma, maybe even ole Pig will come along."

"Now that would be nice dear. After I get through cannin' I'll make a big cobbler and he can stay for supper and..."

'Bout that time Charlie stumbled up the steps onto the porch then slumped to the floor gaspin' for breath. Pa rushed out and knelt down beside him while me and Grandma stared in disbelief through the screen door.

He was deeply scratched all over his face and arms with blood runnin' in ever direction and there were leaves and small twigs and vines in various lengths stuck to his clothing and his hair stuck out in ever direction all tangled up with the same stuff plus big globs of dirt all over him like somebody had slapped it on with their hand. His cotton shirt was tattered, 'specially th' right arm and back and th' ragged blood soaked edges looked like a gruesome crazy quilt. I shivered in spite of th' heat.

"What in tarnation happened to ye, Charlie?" Pa asked as he propped Charlie up against the wall of the house.

"Bring me a dipper of water sprout," Pa yelled.

Grandma was already pourin' water from the waterbucket into the washpan, quickly handin' me the dipper full of water almost before Pa finished askin' for it and as I turned toward the door she was already hurryin'

Pig and a Sack of Stray Cats

through it with a bar of lye soap and a bunch of clean cloths sloshin' around in the pan.

She knelt beside Charlie and began bathin' the bloody scratches on his face and arms while Pa held the dipper of water to Charlie's lips. Charlie drank the whole dipper down like he'd never seen water before and asked for more.

"Not too fast Charlie, else ya might get stomach cramps," Pa admonished handin' the empty dipper to me.

Charlie squinted up at Grandma through bloody, sweat soaked eyes. "I could sure use some of yer buttermilk Net," he muttered hopefully.

"Lets just wait a bit," she said "and see how that water lays on yer stomach."

Pa began to remove the trash from Charlie's overalls and shirt and ever other limb he pulled off would bring a yelp from Charlie.

"These twigs look like blackberry vines to me Charlie what with all these stickers on 'em."

Pa puffed his pipe thoughtfully while he studied the broken pieces of vines.

"Yep, I'm sure thats what they are."

Charlie turned a baleful look on Pa his eyes poppin' with irritation.

"Well now thets right bright of ye Almus," he spat. What in tarnation do ye think I'm yellin' about when yer draggin' them thorns across me hide. Been a farmer all yer life and don't hardly know a blackberry vine when ye see it," he mumbled irritably, "special when its buried in yer best friends hide."

"Reckon he'll live Net," Pa drawled, grinnin' down at Charlie. "Anybody with such a vile temper has to be tough."

He studied the apparition of leaves, dirt and thorn-studded vines slouched on our back porch.

"If I hadn't heard ya speak Charlie I reckon I'd a swept ya off the porch as trash." Charlie's eyes burned with irritation at Pa then they softened as he gave Grandma a sweet, grateful look then addressed her as though Pa wasn't even there.

"It beats me how Almus ever snagged a saintly lady sech as yerself Net, what with his sinful ways and all." He sniffed peevishly. " Peers he didn't hear the preachers sermon on piety and charity two Sundays ago else he'd have a mite of care for the pain and sufferin' of an old friend."

"Yer absolutely right Charlie," said Grandma sternly, givin' Pa a witherin' look. "I've heard 'bout enough of yer foolishness Almus."

Charlie beamed at Grandma then scowled at Pa like a little child. He was breathin' a little better now but he was still very red with white pided serpentine blotches on his face and neck from the heat and his veins were standin' out like balloons.

Grandma laid the wash cloth in her hand aside then took Charlie's hand and pressed two fingers against his inner wrist.

He watched her every move and had as much trust in Grandma's doctorin' as any real doctor he'd ever seen.

After a long moment she released his hand and studied his scratched face which looked some better since she'd removed the blood." Your pulse is a bit fast,Charlie, but walkin' up that hill from the creek in this heat would account for that."

Charlie gave a long drawn out moan. "Gracious sakes alive, Net, ye don't know the half of it. Walkin' up thet hill with them thorns diggin' in me hide ever step I took, jest about wore me patience down to a nub."

Course Pa couldn't let that outlandish statement pass without comment.

"That must'a been tough Charlie, specially since ya don't have hardly any patience in the first place. I bet there's not a clod of dirt on that hill that didn't feel the wrath of yer boot and I won't try to guess how many cuss words got scattered along the way. I reckon if them cuss words were rocks, we'd have ourselves a nice stretch of gravel road from th' creek up that hill."

Pa warmed to his fantasy, his blue eyes full of mirth and affection for Charlie. Course we didn't yet know what had happened to Charlie but we'd soon learn why his usual sense of humor was still down the road somewhere along with a fair amount of his skin.

"Imagine walkin' on that nice gravel instead'a slippin' and slidin' in all that mud when it rains. Why we could wear our shoes all the way to th' creek and if ye'd jest cuss yer way on up the road a piece to th' church we could eliminate th' Sunday foot washin' at th' creek altogether."

Pa was completely captaivated with the idea, his face bemused with pleasure.

Charlie was starin' at him, open mouthed and angry, his eyes dartin' from Pa to Grandma. He set great store in Grandma's oponion of him and her respect was of vital importance.

She had that effect on most folks for she was genuine and carin' and deeds spoke for her instead of words.

Grandma smiled at Charlie, givin' Pa a look of disapproval, which brightened ole Charlie's mood considerable.

"Thet's right, Almus. Kick a hurt man when he's down. Never mind he's yer best friend." or mebbe thet's changed now I cain't defend meself. Ye know right well I give up cussin' some time back and I've kept to thet bargain too. Well... mebbe.... cept fer a slip or two when thet fool Sampson kicked me in the shin and thet dag-blamed mule of yer'n bit me on th'... he hung his head in embarassment before Grandma- " wal, ye know very well whar he bit me. Most anybody wud'a let loose a few cuss words I reckon...cept'n you Net, what with bein' th' angel ye be and all."

"Grandma ignored the two bickering men and told me to fetch the yarrow root ointment she'd just made up. I wondered if she'd heard the angel compliment but her face showed no sign.

Pa scratched his head and contemplated Charlies battered form for a long time. So long in fact, Charlies face reddened and he squirmed about uncomfortably. I could hear ever word from the kitchen while I studied the many bottles of medicine Grandma always made up from roots and leaves and bark and such, lookin' for th' yarrow ointment.

"Well, out with it Almus." he growled. "Somethin's stickin' in yer craw and I'd lay odds it be a bunch of nonsense as usual."

"Nothin' too important Charlie. Just thinkin' on how this Sunday we'll have to pray ye through all them cuss words ya spent on ole Sampson and them clods of dirt comin' up the hill. Sorta renew yer ticket to heaven ya might say. Course there's that other time too when Sampson kicked ya in the shin and Ole Satan bit ye on th..."

"Gol dang it Almus! Never mind whar he bit me. Ye don't have no respect fer nothin' and where do ye get off sayin' that prayin' me soul inta heaven ain't important and never mind tother time when Satan bit me. I already squared thet with the Lord."

"No doubt ya did, Charlie," Pa sighed. Yer knees have scrubbed that altar so many times its slicker'n a banana peel but I reckon thats what it's there for and it does a body good to see it in such regular use specially by my best friend. I heard Mrs. Denton say Sunday its so slick she nearly slid off it onto the ground and could hardly concentrate on her prayin' from then on."

I giggled at the picture of the enormous Mrs Denton slidin' off the prayin' bench, grabbed the bottle of yarrow ointment and another dipper of water and hurried back to the porch.

Charlie snorted and carefully dragged himself to a sittin' position against the wall and reached for the dipper. He drank half th' water then smacked his lips and looked at th' sky dreamily.

"Best water I ever drunk in me whole life," he said.

He stared at the sky some more while we waited politely then he fixed Pa with a dour look.

"As fer thet prayin' bench Almus; I expect if we cud see old lady Denton's prayers they'd jest be so many fly specks on the arbor roof anyhow. Beggin' yer pardon Net but I don't see the good Lord listenin' to long-winded prayers on Sunday from a body who carries gossip all over the county durin' th' week."

Grandma pursed her lips to hide a smile but Pa just laughed out loud.

"I'd say ya got a good point there Charlie but I'm gonna bust if ye don't get around to tellin' us what happened to you."

Charlie drained the dipper of water then again gazed up at a patch of sky as though he was seein' what happened to hisself all over again.

"Well, I was ridin along loose in the saddle, happy as a June bug, dreamin' of Net's fine cookin' and how lucky I wuz fer havin' sech good friends as ye be when suddenly right outta the blue and fer no good reason a'tall thet gol danged, cowardly, weak-livered Sampson up and shied me off when a snake slithered across the road in front of us; only I couldn't get me right foot out of the stirrup and thet dang fool horse bolted through that big blackberry patch down by the creek and drug me behind him like I was a rag doll. I swear that patch seemed two miles long Almus. Never in me whole life have I had sech a feelin', like ten bobcats all tearin' me hide at the same time."

At that last statement Pa fell back on the porch and started laughin', his deep voice rollin' out on the hot air like thunder. When Pa laughs, everybody laughs for he just has that gift of imparting humor, so I joined him and even Grandma had a twitch to her lips as she strove mightily to restrain herself.

Charlie watched th' struggle on her face then sighed sympathetically.

"Go ahead and laugh with thet fool husband of yers, Nettie, fer I know ye'll be laughin' at me words and not me hurts."

He turned a serious face to Grandma. "Net, do ye 'member when I fell outta thet tree last year tryin' to get thet possum fer Almus... and them dogs all over me thinkin' I'm the possum, layin' there with th' breath knocked outta me and Almus rollin' on th' ground laughin' like a fool? Could'a heered 'im two miles off and th' worst of it wuz them six dog tongues swabbin' me tonsils out and steppin' all over me face with muddy feet.

I remember Charlie, "she sympathized, pattin' his hand. "Friends like you don't come 'round often and Almus is mighty lucky and... I imagine underneath all his foolishness he thanks th' good Lord for ye ever day."

"Mebbe he does and mebbe he don't," Charlie said doubtfully.

"Ill answer that," Pa laughed, slappin' Charlie on the back. "Yer just about th' most entertainin' man I've ever seen and if it wasn't for you I'd never have a good laugh. Why, life around here would be as dull as dish water without you Charlie and thets a fact. Now you answer me a question, Charlie. What about that snake?"

"Ya mean th' one what spooked Sampson?"

"The very one," Pa sighed, rollin' his eyes heavenward impatiently.

Charlie studied th' same patch of pale sky as before, then his eyes dropped to his right boot, the one that got caught in the stirrup. It was scratched up somethin' awful.

"Warn't even a pizon one," he grumbled as though it might have been worth it for a poison snake. "Jest a harmless black snake; a black snake mind ye, not a rattler which wud'a made anybody bolt or maybe even a good size copperhead; but thar it wuz, jest a puny little ole black snake mindin' its own business, tryin' to cross th' road ta tother side and here I am all scratched up like I'd been in a cat fight cause thet fool Sampson didn't keep his wits 'bout 'im."

"Well, I expect all the commotion you and Sampson made, raised a few hackles on that snakes back too," Pa grinned. "Where's Sampson now?

"Likely went back home," Charlie grimaced, runnin' a hand gingerly over his face. He studied th' ruined boot sorrowfully. "Reckon he's a mite scratched up too what with all that turnin' and twistin' he done tryin' to shake me outa thet stirrup." He got to his knees and started to stand up but Pa put his hands on Charlie's shoulders and eased him back to the porch.

He puffed on his pipe, clouds of smoke driftin' over his face and up through his hair toward the galvanized bathtub hangin' on the wall.

Pig and a Sack of Stray Cats

Facinated, I watched the smoke clouds swirl and melt into ghostly, writhing spectral shapes, ever changin', driftin' upward into silky wisps of fantasy, teasin' your eyes with their illusion of permanence. Then as if by magic they faded and dissolved into nothingness. Pa stared thoughtfully into space for a long time then he turned a curious eye on Charlie.

"Why didn't ya try to pull yerself back in the saddle?" he asked.

Charlie stared in disbelief at Pa for a long time then turned his eyes beseechingly toward heaven. When no inspiration came from that quarter he turned back to Pa, bristlin' with irritation.

"Pull meself back in the saddle?" he exclaimed. "Why I never in me whole life heered sech nonsense, as tho' I'm some bloomin' acrobat or somethin' with a nice handy rope in me hand instead of jest air. Thar I wus peerin' thru slits in me eyes tryin' to keep an eye on Sampson with them berry vines slappin' me jaws somethin' fierce. Pull meself back in the saddle indeed," he muttered, givin' Pa a malevolent look. "I'll have ye know Almus Hundley thet I pulled ever gol dang thing in sight and some thet warn't, and it all had stickers on it. I'm lucky I ain't blind as a bat."

He groaned miserably just thinkin' on it.

"Them devilish vines had me fore Sampson took two steps and its only by the grace of the good Lord thet thet fool horse didn't stomp me right in'ta th' ground. Reckon it might'a been them vines though," he admitted grudgingly, " thet snagged me away from Sampsons feet and finally tore me outa thet stirrup, if the truth be known. If he'd a made it outta th' berry patch with me still in thet stirrup thar's no tellin'whut might'a happened. Likely been half way ta Burnside by now."

He slumped back against the wall exhausted and Grandma hurried to the well to draw up the buttermilk.

Pa was laughin' so hard he fell over on his back, stuck his boots in th' air and whooped like crazy. Finally he set up, swiped th' tears from his eyes with his shirt sleeve and clapped ole Charlie on th' shoulder affectionately.

"I said why didn't ye try to pull yerself up in th' saddle, Charlie: not why didn't ye; but now that I think on it.... I reckon even tryin' was a mite impossible what with them berry vines slappin' yer jaws somethin' fierce."

Repeating Charlies words sent Pa off in'ta another fit of laughter.

Charlie eyed Pa with contempt. "Try, me arse," he mumbled so Grandma couldn't hear him, "I'd like ta see you try thet little trick, Almus Hundley, while bein' drug behind a horse in a berry patch with one foot caught in'a stirrup, tother draggin' hind-end over howdy, and th' rest of ye bein' sliced like a ripe tomater thru them killer vines. Fact of th' matter is— I'd pay good money ta watch ye demonstrate thet hair brained theory of yers. Yes sir, good money."

Pa went off inta another fit of laughter and Grandma gave him a dirty look as she hurried past them into th' kitchen with th' cooler of buttermilk.

A few minutes later Charlie was sippin buttermilk and tellin' Grandma what an angel she be and how the Lord sent her down to care fer a worthless scoundrel like Almus and save him from the clutches of the devil.... and he reckoned no one else would have a care fer his own miserable welfare while his own dear Norey was away tendin' her sick mother, 'cept Grandma of course, who was known far and wide fer her carin' nature 'bout the poor and sick in her community.

Poor Grandma was embarassed. She purely hated to be bragged on, often tellin' me and my cousins if we weren't careful in our high oponion of ourselves, we'd have our reward here on earth and none in heaven.

Pa asked where his buttermilk was and Grandma said he could just laugh his way into th' kitchen and git his own buttermilk. When grandma said that charlie didn't even try to hide th' big grin on his face.

When Pa returned to th' porch he set down beside Charlie and laid a sympathetic hand on his arm.

"I'd say yer a lucky man Charlie and we're mighty grateful the good Lord looked out for ya, but I sure hope ya didn't do too much damage to that berry patch seein' as how it's one of Net's favorites."

Pa chomped on his pipe and mused thoughtfully on the possible destruction of the berry patch as he continued to pull vines off Charlie's overalls while Charlie gritted his teeth in pain and disgust. Pa took the pipe from his mouth and cupped it in his hand while he studied his old friend kindly. "Tell ya what lets do Charlie. Nets got supper ready and all yer favorites ta boot," he said, watchin' Charlie's face brighten at the mention of his favorites, "so lets eat this good food that Nets worked so hard to fix and when we're finished I'll hitch up the buggy and we'll go to yer house and I'll take care of ole Sampson. How's that sound?"

"Better'n the rascal deserves," he mumbled, "tryin' to kill me over a harmless little ole black snake, makin' me late while Net's good cookin' gets cold. I been lookin' forward to her apple pie fer two days now and here I am all dirty and bloody and not fit ta put me feet under her table."

He looked at Grandma apologetically.

"Iffen ye can stand to look at me all wrecked up like I be Net, I'd shore love to eat thet fine supper ye prepared."

Despite Charlies injuries and wounded pride at bein' thrown off Sampson's back he managed to put away an enormous amount of Grandma's good cookin', smackin' his lips and tellin' Grandma what a wonderful cook she be. Futhermore, he declared her home-made ointment had taken away all his pain and he allowed as how he'd be fit as a fiddle in a day or two. He ruminated all through supper, sometimes exclaimin' to himself and shakin' his head in disbelief.

"I cain't git over thet Sampson" he said out loud, starin at the woods through the kitchen window behind Pa's chair as though he'd see the answer floatin' around out there somewhere; "lettin' thet puny little ole black snake spook him when I seed him stomp the daylights out'uv a bunch of wild dogs thet was chasin' one of our cows. Fearless as anythin' he was, even takin' a bite from th' rump of one of 'em, a big vicious beast who was obviously the leader. I fancy I seed ole Sampson grin at thet dog's humiliation, stompin' his feet and bellerin' out threats as he chased 'em outta sight."

Charlie laughed at the memory, his fondness for ole Sampson obvious in spite of his irritation over the berry patch incident.

Pa's face became serious as he forked a big piece of roast pork in his mouth. His eyes narrowed thoughtfully as he chewed, then he lifted his coffee cup to his mouth and sipped the hot liquid for a long time. He had a way of doin' that during the tellin' of a story, leavin' you hang in suspense.

"As I recall," Pa says, "them dogs got to be too dangerous to let go and we ended up huntin' 'em down for killin' stock. I know the women folk were mighty worried they just might attack a child or even a lone adult, for that matter. You were ridin' Sampson at the time and he purely enjoyed the whole thing."

"Right ye be Almus. Them cowardly dogs warn't so brave when the odds went agin' 'em. We had the devils own time diggin' them critters out-'uv their hidin' places though, what with all the brush piles scattered over the county".

Pa's face was solemn, his eyes going to ole Streator lyin' by the kitchen door. Remember that big burly brute that took us three hours to ride down and bring to bay in the corner of a fence? Must'a been th' leader from th' size and savvy of him. 'Member how he looked 'round fer th' rest of th' pack, knowin' all th' time he was alone; then how he faced us, his head high, eyes steady, knowin' his time had come? In that moment," he murmured sadly, "I felt a tremendous sympathy for his aloneness and admiration for his courage. I suddenly had no heart to kill the beast."

Pa stared vacantly at th' stove pipe above th' kitchen range for a long time and I wished I could see th' picture in his mind of that brave dog standin' all alone in a fence corner facin' certain death with no way to escape, on that long ago day before ever I was born. Pa sighed with sadness closing his eyes on a scene he'd never forget.

"Then Elmo Jackson raised his rifle, th' head of the dog turned to the movement, eyes blazin', lips curled, his teeth bared in defiance as he crouched to spring. Before I could blink Elmo dropped him just as his feet left the ground. I reckon no man could show greater courage than that dog did that day. Him and his pack had killed to feed themselves, somethin' we all would have done under similar circumstances."

There was a long silence while each of us studied the lonely picture in our mind. Then I heard Grandmas voice, quiet and sad. "Things have a way of turnin' even, for man and beast; but the way between bravery and cowardice is survival and I reckon that's the hardest way of all."

Pa and Charlie stared at Grandma intently as they thought on what she'd said. Pa reached over and laid his hand on hers and Charlie's face was full of puzzlement as he dropped his eyes to his plate.

I'd long ago seen the depth of Grandmas wisdom and knew she understood things a lot of folks could only wonder about.

Pa finally broke the silence and smiled at Charlie.

"After all th' food ye've put away old chap, I reckon ya don't have much room left for Net's apple pie." he drawled as Charlie sopped up the last drop of pork gravy with one of Grandma's good biscuits.

"Room and to spare Almus," said Charlie, smilin' sweetly at Grandma who was cuttin' pie on the side board, "and if ye think ta jab me outta me pie then ye can save yer breath."

When Grandma set a hugh piece of apple pie in front of Charlie his face crinkled in delight and when everbody had pie in front of them Charlie closed his eyes and raised his voice to the Lord in unaccustomed prayer, since he believed some folks like hisself who didn't know the proper words ought to, as he put it, keep their traps shut.

"Oh Lord," he said reverently, "bless the hands what made this fine meal, special this apple pie. AMEN."

Pa cast a jaundiced eye on Charlie while Grandma said nary a word and ate her pie as though not another soul was in the kitchen, her face a picture of serene modesty.

Charlie considered himself ignorant compared to those with a little schoolin' but Pa always said Charlie had more common sense and intelligence than most educated people he'd met; so this unexpected prayer was just part of his charm and appreciation for a kindness rendered him and he simply asked the Lord to bless Grandma as she had blessed him. We'd no sooner swallowed the last bite of pie when a nicker came softly from out by the back porch. There stood Sampson lookin' like sometnin' out of a nightmare, his hide all covered with the blackest mud I ever seen and smellin' like rotten' hay thats been in the rain too long.

Charlie and Pa rushed out to look him over while me and Grandma watched. Finally Grandma rose, walked out onto the porch and studied Sampson closely. She ran her finger along his neck scoopin' up a bit of mud, then sniffed it curiously as she rubbed it between her fingers.

"Did ye ever see the likes of thet Net?"

"Well, not very often Charlie. He's a smart horse, no doubt of that," she murmured, strokin' the stallions muzzle.

"He don't look none too smart right now," he mumbled, scratchin' Sampson's ear.

"Well Charlie, this horse has got a lot of what most folks are in bad need of."

"Whats thet, Net?"

"Horse sense Charlie, just plain ole horse sense; and if you'd followed Sampson to that swamp down by the narrows you wouldn't have needed my ointments for your wounds a'tall. Thats where I get most all my herbs for the medicine I make." Charlie studied Grandma for some time then shuddered. "Thet swamp's a dangerous place Net and I purely hate to think of ye wanderin' 'round down there. Thar's sink holes galore, not to mention snakes... and I heered tell several folks seen headed in thet direction never turned up agin."

"It's a good place Charlie if you respect it and obey the rules; and I been doin' that all my life so theres no need to fear. Sampson knew where to go by instinct, which makes him a lot smarter than us."

"Now that you mention it Net," said Pa, "thats where ole Streator went when he was snake bit, only he didn't come home for two days. Sampson's only been gone three hours."

"Three hours was enough for what ails Sampson. Snake bite takes longer."

"Tarnation!" Charlie exclaimed, runnin' his hands affectionately over Sampsons face. "Ye ole son-of-a-gun. All this time I'm feelin' guilty here eatin' Net's good cookin' and thinkin' ye might be home all cut up jest waitin' fer me to come doctor ye and yer down yonder in the swamp gettin' yerself all fixed up in a mud bath." He ran his hand over the mud on Sampson's back. "Yer sure gonna be a sight in the mornin' when thet mud dries on yer onery carcas."

"No need puttin' him through that Charlie," said Grandma, strokin' Sampson's velvet nose. He nuzzled as close as he could get to Grandma, his body tremblin' with joy at her touch. No animal could resist Grandma and we'd seen her gentle th' most ferocious dog. Even ole Satan would stand in a corner of th' feed lot and look on her with what could only be described as grudgin' approval.

"He's ready to be washed off right now and I reckon you and Almus can tend to that soon enough. He'll sleep like a baby tonight, and I expect his cuts won't look bad a'tall by mornin'. You two might even work up enough appetite for another piece of pie."

Charlie let out a war whoop and headed for the well with an enthusiasm that belied his stove-up condition.

It took a dozen buckets of water to clean all the mud off Sampson and when he was clean we looked him over real good. His wounds were already healin', even the deepest cuts and he kept nuzzlin' charlie and bumpin' him around and stompin' his feet impatiently to go home.

"I'd say ya got a hungry horse on yer hands Charlie and if we keep standin' here he might stomp on a few toes." Pa turned to me. "Take 'im to the barn sprout and give 'im some oats. He's earned a treat today by providin' me with a prize story for future tellin'. Course I'll have to add a thing or two jest to make it interestin' but I expect Charlie won't mind that since he'll become famous, leastwise in this neck of the woods."

Life returned to normal in the next few days if one could say the continuation of the severest drought Pa and Grandma could remember was normal.

Crops cooked under the relentless heat of the sun, gardens turned brown, pastures wilted and died, and creeks were dryin' up so fast you could almost see the water level droppin' lower and lower in the creek bed. What was left stood in small sluggish pools, growin' rancid and dark with decay from lack of circulation.

Wildlife stopped comin' to the creeks, seekin' out larger ponds whose water was still drinkable. Even these were rapidly dryin' up and some farmers were forced to buy water from towns that still had enough to spare.

Word of mouth reported more and more rationing as the drought slowly sucked the State dry.

Worry was turnin' to panic and folks talked of a crisis the likes of which no one could remember in their lifetime.

Faces were turned heavenward in silent speculation that God's wrath was fallin' on them and folks started prayin' all through the day wherever conviction found them.

It wasn't unusual to see a farmer kneelin' humbly on the burned earth amid the desolation of a ruined crop askin' God's mercy on a desperate land whose people would suffer the ravages of hunger in the comin' winter, unless He intervened.

Grandma and Pa continously gave thanks to th' good Lord for a well that never ran dry. It was fed by an underground stream whereas most wells depended on rainwater runnin' off the roof into gutters that drained into the well. One mornin' Pa saddled Dimple and rode into town to put out th' word that folks were welcome to all th' water they needed for their families as long as his well had water. He tacked up notices all over town, along th' roads, on trees, fence posts, anywhere folks traveled.

The next mornin' people started comin' from all over the county in everthing from cars loaded with buckets and fruit jars to small trucks and wagons loaded with barrels, and as Pa put it, they hauled away the sweetest water this side of heaven.

"I reckon it ranks right up there with what Moses got when he struck that rock," he would tell folks, who, after they'd drunk one dipper full, happily agreed.

After a few days of this a worried Charlie took to measurin' the water level by the odd shape of a branch rock that was at that time even with the water line. Ever day or two he'd come over and peer into the well over and over again just to be sure his eyes hadn't fooled him, shakin' his head in wonder that th' well wasn't dry.

One evenin', after a week of steady traffic to the well, Charlie rode ole Sampson over to swap a few tales with Pa, as he put it, but mainly we knew he wanted a look at th' rock that marked the water line.

We were sprawled on the well curb, our backs against the wood cubicle that enclosed the well, watchin' th' sun sink behind the trees in the west.

Pa had built the curb out of branch rock a few feet off the ground, exactly like a bench so folks could sit and visit while they refreshed themselves. The bench encircled the well and was a favorite place for coolin' off after supper.

This particular evening the air hung still and heavy, clingin' to our skin like cobwebs. The pond frogs were croakin' half- heartedly, the locusts seemed dispirited, their usual shrill renditions tentative and weak and only a few mosquitoes buzzed about to plague our tranquility. The heat was takin' its toll not only on th' crops but on every livin' creature as well.

Pa had just drawn up a bucket of cold water to quinch our thirst and I was pourin' some over my head, runnin' my tongue round my mouth to catch th' drops slidin' down my face, relishin' th' wonderful coolness as it soaked into my overalls.

Charlie slid outta' th' saddle, tied ole Sampson to one of Grandma's lilac bushes then set down beside me.

"Now thet's a right fine idea sprout," he grinned. "Might jest try it meself."

"This water's a mite too precious ta waste on yer ornery hide, Charlie," Pa smiled, handin' a dipper to Charlie who drank the cold sweet liquid slowly, his eyes closed in enjoyment. After a minute he smacked his lips and sighed as he handed the dipper back to Pa.

"Nothin' in th' whole world better'n this here spring water," he murmured, lookin' up at th' sky as though to acknowledge th' giver of such a special gift. "You been keepin' an eye on this well, Almus?" he asked, standin up on th' bench, peerin' into the darkenin' well.

"Yep! Checked it last night."

"And?"

"Still even with that rock of your'n."

"Thet don't hardly seem possible," Charlie muttered. "How many barrels ye figure come outta here yesterday?"

"Bout twenty, I reckon, not countin' what we used fer th' cattle and Net's kitchen which probably don't take more'n a couple barrels."

"Thet'ud be twenty-four or five plus 'bout three more fer th' live stock."

"Sounds about right," Pa answered, suckin' contendedly on his beloved pipe.

"Thet's crowdin' any well ta take thet much in one day," he mumbled. "What about today?"

"Well today picked up some," Pa said, rubbin' his back against th' rough wood. "My shoulders are about to fall off and that's a fact. Thank th' good Lord for that pulley. It'ud be impossible to draw up that much water without it"

"Ain't it enuff to give folks yer water without drawin' it up to boot? Charlie grumbled. "Sometimes I wonder 'bout yer thinkin' apparatus, Almus."

"Don't be too hard on 'im Charlie," Grandma replied. "The widow Jackson come over with just her twins to help and haulin' up enough to fill three barrels even on th' pulley is might nigh impossible for two skinny ten year olds, much less their mother who's skinner than them."

"Thet woman has a hard time alright," he murmured. "Norey helps her all she can and I know ye do too Net, bein'..."

"Bein' the angel she be," Pa interrupted, smilin' wickedly up at Charlie.

"Charlie cast a sour look at Pa. "Peers like thet prayer bench could stand some scrubbin from yer boney knees, Almus, seein th' way yer sins been pilin' up here lately. Mebbe me ticket to Heaven ain't th' only one what

159

needs some renewin'. I expect ya outta' square thet sharp tongue of yers with th' Lord before ye stick yer nose inta me own Spiritual affairs. Besides, Net here be th' only one I'd allow ta handle me ticket to Heaven, bein'...

"Th' angel she be," interrupted Pa again, roarin' with laughter.

Grunting mightly Pa eased his tall frame up beside Charlie and placed his arm around th' skinny shoulders.

"Charlie," he said sincerely, "I love ye as much as any of my brothers, sometimes more I reckon and I want ta tell ya that life without yer friendship would be intolerable."

Charlie raised his head from th' well and looked at Pa in amazement then opened his mouth to speak.

"Hold yer 'tongue 'till I'm finished," Pa grinned good naturedly. "Didn't I tell ya a few days ago that life 'round here without yer onery hide would be dull as dishwater? I hate ta admit it but I'd be hard up fer laughs if it wasn't for yer foolishness. And..." Pa hesitated, lookin' down at th' water then up at that patch of sky Charlie always seemed to look to for answers. "I reckon I'd lay my life down for ya' if it ever come ta' that." he said softly.

Charlie stared silently into th' well for a long time then cleared his throat.

"Net, thet man of yers has th' tongue of a serpent what eats more honey then's good fer im'. Now Almus," he said, not once lookin' at Pa, "if ye'll jest hold onto me knees I'll have meself a good look at thet thar rock."

He leaned into th' well confidently and Pa wrapped both arms around his legs then Charlie slid slowly downward grasping the rocks for support until he could hook his boots over th' top of the well.

One minute went by, two, not a word from Charlie; just grunts and groans and two dusty boots starin' us in th' face. One was scratched beyond tellin', little curls of leather stickin' up like new bean sprouts; a comical reminder of Charlie's wild ride through th' blackberry patch.

Pa looked at Grandma, rollin' his eyes heavenward and she smiled indulgently at Charlie's boots, knowin' Charlie wasn't a man to be rushed.

"Can ye see it?" Pa finally asked impatiently.

"Cain't hardly see a fool thing down here," Charlie gasped. "Let me down another six inches Almus, while I try ta turn around. Mebbe thet'll do it."

Pa hung on to Charlie's legs his pipe clenched tightly in his teeth, gruntin' under his breath as Charlie slid deeper into th' gloom to have a real close look at his special rock. His boots were no longer hooked over th' curb but were now anchored in Pa's arms as he dangled freely over th' water his only other support bein' his hands graspin' th' rocks linin' th' well.

I looked at Grandma whose face was concerned as she realized that Pa was supportin' nearly all Charlie's weight, head down in a darkening well.

Pa and Charlie weighed pretty near th' same but Charlie's twistin' and turnin' was strainin' Pa's strength and throwin' him off balance.

"Ain't ya seen that rock yet?" Pa yelled.

"I'm doin' th' best I can. It's hard ta see, what with it bein' so dark and all."

"I'm havin' a hard time holdin' on to ye Charlie, so get a move on or I'm haulin' ya up."

"For Pete's sake, Almus, hold yer horses."

"I ain't doin' this fer Pete's sake, Charlie; and I can tell you yer beginnin' ta weigh as much as any horse," Pa grated, tryin' to talk thru clenched teeth that was holdin' his beloved pipe. His face was purple with strain and from th' omnious sounds comin' from his throat I could tell he was close to losin' his temper.

"Bout that time Charlie started kickin' his feet and yellin', "Pull me up quick, Almus. I seed it, I seed it and ye ain't gonna believe what I'm gonna tell ye."

Charlie was laughin' and kickin' like a bull frog and Pa was hangin' on for dear life until one of Charlie's boots thrust upward and knocked Pa's pipe out of his mouth. For a second there was complete silence then we heard a thunk as th' pipe hit something solid then a heart-stoppin' splash.

Pa's tall frame became rigid as he stared hopelessly into the dark shadows of the well then raised his shocked face to Grandma.

"I've lost my pipe, Net, I've lost my pipe," he moaned miserably, his arms still locked around Charlie's boots.

Grandma said nothin', just stood there lookin' at Pa's distraught face, then she turned on her heel and ran toward the back porch. "Don't fret, Almus!" she said over her shoulder, takin' the steps two at a time.

It didn't take five seconds for all this to happen yet it felt like we'd been starin' down in that well for hours. I couldn't see anything past Charlie's knees which were now slidin' up and down in irritation but I could hear him splashin' frantically and reckoned in all the commotion Pa had let 'im slip under th' water.

"What in tarnation's goin' on up thar, Almus?" he sputtered. "Yer 'bout ta drown me down here."

The splashin' sounds became desperate with Charlie choakin' and splutterin, and yellin' for Pa to pull him up but Pa made not a move as he stared toward th' screen door that had just slammed shut on Grandma.

Down below it sounded like a ragein' river as Charlie splashed desperately to keep his head above water. He was now yellin' for Grandma at th' top of his lungs, which wasn't very loud considerin' how much water he was spittin' thru.

I tugged on Pa's shirt and pointed to his hands locked around Charlies boots which were now at least a foot lower in th' well which meant Charlie might this very minute be peerin' at that rock marker of his from under ten inches or more water; but Pa's eyes never left th' screen door nor did he appear to hear the angry, desperate sputterin' from below.

"Help me, Net," Charlie squalled, his voice tinged with panic. "Thet fool husband... o... of yers is tryin'...t... ta drown me. Consarn yer... o...nery hide Almus." he yelped, coughin' and choakin' between words. Iffen I git...

outta'... h...ere... I'll... nev...er speak... t...to ye agin... as l...long as I...l... live... and Nor...ey won't ne...ither."

'Bout that time Grandma burst thru th' screen door with a lighted lantern and a coil of rope.

When Pa seen Grandma he suddenly come alive, reached for th' lantern and dropped Charlie in the well. Ole Charlie didn't even have time to yell or maybe he was all yelled out cause all we heard was a splash, then silence as Grandma's white face turned on Pa accusingly.

"In th' name of Heaven, Almus," she thundered, furiously unrollin' the coil of rope into the well, "git that lantern down there so we can see Charlie. Mercy sakes alive," she worried. "If his head hit them rocks he's likely on th' botton by now."

Pa doubled his frame over the edge of th' well, th' lantern swingin' from one long arm, his eyes tryin' to pierce th' darkness.

Me and Grandma held our breath, listenin' for some sound from Charlie; but no sound could be heard, not even a small gurgle and I feared ole Charlie had gasped his last and was likely crumpled on th' bottom, his grungy old boots pollutin' th' sweetest water this side of Heaven.

I wondered sadly what Miss Norey would say when we told her Charlie had drowned in th' well; then there was ole Blue, his faithful coon hound who thought the sun rose and set in Charlie. Hadn't Charlie told us that a thousand times over, his hands restin' fondly on ole Blues head with Blue's eyes so sad I swore I could see tears about to spill down his face.

"This dog wud die without me," he'd tell us solemnly. "We're closer then brothers, me and ole Blue here and I reckon I couldn't hardly make it without him neither."

Pa would wink at Grandma and I'd wonder what Norey would say if she knew what Charlie said. Course no one would ever tell Norey how low on th' totem pole she was, with ole Blue perched right up there at th' top cuddled up in Charlie's arms.

Pa raised up, his face pale and worried and handed th' lantern to Grandma. "I'm goin' in after 'im Net. Charlie's a good swimmer and ought ta' 'uv come up by now."

Grandma was just reachin for th' lantern when a terrible splash come from th' well as ole Charlie broke th' surface, coughin' and wheezin, a string of angry, water logged threats to Pa sputterin' from his mouth.

Grandpa strained over th' edge swingin' th' lantern back and forth tryin' to see and about that time Grandma dropped the coil of rope which must have hit Charlie in th' face for the well suddenly exploded with a repotorie of cussin' so elequoent it bespoke long years of practice and from the stricken look on Grandma's face, I reckoned ole Charlie was now in a back-slidden state so perilous it would require years of scrubbin' on that prayer bench with his boney knees to redeem hisself; and I wasn't at all sure that even Grandma, who was a personal friend of the Lord's, might have a hope of talkin' th' Lord into givin' Charlie another chance.

Course right now nobody was worryin' bout renewin' Charlie's ticket to heaven. He had to be rescued first.

Pa leaned over th' curb and spoke to Charlie. I'm gonna let th' water bucket down, Charlie. Do ye think ye can hang onto it?

A weak, angry reply come up out of th' darkness. "Wal now Almus, what's me other choice? Stay down here and turn into a bloomin' frog?"

Pa ignored th' irritation comin' from below as he tied an extra knot in th' rope above th' bucket to hold Charlie's weight.

"What in tarnation aire ye doin' up thar Almus, havin' a smoke while yer best friend turns ta a prune down here."

"Wal now Charlie, I might just have me a little smoke if I still had a pipe," Pa spat, "but my so called best friend who I always thought had half a grain of common sense, comes over here and climbs into my well, asks me to hang onto his onery carcus with his number fifteen boots in my face while he checks th' water level of my well. Then he starts havin' a canipution over somethin' or other, laughin' and kickin', and one of them number fifteen boots knocks my pipe outta my mouth and now its at th' bottom of th' well and if I hear any more smart aleck remarks outta him, thats where he's gonna be...AGAIN!"

Pa waited a minute to let Charlie think on the threat then he spoke quietly. "Now I'm lettin' this bucket down on th' left side of th' well Charlie and if ye get knocked on yer head then it's no skin off'a me."

A weak voice drifted upward. "Consarn it Almus, thar ain't no left nor right down here in all this dark so iffen ye'd kindly scrape thet bucket along th' sides so's I can tell whar it is I'd be obliged ta ye. As fer yer pipe...wal I'm purely sorry 'bout thet, knowin' how much ye prize it and all... but I'll get ye another one jest as soon as I can get ta Burnside."

"Pa's face went purple with rage.

"There ain't another pipe in th' whole world that can replace that pipe Charlie, specially not in a one horse town like New Burnside. Ye know very well that that pipe belonged to my Grandaddy, whittled out by his own hand from the finest briar England had to offer. Sides... I reckon that pipe means nearly as much ta me as ole Streator."

Charlie's voice come up outta th' dark, low and mournful. "Don't ye think I knowed thet Almus? Thets why I'm goin' back down thar to find it."

Pa yelled but Charlie was already on his way back down to th' bottom of th' well. We held our breath waitin' for what seemed like hours with not even a ripple to be heard. Grandma's lips were movin' and I knew she was prayin' for ole Charlie. Pa's face was white with worry and I knew he was feelin' mighty sorry 'bout losin' his temper with Charlie even if it was over an important, sentimental, priceless heirloom like his Grandaddy's pipe.

Th' only sound to be heard was ole Streators toe nails scrappin' on th' rock curb as he moved nervously 'round Pa's legs. Then we heard coughin' and splutterin' as Charlie broke th' surface and th' relief on Pa's and Grandma's face was somethin' wonderful.

"Almus!" he called up weakly. "I couldn't find hide nor hair of it and I tried 'till I didn't have anuther breath left... I'm not a very good friend I reckon.

"Nonsense Charlie! Yer th' best friend any man ever had. Now grab that bucket and git yerself up here before we die from worry."

Pa pulled th' bucket up with Charlie hangin' on fer dear life and lifted him out of th' well.

He was wetter than a drowned rat, his skin wrinkled and purple with th' cold.

Pa helped him into th' house for dry clothes while I stirred up th' fire and Grandma put on a fresh pot of coffee. In spite of th' heat we all set around th' supper table, Charlie drinkin' th' hot coffee thru chatterin' teeth, Pa' and Grandma sayin' nothin', waitin' for Charlie to warm up so they could ask him some questions.

Charlie noisily slurped th' hot coffee his hands wrapped tightly around th' big white mug. He was dressed in a flannel shirt and overalls, plus Pa's favorite winter sweater that always hung from its peg on th' closet door. In fact it was his only sweater, what with them bein' so dear and all.

Me and Grandma had picked that sweater out of th' Sears Roebuck catalog one year for Pa's christmas present, dreamin' over it for hours at a time, gigglin' over how surprised he'd be with Grandma declarin' it would look ten times more handsome on Pa than th' model wearin' it.

Then we made many trips up th' railroad tracks to Creal Springs with a basket of fresh eggs which Grandma sold to Mc Neals grocery. I'd walk th' rails, white hot in th' sun, their silvery strands miraging into shimmerin' lakes of sparklin' water that always stayed th' same distance ahead of me no matter how fast I ran.

Mr. Mc Neal paid her six cents a dozen for th' eggs and I'd watch her tie the money into th' corner of her handkerchief then press it carefully into th' bottom of her dress pocket. To fortify ourselves for th' long trip back down th' railroad tracks we'd splurge on a bottle of orange pop and a sausage patty between two biscuit halves that Grandma saved from breakfast.

That night when Pa was out checkin' on th' animals me and her would set at th' kitchen table and add up th' egg money and feast our eyes on that sweater.

Genuine lamb's wool, hand made in England- th caption said- for th' Gentleman who demands quality workmanship. It had a large elegant collar and its thick cable stitched length come down over the male models hips, who stood in front of a cozy rose covered cottage with his hand on th' gate of a white picket fence and he was so tall and handsome I fell in love with him.

The price for this treasure was one dollar and ninety-eight cents, a sum that cost me and Grandma many anxious moments. We'd count our egg money and subtract it from th' cost of th' sweater and little by little we came closer to our goal.

That sweater was Pa's pride and joy, as he so often said, his eyes on Grandma's face.

"Why, I cain't get over you two savin' all that money for this sweater," he'd exclaim, huggin' me close to his chest.

It's rich forest green color brought out th' sparkle in Pa's blue eyes and set off his brown hair and deep tan to perfection. That he let Charlie wear it was a measure of his affection for his old friend.

"Wal, now Charlie," Pa said, "what took ye so long ta come up when I first dropped ye in th' well?"

Charlie shook his head in disbelief. "I never was so surprised in me whole life, Almus, when ye dropped me like thet. 'Fore I knowed it I wuz half way ta th' bottom, choakin' and tryin' ta git me wits 'bout me.

Do ye know how deep thet well is, Almus? he asked incredulously. "And cold!" He shivered at th' thought of it. "I ain't never been this cold in me whole life and I can tell ye I thought I wuz a gonner when I got me feet tangled up in thet rope down thar. Fer a minute I thought th' grandaddy of all snakes had me and I reckon what with th' quart of water I swallowed when ye dropped me and th' quart when thet snake had me, I musta downed a half gallon of th' sweetest water this side of Heaven; and thet's what took me so long ta come up."

"What rope?" Pa exclaimed settin' up straight in his chair.

"Thet rope hangin' down there," Charlie replied impatiently.

"After I got me feet untangled I discovered it was rigid when I pulled on it so I climbed it all th' way back ta th' top. Durn thing nearly drowned me; on tother hand it helped me git back ta th' top too. I was so stiff with th' cold, reckon I might not have made it otherwise."

Without a word, Pa suddenly sprang outta his chair, thru' th' screen door and down th' steps to th' well with me and Grandma right behind him and Charlie's voice yellin' in surprise as he brought up th' rear.

Pa was fumblin' with a rope tied to th' two by four that supported th' pulley then he started easin' th' rope slowly upward like it was a stick of dynamite ready ta go off. He was hardly breathin' as he stared into th' dark well.

"Why, thats my buttermilk rope, Almus." exclaimed Grandma.

"Exactly" Pa whispered, his breath comin' in short excited gasps. "Got me an idee Net. Its a wild chance, a hope really but if I'm right... this day will have a happy ending. Lord, what a story that would make," he laughed softly.

"Charlie, if what I'm prayin' for comes ta pass, yer name'll be famous from Chicago to Memphis."

"Tennessee?" Charlie asked.

"Th' very same," laughed Pa, "and unless I miss my guess we're gettin' close ta findin' out."

The moon had risen in th' sky just above th well and as we all peered anxiously downward, its pale light glowed soft and silvery on somethin' just beneath th' waters surface, its paleness clingin' gently to th' wet rope in a soft blur of light.

Th' end of th' rope rose drippin' above th' water, knotted firmly around th' handle of th' steel cooler containin' Grandma's famous buttermilk and layin' smack dab right in th' middle of th' recessed lid was Pa's beloved pipe, its rich surface gleamin' dully in th' moonlight.

Pa's baritone whoops of joy pierced th' darkness in reverberating waves, echoin' through the woods like eratic gunfire and ole Streator bayed joyously as he sprinted around th' yard, his nose to th' ground for scent.

Charlie stared at th' pipe in amazement.

"No wonder I couldn't find it on th' bottom. It wuz right thar safe and sound on Net's buttermilk all th' time. Thank th' Lord," he breathed, his face wreathed in smiles as he looked at Pa.

Pa lifted th' bucket to th' curb, and reached for th' pipe, holdin' it in his hand like it would disappear any minute. Then he set down on th' stone bench and buried his head in his hands.

Charlie laid a boney arm around his shoulder while ole Streator wriggled and squirmed his way between Pa's legs with his fine head up against Pa's face.

Grandma untied th' knot on th' handle of th' buttermilk pail, picked it up and walked toward th' patch of light spillin' from th' kitchen onto th' back porch.

I followed her and just before th' screen door closed I looked back toward th' well. Pa and Charlie hadn't moved. Two old friends illumined by th' moonlight.

Early the next mornin' Charlie rode Sampson into th' yard yellin' at th' top of his lungs. He slid off Sampson, looped the reins carelessly over Grandmas Lilac bush then sprinted for th' back door where Pa waited, a puzzled look on his face.

"Reckon nobody's dead, else ye wouldn't be so happy," Pa said, holdin th' door open for Charlie. He pulled a chair out for him then propped his own back against th' wall on two legs where he'd been sippin' Grandmas good coffee while she cooked breakfast.

Grandma poured out a cup of coffee and set it before Charlie then set down beside Pa and waited for him to speak.

Charlie drank half th' cup, his eyes closed in pleasure, then sighed happily as he looked impishly from Pa to Grandma, clearly savoring some secret.

'Course I was fit ta be tied and squirmed impatiently but Charlie seemed determined to squeeze ever ounce of suspense from th' moment and refused to be hurried. He finished his coffee, wiped his mouth with th' back of his hand then smiled happily.

"Almus, in all th' excitement last night I clean forgot what got me so excited in th' first place before I knocked yer pipe outta yer mouth. I went home ta bed and slept like a baby 'till four this mornin' when I set straight up in bed like a bolt of lightenin' had struck me and thar it wuz before me eyes plain as day, so wonderful and unreal I scarsely believed I wasn't dreamin' th' whole thing. I'm still afraid I might be dreamin' and I want ta tell ya what I seed before we check it out so thet you and Net can share th' miraculous joy I felt down thar in thet well yesterday."

He shook his head in disbelief. "I still cain't figure out how I could'a fergot sech a thing."

Pa was on th' edge of his chair and Grandma's eyes burned like lights was in them and I thought I'd die if Charlie didn't quit stallin' and git on with it.

"Ye member when I couldn't find thet rock and wuz turnin' ever which way tryin' ta see in all thet dark? Well, jest afore I started kickin' and knocked yer pipe outta yer mouth I looked down and it wuz like th' Lord wuz shinin' a light on them rocks and special on thet rock fer thar it wuz not even with th water line, but ten inches below th' water line."

"Know what thet means, Almus?"

We stared at Charlie dumfounded, afraid our ears had heard wrong; but there it was plain as day, wonderful beyond countin'.

Th' room seemed filled with an invisible light we couldn't see but which filled our hearts with an incredible joy.

"Praise th' name of Jesus," whispered Grandma.

Pa just stared at Charlie with such a look of wonder on his face I ran round th' table and threw myself in his arms. He hugged me to him then slowly got to his feet and moved through th' back door, across th' porch and down th' steps toward th' well.

We all followed silently, our thoughts whirlin' like leaves in th' wind.

Charlie watched Pa's face as he stared down into th' well, anxious and afraid that what he'd seen yesterday might not be there today. He felt he couldn't bear it if they didn't see how th' water had risen above his rock and maybe it'ud gone down

durin' th' night and he was so scared he couldn't breathe cause th' hand of doubt wuz squeezin' th' life from his heart. He prayed a silent prayer, forgettin' his fall from grace th' day before, with nary a thought fer th' well roof overhead which might be covered with th' fly specks of his unheard, unworthy prayers.

"I'm goin down there Charlie," Pa whispered, "to see fer myself." Charlie nodded and Pa swung over th' side and grasped the buttermilk rope which hung from it's anchor at th' top of th' well. He let himself down slowly, scannin' th' rocks then he fastened his gaze on one spot leanin' closer and closer 'till his face was in th' water.

We watched his head slide lower and lower into th' water then it stopped as he studied th' rocks. After what seemed an hour he rose slowly, his face shinin' like th' sun, his eyes fastened on Grandma face.

"Net, I don't rightly understand this but that water is now at least fifteen inches above that rock which means it's come up another five inches since last night."

Charlie sucked in his breath; but Grandma was as calm as could be.

"The lord says in Malachi, 'Bring ye all the tithes into the storehouse, that there may be meat in mine house, and prove me now herewith, saith the Lord of hosts, if I will not open you the windows of heaven, and pour you out a blessing, that there shall not be room enough to receive it."

You've shared our water with all who need it and there seems to be no end to how many are in need, so th' Lord is not only supplyin' th' need but runnin' it over. Maybe ye best start diggin' another well, Almus," she grinned.

Th' well continued to fill until it reached ground level and there it held no matter how many barrels were taken each day.

News of th' well spread and folks started comin' just to see th' well and drink its sweet water and Pa and Grandma would set on th' curb and visit with friend and stranger alike. Pa would tell them th' story of Charlie and th' well and everday there'd be a yard full of people come ta see th' well and hear Pa's stories.

Charlie became famous in them parts with everbody slappin' im' on th' back and buyin' 'im a soft drink ever time he went to Burnside and so many hands patted ole Blue on th' head, got so he'd duck under a bench to escape.

Wish I could say th' drought ended shortly after that but it didn't and while th' well furnished water for cattle and people, its level stayin even with th' top, there wasn't any equipment back then like we have today to irrigate crops.

Grandma carried water to her garden and filled tin cans she'd buried here and there among th' plants. The water would drip slowly thru nail holes in th' bottom of the cans and gradually her garden began to turn green again.

The neighbors soon noticed and followed suit, strainin' th' wells resources and Charlie's nerves to th' breakin' point; but th' well never sank one inch below ground level.

Each day grew hotter, tempers flared and th' kitchen literally became an oven when Grandma cooked. She tried to cook enough before sunup to last th' day but there was coffee to be made at night and dishes to wash and th' smallest fire in th' range heated th' house to intolerable limits.

I took ta sleepin out on th' back porch on a pallet and Grandma and Pa finally joined me cause they said it was easier than gettin' up ever hour ta check on me.

Ole Streator thought it was th' grandest arrangement he'd ever seen, havin' his family all around him at night; but he soon became a nuisance as he patrolled from one pallet to th' next, his long tongue slurpin' our sleepin' faces with indiscriminate joy.

One monday evenin' Grandma was cookin' supper while Pa leaned his chair against th' wall watchin' her as usual.

We'd washed clothes all that mornin', hangin' 'em on th' line under a relentless sun, then we'd cooked lunch for Pa and two neighbors who'd come to help Pa with somethin' or other. We'd hardly stopped for a minute all day and I could tell Grandma was dogtired and in a bad mood.

"Ought to'uv married myself a millionaire," she grumbled, forkin' pork chops from her favorite iron skillet onto a platter, "then I'd be settin' in a cool parlor somewhere readin' one of them Gody fashion magazines while somebody else done th' cookin', instead of me meltin' in this infernal hot kitchen ever day."

Never in his life had Pa heard such a statement from Grandma and he rubbed his ear in confusion, starin' in shocked disbelief at her.

"Why, Net I never heard you say such a thing in our whole life together."

"Wal, now Almus," she sniffed, "I don't reckon its been this hot before either. Right now I'd trade old streeter for twenty-five pounds of ice and thats a fact.

Streeter's face wore an expression of astonishment as he tried to shrink into the linoleum and Pa's mouth dropped open, his pipe hangin' from one lip like a fallen tree. He reached down and laid his hand on Streeter's head all the while regardin' Grandma with a serious look on his face.

"Are ye ailin', Net?" he asked hopefully.

"Jest tired, Almus and weary of this hot spell thats tryin' to kill my garden and everthing else thats livin'. She walked over to the screen door and looked out for a long minute with me and Pa watchin' her anxiously.

"Look at that sky. Not a cloud for a week now, jest a blazin' sun burnin' the land to a cinder." She sighed. "Maybe the whole earth for all we know.

Got a letter from Bess today and its the same up Chicago way. She says there's some really big farms around that area and they're hurtin' as bad as we are."

She turned back to the kitchen and started puttin' food on the table. " In all my years I've never before seen a sky that kind of pale, like its dead and cracked and ready to fall in pieces to the dyin' earth. Ain't natural," she murmured to herself.

She turned to Pa and me, her face shadowed in sadness. "I think we ought to call a special prayer meetin' Almus and ask the good Lord's forgiveness for our trespasses and his mercy on us in our time of need. Seems ta me all I feel like doin' lately is complain and grumble 'bout how hot and miserable I am."

Her mouth set in that determined way we all knew so well.

"Well, no more!" she declared. "Thats just what Satan wants me to do; wants all of us ta do fer that matter and I don't aim ta fall for his connivin' ways a minute longer.

"Lord," she said apologetically, "I thank You for all th' blessin's You've bestowed on this family and I praise Your Holy Name. Amen."

She then addressed th' forked tail monster. "I rebuke you satan in th' name of our precious Saviour, th' Lord Jesus Christ and I don't want ta hear any of yer sly evil whisperins' 'round here from this day on."

Pa was so upset by her mood he was ready to try anything that would make Grandma feel better and when he heard her little prayer to th' Lord and her rebuke to th' devil, his face lit up somethin' wonderful.

"Now, thats a good idee Net. Sometimes we think goin' to church Sunday and Wednesday nite is enough; like a habit we get into without feelin' the real meanin' of worship. We need to dust off the cobwebs and keep our faith fresh and new and I know that sometimes I'm settin' there thinkin' on my crops when the preachers talkin' or my mouth's waterin' over the thought of your chicken and dumplins' waitin' on the back of the stove. Yep. A mighty fine idee, Net and I don't see why we can't start tomorrow night. I'll ride Dimple out tonight and spread the word."

"Grandma set the last dish on the table and we all held hands as Pa bowed his head for Prayer. When the prayer was finished she reached out her hand and laid it affectionately on Streeter's head.

We all breathed a sigh of relief, 'specially Streeter, his long tongue swipin' the side of Grandma's hand as she drew it back into her lap.

Pa smiled and reached fer the platter of pork chops.

The next evenin' our yard was full of friends and neighbors, all come to praise th' Lord, though I heard one or two sayin' there wasn't much to praise Him for seein' as how their crops were done for.

Endless buckets of th' sweetest water this side of heaven was consumed by th' thirsty and it took several men to keep th' water troughs filled for th' good animals that had carried folks from near and far on this hot night.

They settled on pallets around th' yard, some leanin' against th trees, the older ones settin' on our kitchen chairs. Grandma had tenderly helped old Mrs. Knickerbocker into her favorite rockin' chair and placed her very favorite fan emblazoned with th' words 'Jesus saves' into that grateful lady's frail hand.

Th' sun was just before goin' down, restin' on top of th' trees like a giant ball of fire, it's radience fillin' th western sky and softly illuminin' th' faces gathered together in our yard to beseech th' Lords mercy in our time of need.

Pa stood, his face toward th' dying sun whose beauty held us breathless with wonder while our hearts beat in dread for th' morrow when that same sun would rise with a white searing fire to again burn th' earth in relentless fury.

"Oh Lord," Pa whispered softly, "as I look on your magnificent creation, I tremble with th' joy and privilege you've given yer children here on earth to worship yer Holy Name. Some of us come here tonight because we're afraid and anxious and, yes, even angry with You cause we don't understand why this terrible time has fallen on us.

Our spirits are low, our faith is weak and pale, like th' merciless sun that beats down day after day on th' fields of our labor.

Our hearts cry out in anguish in th' still hours of th' nite.

We bow our heads in prayer and we search th' good book for verses of comfort and implore th' preacher to pray to You seekin' Yer mercy in our behalf.

Our tempers are short in this terrible heat, our human frailities pitifully evident. I'm sure that many of us Lord pray fervently for rain and when th' cloud burst fails to come down we look at th' sky doubtfully and ask why You have failed to answer our prayers.

We spend much time tellin' each other how bad times are; and they are Lord as Ye already know for th' good Book tells us You know when even a sparrow falls from th' heavens to th' earth."

Every eye was closed, their faces rapt as they hung on Pa's words, some shakin' their head in agreement, others hunched and still with tightly clasped hands.

The knarled, arthritic hands of grandparents lay tenderly on sleepin' children; sunburned, calloused hands of weary husbands and fathers clasped the hands of their wives in unity of spirit and resolve, while others held their Bibles to their heart like shields against evil.

Ole Streator lay at Pa's feet, his head restin' on a dusty boot as his friendly eyes moved from one familiar face to another.

I looked at Pa and Grandma and said my own prayer of thanksgivin' to th' Lord for blessin' me with their love.

Pa studied th' trees, their dust covered leaves silent in th' still air, some of them curlin' and turnin' brown at th' tips, then his eyes moved downward and traced th' faces of th' good friends and neighbors settin' here and there on th' dead grass of our yard. Finally he turned his face back to th' red globe silhouetted in lacey splendor behind th' proud oaks across th' valley on Logans hill. As the sun slid close to the horizon the earth seemed to tilt upward, th' mighty oaks slicin' thru th' molten mass and I imagined all th' fiery red pieces that was killin' our State might fall on th' other side of th' world in some cold ocean and be dead forever.

"Last night I got on my knees," Pa continued, "and talked to th' Lord just as I would talk to any of you. Poured out all my worries and complaints and argued our case in a manner I thought was respectful and, I confess, even pious."

There were smiles and a few titters from Pa's listeners.

"I don't know how long I rambled on, foolishly thinkin' I was gettin' somewhere; but suddenly my mind was filled with th' Holy Spirit.... and remorse and shame filled my very soul as I realized I was impertinantly addressin' th' creator and master of th' Universe whose ways and thoughts are beyond even th' slightest comprehension of our puny ability to understand.

This wonderful Being, our Father, who loved us so much that He gave His only begotten son to take our sins upon Himself and die on th' cross that we might be cleansed and saved and taken to heaven when we die, placed such a burden of conviction and sorrow and revelation on my heart, I cried out -as th' Bible says- in fear and trembling.

I fell on my face and begged His forgiveness and worshiped th' mighty omnipotence of Him in whom we live and move and have our being and my heart was filled with th' knowledge of how blessed we are to worship and love and obey th' commandments He has given to guide and govern our lives here on earth until He calls us home.

Helen Harper

I wish I could say I heard Him speak in a human voice but I didn't; but th' still small voice He places in our hearts is as loud as any we hear down here. As I listened I realized we have been placin' blame on th' Lord for our troubles, askin' Him to take this burden from us, and there's nothin' wrong with that, but we ask amiss.

I believe th' busy hands of Satan are behind this attitude of blame and doubt and frustration we're goin' through and I say this fer myself ever bit as much as I say it fer you for I've scolded th' Lord as much, or maybe more than anybody here."

I was holdin' my breath in wonder at Pa's words and my heart felt like it would bust with love for him as he again lifted his face to th' heavens. There were tears in his eyes and his mellow baritone lifted our hearts as he poured out his love and praise to th' God of us all.

"Dear Lord, I praise yer Holy name and I ask, we ask yer forgiveness for our petty grumblin' and lack of confidence in yer promise to care fer us.

You have told us you would put no more on us than we could bear; You have blessed us all our lives, yet we cry out and struggle against adversity instead of usin' it to strengthen our faith and make us stronger.

I want us to remember our blessings tonight and praise Yer Holy name fer each one and I'll start it off by thankin' Ye for th' wonderful well of sweet water that never runs dry no matter how much is taken from it. When we put out th' word to one and all to take as much water as they needed, Ye blessed th' well and filled it right to th' top of th' curb and its never gone one inch below that level in all these weeks of drought, no matter how many people come to fill their barrels. I thank Ye Lord and I'll be careful to give Ye th' praise and glory due Yer holy name. Amen."

Murmurs of agreement and gratitude rose from th' group with several amens here and there then Pa waited for someone else to speak.

"Well, Lord," Charlie said, hesitant and shy, "I reckon I got lots of things ta be grateful fer. First off, I got a little bit more'n usual left over from last year which will help me and Norey thru th' winter iffen this drought keeps up and I want ta say thet we'll share with them folks not so lucky as long as theres a sack of grain left. We got aire health, good friends, enuff ta eat... and I reckon a body don't need much more'n thet. I'm goin' ta do less fussin', Lord, and more praisin'... Amen."

Mrs Denton, th' prize gossip carrier of th' community, who is known fer her devoted use of th' prayen' bench, shifted her bulk which hung off each side of one of Grandma's kitchen chairs and fixed her eyes on ole Streetor. He squirmed uneasily and pressed closer to pa's leg.

"I aim ta be a better Christian, Lord and maybe mind what Ezra calls a loose lip and read th' word more. I thank Ye fer yer patience with me all these years and I guess thats all fer now. Amen."

It's a good thing she was lookin' at ole Streetor as there was hardly a face that didn't have a big smile on it, 'cept Charlie, whose eyes were rolled heavenward as though ta see th' Lord's reaction ta such a startling proclamation.

Then Mrs. Knickerbocker closed her eyes, a sweet smile on her gentle face and spoke softly.

"Dear Lord, I've served Ye all my life and never have Ye allowed me ta be in real want. What I needed was always provided. Frills and unnecessary wants were often denied and as I look back from my eighty years, yer wisdom was th' best fer my life fer some of th' things I wanted would have brought me grief in th' long run."

"My Hiram and me raised our children on Yer word and they've all turned out tollabal well, one of 'im is even preachin' Yer word. I praise Yer Holy name and I trust Yer plan fer our lives fer theres no one knows better what we need than You. We're in a drought right now and things seem bad but th' drought is on th' land, not in our hearts and as long as we draw close to You nothin evil can befall us."

"Lord, we rebuke th' devil and his evil intent to us, in th' precious name of Yer Holy Son and His loving sacrifice fer us sinners that we may be washed clean of our sins and live forever with You in Heaven. I trust Yer mercy, Lord, to bless these dear neighbors and friends. Amen."

After Mrs Knickerbocker's prayer a comfortable silence spread a warm, sootheing mantle over th' little group and I could almost feel th' spirit of hope touchin' each person as th' essence of what prayer was really all about began to fill their hearts. They were beginnin' to rise above th' despair and anxiety that had taken control of their lives because of th' drought. In all their misery they'd somehow lost sight of God's promise to them, creating a drought of th' soul far worse than what th' land was sufferin'.

Pa had seen it last night when th' Holy Spirit filled his heart with remorse and shame and reminded him of th' great gift he'd been given when God allowed His only begotten son to be sacrificed on th' cross that we might be cleansed of our sins and live with th' Lord in heaven forever and ever.

Grandma had seen it yesterday when she told Pa we ought to call a special prayer meetin' and ask th' good Lord's forgiveness for our trespasses and his mercy on us in our time of need.

Mrs Denton had seen it a little when she promised to maybe mind her loose lip and read th' word more.

Ole Charlie seen it with his desire to share his and Norey's food with those less fortunate.

I had th' strangest feelin' of bein' in another world, peekin' thru a crack in th' Universe at this gatherin' of special, humble, God fearin' folk who asked no more of life than to till th' land and harvest their crops and raise their children to serve th' Lord and carry on that tradition as had countless generations before them.

Then John Burton slowly pulled himself up off th' ground and leaned his back against a tree so he could favor th' club foot he'd been born with. His face was etched with years of pain and hardship but th' kindness and gentle nature for which he was known was all folks seen and th' club foot had long since become almost invisible to those who knew and respected John Burton.

Pa and Grandma had known John ever since him and his wife Sarah had stopped by our farm one hot mornin' in July to ask directions to th' little farm he'd bought, sight unseen, from th' widow Johnson who lived a mile or so off th' main road. There was only a path to her farm now since th' crude road Mr Johnson had hacked out was long since grown over with bushes too big to run over.

Pa and Grandma had insisted the Burtons take a rest and Grandma wouldn't even listen to th' reasons they give for not havin' lunch with us bein' it was already on th' table and all.

Pa led John's horses to th' waterin' trough, took th' bridle and bits from their mouth and after they'd drunk their fill he threw down hay and filled th' grain trough. They buried their heads in th' grain, munchin' hungrily while Mr. Burton looked on in astonishment. Pa waved aside his protests, threw one arm around his shoulder and said, "We'd best get to lunch in a hurry John, cause Net has a thing 'bout food she's labored over gettin' cold." Pa's boomin' baritone laugh drowned out anything Mr. Burton might have said as he welcomed John and Sarah Burton to our home and to th' community.

The Johnson farm they'd bought sight unseen, needed extensive repairs, specially th' house, so th' Burton's had stayed on with us for a week while Pa and John cleared a road and repaired th' house and barn.

Grandma and Sarah had cleaned th' little house until it squeaked and on movin' day we followed their wagon down th' newly cleared road, unloaded their belongin's and helped them set everythin' in place.

Grandma had brought a picnic basket of fried chicken and all th' trimmin's and we crowded 'round their kitchen table with prayers of thanksgivin' and celebrated their new home and dedicated ever nail and board of it to th' Lord.

After we'd eaten Grandma's chicken, Sarah and John stood up, their hands linked and with tears in their eyes prayed a wonderful prayer of thanksgivin' to th' Lord for their new home and for friends like Pa and Grandma and little sprout as they called me.

Now, years later, here in our yard full of burned out grass from a drought that was killin' everthing' in th' state, I looked at Sarah Burton, small and erect, settin' beside Grandma on one of our kitchen chairs, then at th' weathered face and stooped shoulders of John Burton standin' humbly before our Lord, and my heart was filled with love for this man and woman who was as much family to us as any of our blood kin.

Mr. Burton's eyes rested fondly on Pa's and Grandma's face for a moment, then he raised his face to th' heavens.

"Dear Lord: I don't even know where to begin with all th' blessin's Ye've given me and Sarah. The day we come here, hot and tired and scared about th' farm we'd sunk our life savin's in, a farm we'd never seen, was a big step fer us and one we took only after askin' Yer guidance and feelin' Yer peace settle on us."

"I'll never forget pullin' into th' Hundley farm here fer directions and findin' two of th' best friends any man could have and I thank Ye Lord fer them, cause I know Ye put them in our path to help us in our new home and to bless us with their friendship over these many years."

"We love this community and the dear people we call friends and now we look to You in our time of need Lord for You are th' giver of all good things and me and Sarah been prayin' like everbody else that this drought would end and our crops be saved; but last night after Almus rode over and told us about th' meetin' here tonight and how Net thought we ought to ask Yer forgiveness fer our trepasses, we got to thinkin' on it in a different way."

"Sarah said to me, John, th' Bible tells us we are th' salt of th' earth, but if th' salt loses its savor, its no good anymore."

"Maybe we've lost our savor, Lord."

"Everbody's talkin' about th' drought and thats understandable cause we're all facin' hard times if it keeps up; but peers ta me like Net's right and we're doin' more whinin' than praisin' these days and I expect Yer about fed up with hearin' about it all th' time, Lord. So, from now on I'm not goin' ta say a word about this drought, or how hot it is and I'm not gonna walk up and down th' rows of my garden and worry over th' looks of everthing neither."

"I'm gonna walk up and down ever single row of Sarah's scraggley plants praisin' Ye Lord and thankin' Ye fer all th' blessins' we got right now and trustin' You ta see us thru this comin' winter."

Everbody smiled over Sarah's scraggley plants.

"I reckon that speaks for th' both of us Lord and I thank Ye for all th' years Y've blessed us and I thank Ye for th' greatest gift of all: The gift of salvation, bought and paid fer by th' precious blood of Yer son th' Lord Jesus Christ, on th' cross of Calvary. Amen "

Mr. Burton eased himself back down th' trunk of th' tree he'd been settin' under and th' only sound to be heard was th' soft scrape of his overalls against th' bark.

Many others prayed that night and at th' end Pa began to sing Amazing Grace-my favorite song- and it was decided to continue th' meetings and everbody had a long drink of th' sweetest water this side of heaven before they started home.

Th' night was filled with Amens, and goodbyes and th' thunk, scrape, jingle and squeak of harness and th' coarse swishin' tails of impatient animals eager to get home, snortin' and prancin' as th'wagons creaked and groaned behind them on their way down th' long hill into th' night, their lighted lanterns bobbin' behind each other like a long line of fireflies.

As word spread about th' prayer meetin', people began to come from beyond our community to praise th' Lord and turn their worries over to Him.

Helen Harper

Pa made it clear to all newcomers that we weren't there to complain and grumble about th' drought; but to praise and worship th' Lord Jesus Christ and express our gratitude to Him for His love and care for all His children.

They began to come early, bringin' pies and cakes and fried chicken and loaves of home made bread and we'd set on th' ground and eat and fellowship with one another.

The children would bolt their food so they could play before it got dark, then Pa would beat on a pie tin with his fork to get everbody's attention and when they were settled on palets and th' kids were quiet; he'd open th' meetin' with a prayer.

It was a magic time for th' children and for all of us and th' wonderful old hymns soared out into th' night on spiritual wings of praise to a risen saviour.

As th' meetin's progressed, there was a new spirit among th' people as prayers of thanksgivin' were heard.

Some began to give testimonies of healin' which held everbody spellbound. There were spirited discussions as th' Bible was studied to back up this claim and that, and th' shadows of doubt and worry that had lingered here and there when we first started, began to fade away with each prayer.

Th' sweetest water this side of heaven was in even greater demand as more and more people came every night. Th' numbers also increased during th' day as word of th' well spread but th' level remained constant much to everyone's surprise.

Grandma would shake her head in dismay at th' doubtin' Thomas's who would come and stare into th' well in disbelief and Pa would smile tolerantly and go on puffin' his pipe and dear ole Charlie drank numerous dippers of water so he could keep an eye on th' well without bein' too obvious.

Pa and several neighbors laid boards across saw horses for a makeshift table for th' ladies to put their food on and it was like a family reunion ever nite. Friendships were strengthened and new friends were made and nary a word was said about th' drought.

Come Sunday everbody moved from our yard down to th' bush arbor church and th' circuit preacher was amazed and delighted to see so many newcomers. He preached with new enthusiasm and at th' end of th' sermon he started prayin' about th' drought and how bad it was and how th' people were sufferin' and he implored th' Lord to end it with a big rain.

The congregation began to stir restlessly and finally old Mr. Jent, a devout Christian stood up and said, "Beggin' yer pardon, preacher: We appreciate yer prayin' in our behalf and all and I reckon ye don't rightly know what's been goin' on in our community but we ain't botherin' th' Lord anymore 'bout this here drought cause we know thats what th' devil wants us ta do.

We're trustin' Jesus ta care fer us cause he's took care of us all our lives and we decided thet from now on there'll be only praise and thanksgivin' and no complainin' and whinin'." The preacher's head jerked up in surprise and there was just a mite of irritation in his eyes, and who could blame him 'cause it's not respectful to talk in Gods house with the preacher prayin'; but th' preacher seen only an old man, battered hat in hand, standin' respectful in th' house of God askin' that we praise Him instead of complainin' to Him.

The preacher studied Mr. Jent for a second, puzzled and uncertain, his eyes scannin' th' congregation.

"Has something been going on here that I ought to know about?" he asked, lookin' directly at Pa.

Pa explained th' past week and a half, how th' well never goes down no matter how much water is taken from it and how Grandma felt we ought to stop complainin' and trust th' Lord and ask forgiveness for our trespasses.

"Well one prayer led to another preacher and be fore long we were praisin' and givin' thanks instead of whinnin and askin' fer th' drought to go away. Couldn't none of us remember a time when he hadn't provided fer us one way or other and th' more we praised, th' happier we was and th' greater our fellowship and trust grew until...well, no one even thinks of th' drought any more, cept maybe a few hardened sinners here and there," Pa grinned.

"I see," the preacher murmured more to himself than to th' church. He stood still, lookin' down at his Bible so long some folks got restless and looked from th' preacher to Pa fer some direction; but Pa didn't seem bothered and waited respectful fer th' preacher to reach some conclusion.

Finally he looked out over th' large group packed together under th' small bush arbor, a slight smile on his face.

"I'm a circuit riding preacher, as you all know, and I go where I'm needed th' most. I've preached in everything from a barn to this bush arbor and out in th' middle of an apple orchard with a couple of bushel baskets for a pulpit, so I don't see too many things that are surprising; but I believe today will surpass anything I'll ever see.

I looked at your crops as I rode in, or I should say your lack of crops and began devising prayers then and there to the Lord in your behalf. Now I know you don't need my prayers for I seem to be on a different road than that which you're traveling and I don't mind saying it feels rather lonely down here in th' dumps and if you don't mind I'd like to come up and join you."

They clapped and clapped and laughed and welcomed th' preacher to the unusual manner of worship we were enjoyin' and invited him to come to our farm that night and hold th' service there instead of th' arbor.

He seemed delighted; 'specially when he found out about all that fried chicken, corn on th' cob and home made bread, pie and cake that was bein' served by th' good ladies of th' community.

That night when Grandma seen how much fried chicken and all th' trimmins that preacher put away, she allowed as how she'd never knowed God to call a man to preach who didn't have two hollow legs. 'Course th' preacher had drunk dipper after dipper of th' sweetest water this side of heaven and declared he'd never had anything like it before.

Helen Harper

Pa called th' meetin' to order and started to turn it over to th' preacher but th' preacher said he'd like to attend th' service rather than preach it. Pa stood up once more and raised his face to th' Lord in prayer.

"Dear Jesus we come before You on this blessed sabbath night and we thank You fer th' fine sermon this mornin' given by yer servant Rev. Simon, down at th' church arbor and we ask yer blessin' on these fine christian women who prepared this wonderful food fer us this evenin'.

Sometimes I wonder if we men of th' family truly understand how difficult it must be ta run a house with all th' chores needed ta keep it goin' and specially th' many hours labor in a hot kitchen over a hot stove to prepare meals fer th' family and make it possible fer th' men ta tend their chores in th' fields and take care of th' cattle and a million other necessary things. So, we ask yer special blessin' on them Lord and on us as we go about th' business of everday livin'.

Lord we dedicate this meetin' to yer glory and we praise yer Holy name. Amen.

That Sunday night, wonderful old hymns of praise rose triumphantly up through moon drenched leaves and branches of th'old oaks in our front yard, and soared sweetly heavenward through a star studded sky, on wings of Glory to our risen Lord and Saviour. The more delicate voices of th' ladies and th' pure crystal tones of th' children blended perfectly with th' masculine voices of th' men, with Pa's mellow baritone weavin' a thread of harmony through th' rich fabric of praise.

There were many prayers that night but what I remember most are all those many textured voices lifted in song, accompanied by th' pleasin', soft jangle of harness, swishing tails, and stampin' feet of contented animals sighin' gently to one another.

The following Tuesday dawned hot and dry, like all th' weeks before it. Me and Pa were up at five, same as usual and had th' stock watered and fed and th' milkin' done by six-thirty.

Pa carried th' heavy milk pails while I skipped here and there, askin' a jillion questions, just enjoyin' his company. There wasn't anything Pa didn't know, at least I hadn't come across anything yet and not until years later would I realize that he'd started my education long before I'd begun to talk and he made it all so much fun I absorbed his teachin' as naturally as breathin'.

"Today marks th' second week of our prayer meetin's" he told Grandma as we gathered 'round th' breakfast table.

"I know, and I'm glad to say I've never felt better or been happier," she smiled, takin' a big pan of hot biscuits from th' oven.

We ate, mostly in silence, listenin' to th' birds singin, our ears buzzin' slightly from th' risin' and fallin' creschendo of whirrin' locusts in th' woods outside th' kitchen window.

I took long breaths of th' fresh, almost cool air seeping from th' green depths beyond, half listenin' to th' soft voices of the two people I loved most in all th' world, my toes buried in Streators soft fur, my mouth full of grandma's good food and sighed happily.

Pa's beloved pipe lay on th' table beside his plate waitin' to be renewed for th' comin' day.

Soft curls of steam rose from Grandma's and Pa's coffee mugs while big globs of rich yellow butter sank lower and lower into Grandmas special biscuits.

Ham and eggs and milk gravy, pear butter and blackberry jelly crowded each other for room on th' round table.

I listened with sudden awareness to th' sounds of contented chewing, Pa softly sluppin' his coffee from a saucer, blue eyes restin' here and there in random contemplation; a million things goin' on in his head.

Grandma ate silently, nodding her head in answer to anything said, her bonnet hangin' from th' back of her chair, feet anchored on a lion paw leg of th' table.

As I listened to th' familiar sounds, gazed on th' sweet faces of my beloved Grandparents, watched busy butterflies and bees workin' Grandma's hollyhawks and her magnificent snowball bush outside th' kitchen window, I knew I was in th' safest, happiest place in th' world.

Streetor, grown tired of my feet on his back had moved to his favorite spot by th' screen door and fallen asleep. He was now in th' middle of a dream, his feet twitchin' excitedly, tail thumpin' rapidly, his jaws fluffin' in and out like sails in th' wind, while muffled barks and whines issued from his throat. Sometimes Pa would speak to him if th' dream seemed particularly scary and he'd wake, eyes dark and fearful, give Pa an embarassed, grateful look, then doze off again.

After breakfast Grandma broke three or four biscuits into pieces, threw in a handful of ham chunks, then smothered it all with her good milk gravy. Ole Streator waited patiently, his jaws hangin' open, lickin' his chops and tryin' hard to remember his manners. I reckon there wasn't anybody that didn't like Grandma's cookin.

"I kind of look for everbody to come early tonite," she said, "so I'm goin' to do my bakin' this mornin' and just rest and study th' word this afternoon."

"I been thinkin,'th' same thing," said Pa, "so I'll join ya and we'll spend th' afternoon just rockin' under th' trees and praisin' th' good Lord."

"Amen," Grandma whispered softly.

That night the gates of Heaven opened and a soft rain fell on the bowed heads of those humble, God-fearing country folk congregated in our yard. Suddenly every face turned Heavenward, their lips moving in silent prayer to our Lord and Saviour.

Homecoming

I turned off route 45 onto 166, which follows the outer edge of New Burnside on its meandering way through the beautiful lush countryside of Southern Illinois.

A mile out of Burnside I turned left onto the familiar gravel road of my childhood that would take me to the farm of my grandparents-five miles away- my heart pounding with excitement as the car climbed up and down each familiar hill. It had once been a dirt road like all the country roads so the gravel seemed a luxury to me. In my childhood I'd traveled these hills and cool valleys with the trees and bushes shading the road so close I could reach out and grasp handfuls of leaves as we rode contentedly in a wagon behind a gentle team of horses.

At that tender age, happy and content with my world, I little knew that someday life wouldn't be as sweet and carefree as it was then. Nor did I think that one day my beloved Pa and Grandma would be gone forever and that I'd stand desolate and lonely in the front yard of their farm and stare in shock at the crumbled house and barn.

I crossed the weathered bridge over sugar creek and slowly crawled inch by inch up the long hill toward the farm, overwhelmed with millions of memories, savoring each one with a fervent hope that somehow I was back in the past, seeing the same things, hearing the same beloved voices, smelling the same clean country air mixed gloriously with road dust, wild roses, golden rod and dandelion.

The wonderful feeling of cool air drifting through the thick woods crowding each side of the road transported me even farther into the past. I had spent many happy hours in these woods playing hide and seek with cousins and friends but the greatest thrill of all was following close on my Grandfathers heels as he hunted these very same woods for squirrels.

All my life I'd called him Pa or PaPa; but now that he was gone, Grandfather seemed more a title of honor and respect, a reverence of what once was and was no more. Memory had laid a fine layer of gold on the past and nothing would ever tarnish it.

I pulled to the top of our hill and into the little road leading up to the farmhouse, forcing the car through ruts and weeds that scraped and rattled against its bottom.

The yard, too, was choked with weeds and bushes. There were no flower beds, or rows of Cannas or clumps of Holly Hawks growing in rambling profusion and the porch where morning glories had climbed to the roof forming a perfect shade against the sun, had fallen in on itself, just rubble in various stages of decay.

No glass in the windows, just hollow gaping eyes staring out at a future that could never be as wonderful as the past.

The back porch stood shakily on rotting timbers with weeds and bushes filling in the empty spaces, seeming to hold it up for yet a little while. My eyes sought the galvanized bathtub that was no longer there, but to my joy the long nail from which it had hung was clinging tenaciously to one of the loose boards on the decaying wall.

I searched through the grass for the well but found only a large hole in the ground filled with debris; but the rock curb and parts of th' bench that had encircled th' well were scattered here and there among th' weeds, cracked and crumbling around the edges, but still there. My heart rocked painfully against my ribs as I ran my hands over its rough surface, remembering cold baths in the galvanized tub with Grandmas lye soap peeling away the dirt and sometimes my skin.

I sat on the curb a long time, listening to the birds sing and the insects humming in the undergrowth, wondering how many people had sat on this old well curb drinking a dipper of the sweetest water this side of heaven, passing the time of day with Grandma and Grandpa.

I finally rose and stared toward where the home place used to be where my Great Grandmother and Grandfather Hundley had lived. The path was gone but half way across the field Pa's pear trees still grew in a ragged row despite the bushes trying to crowd them out.

Above me the leaves on the old oaks on whose limbs I had climbed as a child, seemed to sigh dispiritedly in the summer breeze and I imagined they somehow missed the folks who had lived busy lives in their shade.

Did they remember the wonderful stories Pa told to a yard full of friends on a Sunday afternoon? Did they miss the folks that drifted in for miles around to listen and laugh and be entertained before going on down to the bush arbor that served as our church? What wonderful revivals were held in that bush arbor: the leaves vibrating with the fire and brimstone sermons, amens going forth from the heart of devout Christians who happily walked for miles to be in God's House and praise His Holy Name.

Sometimes it would storm, the wind-driven rain whipping through the open sides drenching the entire congregation to the skin. I'd huddle between Grandma and Pa, their arms draped around me and Grandma's skirt pulled demurely around my skinny frame.

Recently I heard a fine sermon in a fine church, preached by a middle-aged preacher, and when I later told him it reminded me of the bush arbor preaching of my childhood he didn't know what a bush arbor was. Wish I'd had time to tell him and wish he'd had the time to listen, but the long line of hand shakers behind me prevented an explanation.

I looked down the hill to where Grandmas two seater toilet used to stand and wondered if the wood ash bucket, the water bucket and dipper, the wash pan and a bar of her lie soap might lie hidden somewhere under the thick brush.

"You younguns wash yer hands good when yer through," she'd admonish us as we trotted down to the outhouse, "and don't touch the dipper with yer wipin' hand."

Since most everbody was right handed, grandma's statement prompted pa's contemplation of a left-handed dipper. We'd giggle, plop down and read the catalogs.

As I think on that simple outhouse of the past and it's soothing powers on the intellect, I believe world peace might be achieved if the heads of States spent time together in an outhouse, unashamedly attending to the demands of nature, looking at the catalogs and sharing their most treasured childhood dreams.

The smoke house that was always stuffed with hams and bacon and racks of ribs, was gone.

No familiar animal sounds came from the rotting barn, which leaned precariously to one side.

No sign of the fence around the feedlot where Old Satan had held a three years reign of tyranny.

No Dimple, no Nell, no Marcy (a favorite milk cow) no chickens or ducks or geese. I even missed the selfish indignation from the pig's pen as they squabbled over the feed trough.

No beloved Streator walking politely at your heels, giving unbounded love and devotion, listening to your troubles with a keen intelligence that bordered on the uncanny. Pa used to say Streator was smarter than most folks he knew.

I started walking over the farm, forcing my way through the undergrowth, wrapping my heart in memories that can never die or rot or fall down crumbling to the earth.

I tramped the fields and woods and walked along the fence I used to run and jump over as a child, only now the fence was gone but my memory was real and I knew its path by heart.

I visited the row of pear trees that had given us so much good fruit and found a meager crop hanging from their limbs. Their juicy sweetness amazed me after so many years of neglect and I wondered if anyone ever came to pick the fruit.

I could still hear Grandma admonish Pa to pick only the ripe ones for canning. Her pear butter and preserves spread on hot biscuits are memories that can't be described.

I stood in the open field where Bali and his gypsy clan had lived so many summers, their beautifully carved wagons forming a circle where bon fires leaped skyward and fiddles and guitars played for the square dances we always had. People would come from all over the county, their wagons laden with food for our outdoor suppers. Bales of hay would circle the fire and folks would fill their plates and sit and talk for hours on end. We children would eat hurriedly then swim in the creek nearby. I imagined I could still hear the sound of laughter and splashing water. I thought I heard the faint sounds of a lute being played by the Being whose grotesque form startled you until you looked into his eyes; then all you seen was beauty so ethereal your Spirit soared Heavenward under his healing love. He was the light that guided the clan. He was the carver of impossible things. He also could heal sickness by playing the lute and looking into your eyes. Grandma told me he was a man of God, and not until I was grown did I fully know what she meant.

    I finally made my way back to the front yard and sat on a corner of the fallen-in porch, allowing the tears to wash away my loneliness and despair. I found myself praying in gratitude for all I'd had from these loved ones who tilled the earth, raised cattle and pigs and chickens and geese and guinea fowl to feed their families.

    I had loved the sound of the Guinea's as they conversed excitedly with one another.

    I remembered the hundreds of jars of fruit and vegetables my mom and grandma canned in summer to sustain us through the long winters. Remembered them slumped with exhaustion in rocking chairs on the front porch after supper. They'd exclaim to each other how beautiful the cold packed peaches looked in their jars and marvel that not one jar had broken all that day. I've seen many a jar of peaches lifted from the scalding water of grandma's iron kettle, shimmering like red jewels in the sun then suddenly bursting, spilling the precious contents onto the ground. Their faces would crumple in dismay that so much work and beauty was destroyed in such a few seconds. We finally solved the problem by wrapping a blanket around the jar as it left the kettle, then lowering it into a covered basket to maintain an even temperature. I'd sneak into the kitchen and wash the dishes while they rested, then swell with pride when they'd come in and exclaim in surprise that the dishes were all done. Only years later did it dawn on me that they could hear me doing the dishes since the kitchen had a window onto the front porch. It was a wonderful subterfuge on their part. They nourished my self Esteem and I gave them a much deserved rest. I thought of the hard work and hardships they had endured all through the years and I thanked God for his Grace to them and for the privilege of growing up in a time when neighbors would gather to rebuild a burned house or barn.

    I remembered the women cooking over an open fire to feed the hungry men. We children loved such times, running back and forth to carry lumber up on ladders that seemed two stories high to our young eyes, handing up dippers of cold cistern water to the thirsty men, holding a hammer and a handful of nails while a farmer, turned carpenter, wiped his sweating face with a big bandana handkerchief.

I took special care of Pa, climbing up to him with a tidbit I'd filched from the cook table and a cold wet rag to wrap around his neck. He'd smile, kiss me on the cheek and tell me I was his darlin'.

When the building was done they'd gather in a circle, hands clasped, their faces radiant with joy and thank God for His mercy and Grace to them.

There would be baskets of odd size dishes, pots and pans and food from every woman's kitchen, generously sharing her own meager supply.

These God-fearing folk were the heart of America: its strength, its perseverance, its foundation, whose bedrock was the Lord Jesus Christ, and I'm privileged to have had such ancestors.

Now as my eyes drifted over this strange tangled terrain that was once my home, my heart suddenly leaped with recognition. Pushing itself up through the undergrowth was Grandma's snowball bush clinging valiantly to life in spite of its neglected state. It was alive! A living, glorious monument to all that had been and would never be again. In its roots, its leaves and branches, were generations of memories. Countless hands had plucked its blooms and countless birds had nested and raised their young in its fragrant foliage. All my life it had served as third base for our ball games, enduring slide-ins and wildly grasping hands in silent splendor. It had stood silent and dignified while the ones who were 'it' in our hide and seek games clamped hands over their faces and buried their heads in its leaves and counted to ten; then laughing and peeking thru spread fingers they had yelled, "Here I come ready or not."

I fell on my knees beside it cupping the few scraggly blooms in my hands, remembering Grandma walking 'round and 'round it, pruning and talking and caressing it with her green thumbs.

I also remembered the day we younguns, as they called us, got a glimpse of Grandmas famous temper that Pa was always telling us about. We had all been exposed to her strict discipline and an occasional experience with the whacking stick, but she was always fair and we knew we deserved every lick, so not one of us ever held a grudge or felt we were abused.

On this particular day a wild, competitive ball game was in progress, tempers were flaring, some half-hearted threats were being bantered about and a home run for the down team would even the score.

I was on the down team and my cousin Frankie was up to bat which didn't do anything to raise my hopes.

Various cousins loaded the bases waiting for Frankie to perform a miracle. Frankie's stained record of burned toilets from smoking grape vines, broken windows, dead chickens and terrorized dogs during his sling shot days, wasn't, I reckoned, much of an incentive for asking God's intervention in a rag tag team of country kids.

The ball was thrown, Frankie swung mightily catching just enough of the ball to skitter it along the ground toward first base.

Cousin Lucille, the stumblebum, guarded that base and I knew that unless the Lord intervened in her behalf, we would tie up the game. I skidded into home plate, which was a slab of branch rock, leaped to my feet triumphantly then stared in horror.

Grandma's snowball bush (third base) was bristling with arms and legs. On the ground lay a large limb, its big clumps of blooms clinging brokenly to the severed branch.

A deadly silence fell. Not even a breath could be heard as we all realized what a disaster confronted us. We stood there for what seemed like an hour, then Frankie, white faced and trembling, slouched toward the porch to summon Grandma, but she was already standing in the door staring at the magnificent bush with a gaping slash in its side. The ground was littered with white blooms, like a freak snow in July.

Grandma opened the screen door carefully, stepping slowly and deliberately across the porch and down the steps.

Frankie hung his head as she passed then watched sadly as she approached the bush. We all stood back, holding our breath, watching Grandma's face with fearful facination.

Her normally brown skin was now as pale as the broken blooms on the ground as she knelt beside the bush, gently lifting the ruined branch in her hands. Her eyes caressed the wounded bush and we were all horrified to see tears rolling down her cheeks.

There wasn't a one of us that felt as tall as a snakes belly on that terrible day for everyone knew how special that bush was to Grandma. After what seemed an eternity, she stood, her black eyes raking each one of our faces with frightening penetration. "Not a one of you but what knows how much this bush means to me," she said coldly. "It's part of the family ever bit as much as any pet on this farm, includin' Old Streator."

That was a revelation to us for we all knew how much she loved Ole Streator; almost as much as Pa if that was possible but we'd never have thought that included the snowball bush.

"This bush don't just belong to me," she sighed. "It belongs to everyone of you and to every friend or stranger who sees and admires its beauty. It belonged to my own dear Grandmother, God rest her soul, and I've nourished and nursed it through drought and heat and I've shielded it against the bitter winters."

We knew how carefully she piled hay around the bush in the fall wraping it snugly in burlap sacks. Her eyes seemed to have a fire in them and we could already feel the whacking stick that would avenge the snowball bush on our guilty hides. So her next words took us completely by surprise.

"I don't want to know which one of you did this." she said angrily "else I might be tempted to use ever switch on this old oak tree to thrash yer ornery hide. Fact is I suspicion that more'n one of ye had a hand in it."

With that she adjusted her bonnet, cradling the wounded branch in her arms and walked back into the house leaving us to ponder her reaction and our close scrape with a thrashing. She hadn't forbidden us to continue using the bush as third base, nor did we stop using it, but there after scrupulous care was taken to protect Grandma's beloved snowball bush.

Now you might be thinking that Grandma hardly displayed much of a temper on this occasion but if you had seen her black eyes all lit up with fiery indignation you'd change your mind.

I looked at the now scraggly bush clinging to life, my heart aching for that long ago time. Cupping the few ragged blooms to my face I smelled the fragrance that would always remind me of my beloved Grandmother. In my memory I could still see her walking slowly around the bush, pruning and talking and caressing it then sitting on the front porch with a second cup of coffee, her eyes resting fondly on the magnificent snowball bush.

"Thank you dear Lord," I whispered, "for giving me this small miracle." The wind suddenly came up rattling the leaves on the great oaks and it was then I heard a thousand voices on the wind. They swept into my heart, into my own secret chamber of memories, scene after scene, voice after voice.

Pa calling Ole Streator to supper and the red bone answering in his rich voice.

Grandma's voice, soft and sweet, talking to me as she brushed my long hair at nite.

I could hear them all, talking and laughing and singing.

Then a strange voice broke my reverie.

"Aire ye lookin' fer sumthin' miss?"

Startled, I Looked up to see an obvious farm man with earth smeared overalls and batterd hat. Attached to a rein held loosely in his hand was a mare whose eyes were fastened on mine, her ears up and inquisitive. She whinnied softly, took a step forward and nuzzled my face knowingly.

Now, now Dimple" the farmer said kindly, "lets not be forward with th' young lady."

I wrapped my arms around her head, tears of joy filling my eyes. "Did you say Dimple?" I asked in disbelief.

"Yes miss, thets her name."

"How did you come to name her that?" I inquired eagerly.

"Well," he said, easing down on a corner of the porch, " my daddy knew a man by th' name of Almus Hundley, who lived right here on this old farm, as a matter of fact. He had a fine mare named Dimple thet my dad purely admired. After dad worried Mr. Hundley to death, he finally let him breed her to a nice stallion we owned. She dropped a fine lookin' foal which dad bought and of course he named her Dimple. This Dimple here," he said, "fondly rubbing the mare's nose, "is about the fifth generation of Dimples."

He looked at me quizzically. "You seem mighty interested miss, if ye don't mind my sayin' so."

"I certainly don't mind," I smiled. "You see, Almus Hundly was my Grandfather."

"Pawn my word," he exclaimed, studying my face intently.

I could see his thoughts skimming over a distant road map looking for the key to my identity. Then a slow understanding spread over his face and he laughed excitedly.

"Unless I miss my guess yer Ruth's girl. Got the same features," he mused, "only different, if ye get my meanin'."

I nodded, silently enjoying this glimpse of my family through this man's eyes.

He chuckled softly, his eyes searching my face, then he thrust a sunburned hand toward me.

"Pleased to meet ye miss. I'm Yancey Newbold."

"Why, I remember hearing my mom mention you, Yancey."

"I expect thets a fact," he smiled. "I was underfoot a lot. Even though yer mom was five years older'n me, I still had a terrible crush on her, standin' 'round in th' background watchin' her antics."

"Antics?"

"Beggin' yer pardon, miss," he blushed. "I meant nothin' wrong in thet. It's jest that Ruth was always up to sumthin', sorta keepin' the community on its toes you see. She was some looker, that one," he said softly. "Could'a had her pick of anyone anywhur".

"My mom allus said she should be on the stage with all them lights on her, singin.'and pickin' her guitar."

"She could play hoedowns on that fiddle of her'n with the best of em'. Taught herself too," he said proudly. "Many's the time I'd ride by here and Ruth'ud be settin' in the front yard playin' and singin' as though she had a thousand people listenin'. I'd tie my horse to a limb and set on the ground with my back to a tree. She'd smile at me and go right on. She never met a stranger or had a bashful bone in her body."

"That's never changed," I said. "She's as outgoing today as she was then and your mother was right when she said she should have been on the stage. She truly could have been a star if she'd had the right chance."

He was drinking in every word, a glow on his weathered face.

"Did you know she was once invited to the White House and entertained President Kennedy?" I asked.

"Reckon I missed that," he said in astonishment;" but I do remember you and her campaignin' with them politicians, specially Paul Powell. I shor did like thet man, voted for 'im ever time. I went to ever speakin' here abouts jest to watch you and Ruth sing and you dance. Imagine our Ruth singin' for the President," he mused. "Shor makes me proud that I knowed her and I reckon she's a celebrity now, what with all thet publicity and all."

"Same common outgoing person," I laughed, "cept she's still outspoken. I guess thats her biggest fault, opening her mouth and putting both feet in it."

Yancey laughed and laughed over that, slapping his overalls in delight as Dimple stared at him.

We spent the next hour sharing memories, with Dimple soaking up a fair amount of love and a couple of apples I had in the car.

"I used to come here a lot," he said. "Yer Grandpa was a prize tale spinner and he'd have a whole yard full of people come to listen to his yarns; specially on Sunday afternoons. Ever now and then I'd carry a bucket of(as yer Grandpa put it) th' sweetest water this side of heaven, from th' well and pass it 'round about. Almus wud take a swig, hardly missin' a word of th' story he wus tellin'. I've often thought them tales of hiss'en would be worth a fortune today iffen' they'd been put on a record. Course such foolishness wuz beyond us country folk then. No one hereabouts even had a radio in them days."

Much to my surprise he turned and pointed to the snowball bush.

"See that bush?" he smiled. "I expect you remember how fine it wus when yer Grandma was here. All the women folk loved it and so did I," he admitted, "only I never said so to anyone, bein' a boy and all."

My, I thought, the Lord was sure answering prayer today. I had hated to think of it standing here alone with no one to love it.

"Would you do something for me?" I asked eagerly.

"If I can miss," he replied doubtfully, eyeing my new car looking out of place there in the weeds.

"Would you dig up that bush and plant it in your yard and give it a chance to be beautiful again?"

His eyes feasted on the snowball bush just as the Parsons eyes had feasted on old Satan so many years ago.

"Why I'd be purely proud to do thet, miss. Martha will be so happy to have Net's bush in her yard. She'll fuss over thet bush somethin' awful," he smiled.

The sun was getting low in the sky and Dimple was fidgeting to get home. Yancey gathered the reins in his hand and looked at me sadly.

"I can't tell ye what it means to me findin' ye here and all. Sometimes I pine for all th' long gone yesterdays and I expect thet's why yer here today." He looked around at the ruins then smiled wistfully. "This was a happy place miss and you were a happy little girl." His eyes rested on me fondly. "You were the tinest little child I ever seed. My mom used to say ye looked like a movin' haystack with all that red hair hangin' down yer back. I'd purely give a lot if she could be here today to see ya.

My heart was overwhelmed with longing and I knew he felt the same sadness and lonliness I was feeling; but for this brief time on a spring day filled with country sounds and the sweet smell of freshly turned earth, we had shared that most precious of gifts: our memories. His eyes were on the snowball bush and I knew it would soon be resting in Martha's yard, tended carefully by loving hands.

"Come see the bush anytime yer in these parts," he said, extending his hand, "and I'm much obliged for it." The weathered face smiled fondly as he studied me. "It's not often you get a chance to renew th' past and help it to a new beginnin'. Me and Martha live down the hill 'bout a mile. Our names on the mailbox so you can't miss us."

As he turned the mare and started to walk away I suddenly remembered something.

"Yancey!"

"Yes miss."

"Remember how you had a crush on my mom? Well, I used to have a crush on you and thought you were the best looking fellow I'd ever seen."

His face was wreathed in smiles as he stood beside Dimple, the afternoon sun glowing behind them.

"And," I laughed happily, "you're still a nice looking fellow."

He chuckled delightedly.

"Thank ye miss, you've made an old farm boy happy today and I'll be sure to remind Martha what a lucky woman she is."

I watched him and Dimple walk down the hill in solitude, enjoying each others company, the tired man walking the tired mare instead of riding. My Pa always said any man who rides a tired animal home from the fields is not a man. He would have approved of Yancey.

A lump rose in my throat as I watched Yancey and the mare come to a curve in the road, then they both stopped and looked back; the man waving his battered hat, the mare's head held high, her ears erect.

I took one last look at the crumbling farm, saying goodby to it all, knowing it was still alive in my heart and would be forever, but I now realized there were others who remembered fragments of those years and somewhere in the hearts and minds of good folks I had known and some I had never known, were enough fragments to make a whole memory.

I got into my new car and drove slowly down a road that was not quite the same as it once was, yet the same old dust billowed up behind me as it had behind Uncle Bill's new emerald green packard sedan on that long ago day, and the dust covered bushes lining the narrow road still clacked and twisted in the cars wake, and fat grasshoppers still sounded like rusty hinges as they sprang in confusion through the long grass.

I stopped the car on the sugar creek bridge where I'd known so many happy hours, got out and climbed up to the top of the guardrail. I sat watching the water move sluggishly toward Parker where my mom had hopped on and off freights for fun and where on this very creek she had broken her big toe swinging across on a grapevine.

I looked up at Massive white cloud ships sailing on a cobalt sky just as they had done for generations past and would for generations to come. I closed my eyes and let the memories fill all the lonely places in my heart.

Across the creek a herd of cattle grazed quietly and from a distant farm the faint sounds of a barking dog drifted on the late afternoon breeze. Someday, I thought, caressing the steel beam of the old bridge fondly, I'll buy back some of this land and I'll plant a garden and raise some chickens and pigs and cows for milking and of course some horses.

Maybe I might even get a colt from Yancey's Dimple and carry on the beloved line. Of course I could never replace any of them, especially ole Streator but I'd have a coon hound or two and I'd take them hunting on a cold night and I'd sit on a downed tree and listen to their rich voices as me and Pa used to do.

I touched the worn surface of the old bridge and wondered if the weathered, steel structure contained all the voices and laughter and good times of which it had been a part.

I don't know how long I sat on the bridge, my mind racing back through the years before the sound of a wheezing motor brought me back. A pick up truck was chugging down the road in a leisurely fashion, the dust swirling up behind it and I imagined it might be Pa in his Model A if I just wished it hard enough.

I'd sat on this very bridge as a little girl and watched for dust on a friday night when my mom would come home from her job in a distant town to spend the week-end with me. I'd ride back with her as far as the bridge on a Sunday afternoon and with heavy heart watch her out of sight until not a speck of dust hung in the air.

The pick up slowed to a crawl as it got closer, finally coming to a stop on the bridge. "Sorry 'bout th' dust, miss?" smiled an old man whose brown wrinkled face reminded me of a rare painting. Sitting beside him, a red bone hound studied me, his brows beetled in curiosity.

"Don't give it another thought," I grinned at the hound. "I was raised on this dust."

"Is thet a fact?" he said, squinting at me curiously. "Whose kin be ye then?"

"Well, I don't have kin here anymore, but Almus and Jeanette Hundley were my Grandparents. I pointed back to the cross roads I'd just come through. You turn right back there by Birdwell school and go up the road from Birdwell about..."

"Yeah, yeah," he interrupted excitedly, "know jest whur it be." He tugged at his chin, "Been there many a time. Yer Grandaddy was a mighty fine teacher and I could say the same 'bout his farmin'. Course story tellin' wuz his special gift. I used ta set and lissen by th' hour." His eyes looked off into the past. "He'd rattle thet old pipe 'cross his teeth from one side of his mouth ta tother and never miss a word. Why, he kept the whole community entertained. Better'n thet movie stuff they call entertainin' these days," he snorted disdainfully; then the seamed face softened and a gentle smile tugged the corners of his mouth.

"And then there wuz Net, yer Grandma. She be an angel in Heaven now, jest as she wuz down here on this lonely ole earth. Tweren't lonely though when she be here, helpin' folks, keepin' yer Grandpa in line and lettin' me come to supper more times then I deserved. Her apple pies were pure majic and I'll let ye in on a little secret," he whispered, crooking his finger for me to come closer. "Thar wuz a genie in thet cook stove of hers jest as sure as day follows night. Oh, I know they ain't supposed ta be sech things," he grinned "but I know better."

He stopped suddenly and searched my face.

"Can't rightly place which grandchild ye be," he puzzled. "Ye don't look like Margie or Mildred," then he chuckled triumphantly, slapping his hands together,"so thet jest leaves Ruth. My, my, thet Ruth," he mused, smiling affectionately at the memories of my mother. Me and Norey luved thet girl like aire own and she stirred up more mischief than all aire boys put together. "

The red bone thrust his head past the old man and tested my smell, his nostrils flaring little snuffing sounds. I reached out and cupped his muzzle in my hand, my face close to his while he sniffed me thoroughly. Then a wet raspy tongue stamped his approval on my face. He could have been ole Streator I thought. He has the same fine head and eyes.

"Charlie Horn I be," he smiled, "and it's mighty happy I am to see ye agin' child. "

I shook the calloused, wrinkled hand he thrust from the window, my eyes still on the hound. " I spent many happy hours playing on your front porch, Charlie, and I can't tell you what a miracle it is to run into you today of all days".

"The feelin's mutual and I reckon it warn't jest whim thet sent me ta Burnside fer vittals I don't need. I believe the good Lord meant us to meet today. Sides, I ain't never see'd Sam here take ta no one right off like he has ta you, miss and I don't lie when I tell ye ole Sam here can read character better'n anybody I ever see'd."

I smiled at the word anybody as though Sam was a person and indeed Streator had been as much a person as anyone I ever knew.

"Well Sam, ye jest met Helen Ruth, Ruth's girl," he laughed, hugging the dog; "and I reckon she knows her coon dogs, havin' growed up with some of the finest." His eyes got a distant look in them then he spoke quietly with awe. "Thar wus one though, the likes of which I never see'd before and never expect to see again."

"That would be ole Streator," I laughed excitedly, not at all embarassed for jumping ahead of him.

"Right ye be girl, the very same. Lord what I would'a give fer thet dog and I reckon ever man in the county felt the same. Once ye heer'ed his voice ye never fergot it. Course Almus could pick his voice out from a hundred others and many's the time me and Almus set on a log on a cold nite and waited fer aire dogs ta tree. As soon as Streator's voice wus heer'ed we'd grab our lanterns and crash through the woods like fools."

I nodded sadly. "Those were good times."

"Mighty good times" he agreed, "and I reckon we didn't know how lucky we wuz. "Well Sam," he said, turning to the dog, "thur's a car comin' over the hill yonder and I 'spect we best move airselves outa' th' way, so go say a proper goodby to the young lady and never ferget thet the hands what carressed ole Streator have now been laid on yer ornery hide."

The dog sprang out and dashed around the truck to where I knelt down, then slowly thrust his muzzle into my open hands.

"Mind yer manners now, Sam," Charlie admonished affectionately, "and don't slobber on the young lady."

I gazed into Sam's eyes and we had a mutual understanding as he walked trustingly into my arms. After a minute Charlie called the dog, scolding him in mock sterness for taking up so much of my time. We both watched the dust swirling up from the oncoming car in silence, then Charlie gazed wistfully at me. "If ye've a mind to miss, me and Sam here wud be proud to have ye take a bite of supper with us." Sams tail wagged in approval. "That is iffen yer not in a hurry er' somethin'."

"Maybe Nora wouldn't take kindly to unexpected company," I said, my heart beating faster.

"Mama's been gone a few years now," he answered, "so it's jest me and old Sam here. Yer mother come ta Norey's funeral and she's been here a few times since then," he said fondly.

"Well, for sure I can't sit on this bridge forever," I laughed" and I've been dreading to leave 'this place where so many years of my life were spent. Charlie, I'd love to have a bite of supper with you and Sam if I won't be a bother."

"It'll pleasure me no end miss to have ye and talk about the years gone by. Seems like the older I get the more I live in the past where life was slower and simpler."

I followed the old pick up back to the crossroads, made a left turn and just before we dropped over the top of Mc Farland hill I stared in the rear view mirror at the road behind me. Half a mile up that road, among the ruins of rotting timbers, lay the memories of my childhood and countless generations before me. I took one last look as the road disappeared behind the crest of the hill.

We drove past familiar weathered houses of long ago neighbors and schoolmates, on down into the valley where to my amazement, stood the same ramshackled wooden bridge over the creek where I'd once hunted polyglogs. Charlie tooted his horn and waved his arm out over the bridge and surrounding fields. This was his land where my mom had hunted rabbits when she was growing up and he was sharing his memories with me. I knew I'd hear many tales about the past on this night from this wonderful old man and his fine coonhound that looked so much like ole Streetor and I could hardly wait. The creek, its banks lined with trees, meandered this way and that through fields drowsing in the afternoon sun. We finally made our way up the long hill leading to the Horn farm. When we reached the top I was surprised to see the original house standing just as it had when I was a kid.

It was like walking back into the past. The same trees, the same front porch with the same kind of porch swing that surely couldn't be the one I'd swung in when my feet wouldn't even begin to touch the floor.

Pig and a Sack of Stray Cats

There were five or six cane bottom chairs in various positions around the porch, which told me that folks still came by to visit with each other, discuss their crops and pass the news. It was an efficient grapevine and kept folks closely linked with themselves.

"Why, this house is just as it was when I was a kid," I exclaimed, stepping up on the porch from the large slab of branch rock that had been there for no telling how many generations. "If that rock could talk," I murmured.

"It'd have some tales to tell alright," Charlie smiled, kicking it gently with the toe of his shoe. "Reckon it be jest as well it cain't talk tho. It'ud might nigh destroy a body to live life over again, not to mention the hurts and sorrows of all them gone afore us. Course thar'ed be the joys to gladden our heart, and some I'd purely love to see again; but I reckon the good Lord knew what He was doin' to set us on a straight ahead path with no turnin' back."

He smiled warmly at me." I reckoned ye'd like seein' the old house again the same as twas'. Course she's had a board or two replaced from time to time and the roof's been put back twice. I reckon she's wearin' out though, like me," he smiled, holding the screen door open for me.

The living room was sparsely furnished and neat as a pin. Iron bedsteads dressed in colorful quilts were quietly elegant as they peered through the shadowed bedroom doors. I followed him to the kitchen, my eyes hungrily drinking in everything. An old pie safe stood in one corner, the same bulky cabinet for dishes and pans standing beside it; but the round oak table with lion claw feet and the Warm morning cook stove with its hot water resovoir flipped my heart over and sent me crashing into the past. I could almost hear Grandma and Pa talking over the days events at the supper table with me sitting propped on a box between them so I would be comfortable and as tall as they were.

"Set down here miss and I'll make ye a cup of coffee," said Charlie kindly. "Ye've had a hard day with yer memories and all but I believe here in familiar surroundins' ye'll be able to put things right again."

"It's so like theirs," I said, looking around the kitchen.

"Well, its like now," he said sensibly. " Houses and furnishins' are much the same as they wus then, except they be more modern and convenient now. As fer me, I like th' old ways better."

"Is that why you invited me to supper, Charlie, so I could see it again.?

"Jest a small part of it child. It was plain to see yer heart be breakin' and when I see'd it, my heart be breakin' too, fer all the old times gone by; fer yer Grandpa who wuz me best friend and fer yer Grandma who always had a dipper of cold water fer a thirsty traveler, or if ye be lucky she'd pour ye out a glass of her famous buttermilk."

He looked out the window at the rolling fields and woods where my mom had hunted his prize rabbits and squirrels, then chuckled. "Memories be the real treasure, child, and I know ye've got a whole storehouse full of 'em, so I reckon I invited ye cause yer like my family, and it be time to come back to yer roots and renew them memories with an old fossil like me. Sometimes the good Lord spreads balm on a heart in ways beyon' our puny understandin'. Now ye jest set yer bones and drink yer coffee while I rustle up some grub."

Charlie soon had new potatoes frying in an old iron skillet, on a cookstove exactly like Grandma had and I watched in amazement as he stirred up a batch of biscuits.

I tried to help but he would have no part of it and assigned Sam to keep an eye on me. In less than an hour we sat at the battered old table with its oilcloth cover and feasted on slabs of ham, fried eggs and new potatoes and the best biscuits I'd had since Grandma's. We washed it all down with fresh brewed coffee from a speckled porcelain pot that simmered gently on the back of the stove. From its spout issued a soft steamy whistle, filling the room with a fragrant soothing peace.

"I'm disgracing myself Charlie," I said between mouthfuls, "but I haven't had a meal that tasted this good since I was a kid."

"I'm obliged for the compliment," he smiled, "but I'd say bein' back again in loved places among home folks accounts for ninety percent of the taste, and ain't thet the way the good Lord meant it to be?"

I studied the wise old man across the table from me. The kind eyes shining out from a deeply seamed face, bib overalls and cotton shirt just like Pa's that I remembered and loved so well. His life had been spent in this peaceful part of the world. Most of it right in this old house where he married, grew his crops and raised his children.

"Charlie," I said. "You're the most fortunate man I know and the luckiest."

"How do ye figure thet?" he asked, surprised.

"Well Charlie, I've seen my share of the world and the people in it, but I'd give a great deal to go back and live my life over again, right here in this country, close to my roots and my kind of people where you can still hear cattle bawlin' and chickens cacklin' and locusts and tree frogs and the big ole bass sound of pond frogs and crickets chirping you to sleep at night." I took a deep breath. "You know how long its been since I heard a rooster crow? I mean a real honest to goodness country rooster."

His eyes had a lively interest as he looked at me. "How long child since ye heer'ed a rooster crow?"

"Last time was when I was a kid, except at the fair in the poultry house which don't count. Those poor things can't figure out whats happened to them, trying to balance themselves on a wire floor with their toes hanging down, staring out at a strange world with a bunch of people gawking at them. It's enough to make anything crow... but it just don't sound the same."

Charlie laughed loudly, slapping his knee. "Well child, iffen ye want to spend the night with me and old Sam here, I guarantee that a real bonifidee rooster will wake ye up 'bout five in the mornin' and he'll be crowin' with joy to the new day. Fact is thar'll be three of the rascals crowin' their heads off. Ye could even gather fresh eggs fer breakfast," he smiled, "and take a look at me little flock."

His face was sincere and I suddenly wanted to stay on in this familiar place more than anything I'd wanted to do in a long time.

"Charlie, you've got yourself a deal. It'll be heaven to be wakened at five by a bunch of real bonifidee roosters and eat real fresh laid eggs for breakfast. Now I'm going to tend to these dishes and I'll hear no word about it," I laughed.

The old man nodded contentedly, his gaze fastened on the window. The fields and woods were bathed in a warm pink by the setting sun and I could hear frogs beginning to croak in a nearby pond. Maybe in the morning I'd hear a crow -one of my favorite sounds- and maybe I'd even hear a whole flock of them squabbling and talking noisily among themselves in the big oaks down by the creek. When the dishes were done we sat in the swing on the front porch, listening to the sounds of country life, watching the darkness fall slowly from the sky, the swing creaking gently in the night.